In Praise of *Tough Choices* or *Tough Times*

"While *Tough Choices or Tough Times* does a tremendous job in identifying and articulating the challenges we face, what truly sets it apart is the specific and highly innovative policy prescriptions it advocates to reverse the 'education deficit.' I encourage every policymaker, at every level, to read this compelling and comprehensive report." —WILLIAM E. KIRWAN, CHANCELLOR, UNIVERSITY SYSTEM OF MARYLAND

"*Tough Choices or Tough Times* is must reading for policymakers, educators, businesspeople, and citizens who want America to be prosperous and competitive in the 21st century. The report pulls no punches about the economic threats facing our country. The Commission advances thought-provoking recommendations that should stimulate debate and then galvanize every sector of society to muster the will to ensure that America's workforce is the best educated and prepared in the world." —HUGH PRICE, SENIOR FELLOW, BROOKINGS INSTITUTION, AND FORMER PRESIDENT, NATIONAL URBAN LEAGUE

"*Tough Choices or Tough Times* provides a bold and specific road map for transforming all levels of education—preschool through postsecondary education—to meet the challenges of a rapidly changing global economy. It calls for massive fundamental change in education structure, curriculum, teacher compensation, and assessment, as well as in the roles of virtually all our education institutions." —MIKE KIRST, PROFESSOR OF EDUCATION EMERITUS, STANFORD UNIVERSITY

"The steps proposed in *Tough Choices or Tough Times* will move us dramatically forward, fostering a 21st-century skills development pipeline that meets the needs of working adults, and enables them to engage in the lifelong learning necessary to meet the changing demands of the workplace." —MARLENE SELTZER, PRESIDENT AND CEO, JOBS FOR THE FUTURE

"The Commission provides a 21st century formula for workforce development: think regional, eliminate structures that no longer serve our needs, and create universal access to quality education and training." —JOSEPH CARBONE, PRESIDENT AND CEO, THE WORKPLACE, INC., SOUTHWESTERN CONNECTICUT'S WORKFORCE DEVELOPMENT BOARD

"Efforts at bringing together the three integral components of a successful workforce investment system—education, training, and economic development—have been haphazard at best. The recommendation to encourage the creation of high level jobs/skills/economic growth authorities with the ability to issue tax exempt bonds holds real promise for the development of a rational, sustainable, and politically supportable system." —MARION PINES, DIRECTOR, SAR LEVITAN CENTER, JOHNS HOPKINS UNIVERSITY

"Anyone who hopes to hold a job in the next several decades should read—if not memorize—this extraordinary report. Hopefully the report will motivate our nation's leaders to promptly take the steps needed to assure that our nation's citizenry can enjoy a decent quality of life in the years ahead." —NORMAN R. AUGUSTINE, RETIRED CHAIRMAN AND CEO, LOCKHEED MARTIN CORPORATION, AND CHAIRMAN, THE NATIONAL ACADEMIES' COMMITTEE ON PROSPERING IN THE GLOBAL ECONOMY OF THE 21ST CENTURY

"*Tough Choices or Tough Times* is an exciting vision of a reformed and revitalized American education system. It has many important ideas that should generate considerable debate and are worthy of serious consideration." —SUSAN FUHRMAN, PRESIDENT, TEACHERS COLLEGE, COLUMBIA UNIVERSITY

"*Tough Choices or Tough Times* calls into question whether we are willing to invest in the future of America's workforce." —BOB GILOTH, DIRECTOR, FAMILY ECONOMIC SUCCESS, ANNIE E. CASEY FOUNDATION

"This penetrating, scary analysis and astute, far-reaching recommendations amount to *A Nation at Risk* for the next generation, a brave, clear call for top-to-bottom reforms in U.S. education. While overturning plenty of creaky applecarts, *Tough Choices* sketches a bold and efficient new vehicle for equipping 21st century Americans with the skills and knowledge they will need—and that the nation needs." —CHESTER E. FINN JR., SENIOR FELLOW, HOOVER INSTITUTION, STANFORD UNIVERSITY, AND PRESIDENT, THOMAS B. FORDHAM FOUNDATION

"The Commission's report joins a chorus of voices warning us of the looming consequences facing our nation because of the poor level of preparation of students and members of the workforce. What is different is that this report recommends bold steps for action. To do any less will result only in more half-measures that over time have had too little effect and have left us vulnerable as we face growing competition in a changed world economy." —G. WAYNE CLOUGH, PRESIDENT, GEORGIA TECH, AND VICE CHAIRMAN, U.S. COUNCIL ON COMPETITIVENESS

"This is a remarkably bold and refreshing report. It is time for us to stop tinkering at the edges of the educational enterprise. What I find most appealing about the Commission's recommendations is that it represents a total overhaul of how we do the business of education. The Commission is telling us that we need to stop rearranging the deck chairs on the Titanic, reinvest the resources we have, and turn the ship in a new direction." —JAMES W. PELLEGRINO, DISTINGUISHED PROFESSOR OF COGNITIVE PSYCHOLOGY AND EDUCATION, UNIVERSITY OF ILLINOIS AT CHICAGO

"The current public education system at the K–12 level is broken. Can it be fixed? This report says no, it has to be replaced. This is more than a wake-up call. It is a call to arms. The reasons to be alarmed are clearly and persuasively documented. Out-of-the-box, stretch recommendations are offered." —ALBERT J. SIMONE, PRESIDENT, ROCHESTER INSTITUTE OF TECHNOLOGY

From the Commissioners

"The question this report raises is whether our country has the kind of education system that is needed to maintain America's standard of living for our children, our grandchildren, and future generations. I very much hope that it will spark the kind of tough, honest debate on that topic that it so richly deserves." —RICHARD W. RILEY, FORMER SECRETARY OF EDUCATION, CLINTON ADMINISTRATION

"Bold, inventive, analytic, and piercing, the report's recommendations stand to make a huge difference in how America thinks about and enacts its educational enterprise for *all*—including its youngest—students." —SHARON LYNN KAGAN, VIRGINIA & LEONARD MARX PROFESSOR OF EARLY CHILDHOOD AND FAMILY POLICY, TEACHERS COLLEGE, COLUMBIA UNIVERSITY, AND CODIRECTOR, THE NATIONAL CENTER FOR CHILDREN AND FAMILIES

"This report deals with the critical issue of training and educating the current workforce to meet the competitive challenges of the future and indicates the depth of the changes our nation needs to make to change our culture to one of life-long learning." —MORTON BAHR, PRESIDENT EMERITUS, COMMUNICATIONS WORKERS OF AMERICA

"This report offers a radical new blueprint for making America's K–12 educational experience more meaningful and effective. It's a fascinating and thought-provoking read that is sure to get the American educational establishment talking." —CHARLES B. REED, CHANCELLOR, CALIFORNIA STATE UNIVERSITY SYSTEM

"This report shows how states and professional educators can create efficient, high-performance school systems to educate all students to high standards." —RAY MARSHALL, FORMER SECRETARY OF LABOR, CARTER ADMINISTRATION

"A thorough, thoughtful, and timely study. Most important, it goes far beyond the normal conclusions. The recommendations are sweeping and controversial but must be considered seriously as they flow directly from the logic of the study. If not these, what then?" —HENRY B. SCHACHT, MANAGING DIRECTOR, WARBURG PINCUS LLC

"Piecemeal reform of public education in America is insufficient to deliver on the promise that every child will receive an education that leads to a good job, productive life, and responsible citizenship. The *New Commission Report* is a coherent, comprehensive, systemic plan for how to enable public education in America to be the best in the world." —THOMAS W. PAYZANT, FORMER SUPERINTENDENT, BOSTON PUBLIC SCHOOLS

"It is my hope that the report will be heeded at the highest policy levels in every local community. What is at stake for our nation and every citizen is nothing less than the prospect of a plummeting standard of living for our children and American generations to come if we fail to act." —PAUL A. ELSNER, FORMER PRESIDENT, MARICOPA COMMUNITY COLLEGE SYSTEM

"This may be a policy report, but it should be read by every practitioner. Brutally honest, it shows why money alone cannot get all our students ready for college and lays out bold and imaginative solutions to the problems that educators deal with every day, solutions that will take courage to implement, but that are at the same time realistic and practical." —JUDY B. CODDING, PRESIDENT, AMERICA'S CHOICE, INC.

"I become more concerned each day that our students are falling further behind and the people of this nation do not seem to be alarmed. This report lays out the kind of drastic change to the system that is crucial if we are to remain a viable economic and political leader in the world." —DAVID P. DRISCOLL, COMMISSIONER OF EDUCATION, MASSACHUSETTS

"This proposal is radical? Yes. Hard to achieve? Of course. Essential? Absolutely. Our nation's schools are failing to educate our children, and that has to stop—else we condemn our own kids to ever lower incomes. We must act—now!" —WILLIAM E. BROCK, FORMER SECRETARY OF LABOR, REAGAN ADMINISTRATION

"Being a member of this Commission was exciting and enlightening. I emerged convinced that there is an urgent need for precisely the kind of national discussion—probing and thoughtful—that we had and that this report is intended to provoke. It is essential that these recommendations get a full and fair hearing." —BEVERLY O'NEILL, FORMER MAYOR, LONG BEACH, CALIFORNIA

"This provocative report challenges all of us to act now. Entire nations are working harder and studying longer in order to enjoy what many Americans have come to take for granted. The question is: Are there states or communities with the confidence and the courage to act before it is too late? In 1983, we were *A Nation at Risk.* Twenty-three years later, in 2006, the risk is even greater. It is getting late. For the sake of our children and our future, read this report and get to work." —JOHN ENGLER, PRESIDENT, NATIONAL ASSOCIATION OF MANUFACTURERS

"I commend the Commission for a report that presents bold and promising proposals to deal with the issues that our nation and its workforce will face in the 21st century." —JOEL I. KLEIN, CHANCELLOR, NEW YORK CITY PUBLIC SCHOOLS

Tough Choices *or* Tough Times

THE REPORT OF THE *new* COMMISSION ON THE SKILLS OF THE AMERICAN WORKFORCE, REVISED AND EXPANDED

NCEE
National Center On
EDUCATION
And The Economy ®

JOSSEY-BASS
A Wiley Imprint
www.josseybass.com

Published by Jossey-Bass
A Wiley Imprint
989 Market Street, San Francisco, CA 94103-1741 www.josseybass.com

Jossey-Bass books and products are available through most bookstores. To contact Jossey-Bass directly, call our Customer Care Department within the U.S. at 800-956-7739, outside the U.S. at 317-572-3986, or fax 317-572-4002.

Jossey-Bass also publishes its books in a variety of electronic formats. Some content that appears in print may not be available in electronic books.

Credits appear on p. 171

ISBN: 978-0-470-26756-1

Library of Congress Catologing-in-Publication data has been applied for.

Printed in the United States of America
REVISED EDITION
PB Printing   10 9 8 7 6 5 4 3 2 1

NATIONAL CENTER ON
EDUCATION AND THE ECONOMY

The National Center on Education and the Economy is a nonprofit organization created to develop proposals for building the world-class education and training system that the United States must have if it is to continue to be a world-class economy. The National Center engages in policy analysis and development and works collaboratively with others at the local, state, and national levels to advance its proposals in the policy arena.

National Center on Education and the Economy
555 13th Street NW
Suite 500 West
Washington, DC 20004
(202) 783-3668
www.ncee.org
www.skillscommission.org

THE *NEW* COMMISSION ON THE SKILLS OF THE AMERICAN WORKFORCE

CHARLES B. KNAPP

PAUL A. ELSNER

MARC S. TUCKER

JOHN ENGLER

MORTON BAHR

STEVE GUNDERSON

WILLIAM E. BROCK

CLIFFORD B. JANEY

JUDY B. CODDING

SHARON LYNN KAGAN

MICHAEL DOLAN

JOEL I. KLEIN

DAVID P. DRISCOLL

DAL LAWRENCE

Ray Marshall

RAY MARSHALL

Richard W. Riley

RICHARD W. RILEY

Marc H. Morial

MARC H. MORIAL

Henry B. Schacht

HENRY B. SCHACHT

Beverly O'Neill

BEVERLY O'NEILL

Susan Sclafani

SUSAN SCLAFANI

Roderick Paige

RODERICK PAIGE

Harry A. Spence

HARRY A. SPENCE

Thomas W. Payzant

THOMAS W. PAYZANT

A. William Wiggenhorn

A. WILLIAM WIGGENHORN

Charles B. Reed

CHARLES B. REED

Contents

INTRODUCTION TO THE REVISED EDITION...................................XV
Marc Tucker, President, National Center on Education and the Economy

EXECUTIVE SUMMARY XXI

PREFACE..XXXIX

PROLOGUE XLI

PART I :

The Nature of the Challenge Now I

PART II :

*The Scenario: The Recommendations as They Might
Look from the Vantage Point of an Observer in 2021* 47

COMMENTS 96

BACKGROUND PAPERS

Estimates of the Additional Expense and Savings Associated
with the Commission's Proposed Reforms in Elementary
and Secondary Education...98

Teachers and Teaching Policy......................................127

Early Childhood Education...136

The Adult Workforce...139

COMMENTARY ON THE REPORT

"Tough Choices": Change the System, or Suffer the Consequences 150
Marc S. Tucker

"Tough Choices": Radical Ideas, Misguided Assumptions 154
Diane Ravitch

Education's "Grand Departure": Defending the Skills
Commission's Vision for the Future 158
Thomas W. Payzant, Charles B. Reed

Making Tough Choices 160
Marc S. Tucker

The *New* Commission on the Skills of the American Workforce:
Old News or New News? 166
Denis P. Doyle

Big Challenges, Bold Ideas 170
Michael J. Petrilli

False Alarm 174
Lawrence Mishel, Richard Rothstein

The Economic Case for Education Reform 180
Marc S. Tucker

Improper Diagnosis, Reckless Treatment 185
Lawrence Mishel, Richard Rothstein

Reckless and Wildly Exaggerated? We Don't Think So!
A Response to Mishel and Rothstein 193
Marc S. Tucker

APPENDIXES

The Study 200

Trustees of the National Center on Education and the Economy 209

Biographies of the Members of the Commission 210

Commission Staff and Associates 220

Introduction to the Revised Edition

We began to brief the press on *Tough Choices,* as our report has come to be known, a few days before it was formally released on December 14, 2006. Almost immediately, we could feel a sense of excitement among the press.

Just before the report was released, it was featured in a cover article in *Time* magazine. The day it was released, Tom Friedman, the legendary *New York Times* columnist, urged the readers of his column to read it. The next day, articles, op-eds, and editorials appeared in the *Wall Street Journal,* the *Washington Post,* the *New York Times* (beyond the Friedman piece), the *Chicago Tribune,* the *Los Angeles Times,* and many other dailies. It was featured on *CBS News* and the Lou Dobbs show on CNN and on NPR. And the press just kept on coming, week after week, month after month. The Web site we set up for the commission report was overwhelmed by the flood of hits, and our Internet provider had to upgrade its server before it recovered. Within a week, Amazon.com had to place another book order to our grateful publisher to keep up.

Part of the excitement, I think, had to do with the fact that this report was proposing not a new set of education policies or programs but was, in some sense, proposing a new "constitution" for the education system itself, a new set of agreements on a different way to structure the entire enterprise. It seemed to meet an enormous hunger for a way to get beyond the tired arguments of the education reform debate, to reframe that debate in a new way—a way that would, as some put it, make for some proportionality between the scale of the problems that we face and the scale of the solutions that are offered.

Andrew Romanoff, the Speaker of the House of Representatives in Colorado, in remarks he made at our release event, may have captured at least one dimension of what made this report different. In Colorado, he said, the debate about education had long been a dialogue of the deaf. There was no problem in education, according to the Democrats, that could not be solved with more money (he is a Democrat). And as the Republicans in his state saw it, the best solutions to all problems with the education system were market solutions. The two sides, he said, had engaged for years in a dialogue of the deaf. But *Tough Choices* had made possible a whole new conversation, a much more constructive one.

This is no accident.

Social change almost never happens in small, easy increments over long periods of time. To the contrary, the process of social change is much more explosive than that. There are long periods of stability in policy and structure, and then an eruption. At some point, a new set of ideas is put forward that catches the wave and becomes institutionalized. Various public and private interests grow up around the new institutional structure. People are employed by that structure and learn how to protect their job security in the new system. Contractors learn how to get contracts for themselves in that system. The public learns how to negotiate the systems for themselves and their families. Over time, the whole system develops an aura of inevitability and tradition that further sanctifies it—until, finally, more and more people realize that circumstances have changed and the system no longer works for them.

The interests that have grown powerful under the established system, however, do not give up without a fight, even though they themselves often think privately that the old system no longer works for them either. They will protect the old system because the revolutionaries are holding those who appear to benefit from the old system responsible for all the problems, and they are afraid that they will get swept away by the flood of reform. So they hang on ever tighter.

The solution to this problem is not a war between the revolutionaries and those with vested interests in the system. It is to come up with a set of proposals that will change the shape of the negotiating table so that all, or almost all, of the major parties see ways to get something they never thought they would be able to get; but in order to get it, they would have to give up something a little less important that they never thought they would be willing to give up. That is just the way in which the report was constructed.

Why am I saying all this? Because the smart money in Washington had a fairly consistent view of this report when it came out: accurate analysis, maybe the best one we have seen so far, they said, and a good set of recommendations, maybe the only ones that will get us out of this mess. But it will never happen. "They" will never let it happen. Pie in the sky, they said.

If that was so, these commissioners would never have signed the report. They signed it because they were persuaded that the old ways were not working, and the United States had to make a clean break from the system we all grew up with if our children were going to have a chance. These are very experienced people. None are revolutionaries. None needed the notoriety of producing a revolutionary report. The commissioners, in the end, turned out to be exactly what they were recruited to be: a representative sample of mainstream Americans who were the kind of leaders who have always turned up when we needed them the most.

So we thought we had reason to believe that if this commission could convince itself of the merit of these ideas, we and they could convince others, not in the cynical capital perhaps, but out where it really matters, out in the states.

Education in the United States is still mainly a state responsibility. Groundbreaking changes in social policy usually start in one or two states, then spread to others, and are finally embraced by the nation as a whole. The commission never imagined that we could sell the kind of changes being proposed to all of the states at once, but it seems quite possible that a few states would agree to pioneer such proposals. The nations from which we took most of the ideas in the report are the size of American states. If the ideas work there, we thought, they can work in our states, for the states have all the authority they need to adopt them.

We set out to find some dozen to fifteen states that might be seriously interested in the ideas presented in the report. We did not imagine that any state would

treat our report like a set of engineering drawings, a detailed guide for precise replication. What we were looking for were states in which a broad cross-section of government and private sector leaders want to use the framework laid out in the report as a general framework to organize their own reform program over a period of many years, incorporating under that framework both our ideas and their own, in a coherent, forceful approach to the whole range of problems we had identified in the report. Each state, we thought, would and should go at it very differently. What would be essential would be a steady focus on the system as a whole and a readiness to adopt the most powerful system possible, notwithstanding all the pressures to cut corners and meet the constituencies halfway. This would take great leadership, but also the concerted actions of many, many people in the state.

There was only one way to put such ideas to the test, and that was to go out to the states that would have us and begin the conversation. And that is what we did.

In January, a few weeks after we released the report, we were invited by two Colorado foundations to come to the state for three days to talk with many different groups interested in the report, make a presentation open to the public, and talk with the press. By that time, former senator Bill Brock, one of the commission members, had agreed to co-chair the implementation phase with me, and so the two of us flew to Denver.

We began with a meeting with the top legislators in the state. Then that afternoon, we went to the only public meeting of the visit. The organizers had expected maybe 50 people to show up and had gotten a room that seated 200. But that number had signed up two weeks before the event, so they moved us to a room in the convention center that seats 600 people. When we walked in, all the seats were taken, and there were many people sitting on the floor. When this two-hour meeting was over, Speaker Romanoff stood by the door and asked participants as they left what they thought of what they had heard. Overwhelmingly, he reported, they wanted to know when Colorado could get started.

The next day, we met for two hours with the Colorado Education Association, the state affiliate of the National Education Association, then for another two hours with the Colorado School Boards Association. Both meetings started out a bit frosty, but in both cases, they ended with many of those present asking how they could help. We discovered in the process that when we had enough time to get over the sound bites and move into the substance, we had very different reactions than the Washington analysts had predicted. Over the course of the three days, we met with the governor, the lieutenant governor, several key business leaders and business groups, higher education leaders, senior legislators, and key players in elementary and secondary education, as well as the general public. In almost every case, these meetings took place in small groups and were long enough to enable productive conversations.

And we met with the press. Before we arrived, the advance press had not been particularly favorable. But as the three days unwound, it was progressively positive, because the press too had been able to see a lot of tough questions thrown our way and to hear the exchanges that followed.

We have now had a chance to do this in a growing number of states. We have been back to Colorado and to other states, in some cases a number of times. In each case, we have been able to continue the conversation with a growing number of people and to get a growing number enthusiastic about the report and the prospect of a longer-term relationship with our organization. There are now about a dozen states that we have either barnstormed in the way I have just described or have plans to do so.

We set out to barnstorm at least a dozen states at least once by the close of calendar year 2007. During the first couple of months in 2008, we will narrow the field to the four to six states in which we are going to concentrate our efforts for the next five years or more. We will, of course, provide at least some help to any state that asks for it, but our time is limited, and it makes the most sense to concentrate it on those states that have made the greatest commitment and appear to have the greatest capacity to go the distance.

We are seeking foundation assistance to enable us to draw on experts from all over the world, in particular those countries that have had the greatest success in educating their students—the same countries we drew on for the ideas we offered in the commission's report.

But there is another kind of help that we also want to provide if possible. In our report, we showed how it will be possible to get great gains in student performance for a trivial net increase in cost. But the savings that make this arithmetic possible are realized only after states have made a large initial investment in the areas we have highlighted. So there is a large transition cost. The magnitude of this cost will vary by state, depending in part on which of our proposals any given state has already embarked on and funded and which have yet to be initiated. But in any case, the transition costs are likely to be nontrivial.

We have drafted federal legislation that would create a competitive program for the states, to be administered by the U.S. Department of Education. The competitive program would provide funds to states with winning proposals that convince the secretary of education that their commitment to the ideas put forth in our report and their capacity to carry them out are superior to those of their competitors.

As in our direct efforts with the states, the legislation would encourage states to create a parallel universe of policies reflecting our recommendations that would apply only in a carefully chosen set of volunteer districts. Winning states and their volunteer districts would also be eligible for waivers from key features of the No Child Left Behind (NCLB) legislation if they could demonstrate to the satisfaction of the secretary of education that they had successfully implanted the relevant features of our proposals. These waivers would not be of interest to states that simply wish to be relieved of the accountability requirements of NCLB, because the bar they will have to reach to get these waivers is set to a very high standard. But for states that are committed to high standards and are genuinely interested in alternative ways to demonstrate that they have attained them, this legislation will be very attractive. As this is written, we do not know what the fate of these proposals will be.

At the beginning of our report is an extended quotation from a book by Corelli Barnett, the eminent British historian, in which Barnett reflects on the British fall from great power status. The book, Barnett says, "documents how Britain failed to match the education and training efforts . . . being made by her challengers to supply the highly skilled and motivated workforce . . . essential for continued industrial success . . . and so by default left the way clear to the fall that was to come after the pride. Although this history concerns itself with a particular nation in a particular time, other nations in other times might profit from the moral."

And that is our hope: that our great nation might profit from the experience not only of those countries that have failed to educate their young people to the highest standards but, even more to the point, from the experience of other countries that have succeeded in doing so, in order to create an education system second to none. Without question, we can do it. But will we? That is up to you.

Given the nature of our recommendations, we expected a wide range of reactions to what we had written. In fact, no small part of our purpose was to stimulate a debate on the issues we had raised and the solutions we offered. And debate is what we got. Since the release of *Tough Choices* in December 2006, many people have commented in print in reaction to our analysis and recommendations. And in some cases, we have had an opportunity to respond to those comments. In this revised edition of the report, we offer readers a chance to sample some of those commentaries and our responses.

Marc Tucker
President
National Center on Education
and the Economy

Executive Summary

When the report of the first Commission on the Skills of the American Workforce, *America's Choice: high skills or low wages!*, was released in 1990, the globalization of the world's economy was just getting under way. That Commission understood the threat in the straightforward terms captured in the report's subtitle. A worldwide market was developing in low-skill labor, it said, and the work requiring low skills would go to those countries where the price of low-skill labor was the lowest. If the United States wanted to continue to compete in that market, it could look forward to a continued decline in wages and very long working hours. Alternatively, it could abandon low-skill work and concentrate on competing in the worldwide market for high-value-added products and services. To do that, it would have to adopt internationally benchmarked standards for educating its students and its workers, because only countries with highly skilled workforces could successfully compete in that market.

A swiftly rising number of American workers at every skill level are in direct competition with workers in every corner of the globe.

★ ★ ★ ★

If someone can figure out the algorithm for a routine job, chances are that it is economic to automate it. Many good well-paying, middle-class jobs involve routine work of this kind and are rapidly being automated.

The first Commission never dreamed that we would end up competing with countries that could offer large numbers of highly educated workers willing to work for low wages. But China and India are doing exactly that. Indeed, it turns out that China and India are only the tip of the iceberg. Whereas for most of the 20th century the United States could take pride in having the best-educated workforce in the world, that is no longer true. Over the past 30 years, one country after another has surpassed us in the proportion of their entering workforce with the equivalent of a high school diploma, and many more are on the verge of doing so. Thirty years ago, the United States could lay claim to having 30 percent of the world's population of college students. Today that proportion has fallen to 14 percent and is continuing to fall.

While our international counterparts are increasingly getting more education, their young people are getting a better education as well. American students and young adults place anywhere from the middle to the bottom of the pack in all three continuing comparative studies of achievement in mathematics, science, and general literacy in the advanced industrial nations.

While our relative position in the world's education league tables has continued its long slow decline, the structure of the global economy has continued to evolve. Every day, more and more of the work that people do ends up in a digitized form. From X-rays used for medical diagnostic purposes, to songs, movies, architectural drawings, technical papers, and novels, that work is saved on a hard disk and transmitted instantly over the Internet to someone near or far who makes use of it in an endless variety of ways. Because this is so, employers everywhere have access to a worldwide workforce composed of people who do not have to move to participate in work teams that are truly global. Because this is so, a swiftly rising number of American workers at every skill level are in direct competition with workers in every corner of the globe. So it matters very much that, increasingly, it is easier and easier for employers everywhere to get workers who are better skilled at lower cost than American workers.

Another important trend in the global economy bears on this point. A century ago, the United States led the world in the process of vertical integration, where corporations performed every function necessary to get their products to market, from the mining of the raw materials right through to the sale of those products through retail outlets to the final customer. Today, the United States is once again a leader, this time in the deconstruction of the vertically integrated firm. Corporate analysts identify each step in the process and ask whether the firm is a leader in that step, and, if not, who in the world can do that work at the needed level of quality at the lowest possible cost. The firm then contracts with the best providers of each of those services and keeps only those functions that it can do best. This is outsourcing. Firms that do not do this will inevitably be put out of business by firms that do. In this way, many functions that have always been performed by American workers in American firms will

be outsourced to workers in other countries who do them better and cheaper.

In many cases, the work will be done not by people in other countries, but rather by machines. With the rapid advance of new technologies, it is becoming progressively less expensive to automate functions that used to be performed by people. As the cost of labor rises and the cost of automating jobs continues to fall, it becomes both possible and necessary for firms simply to eliminate job after job now being done by humans. Earlier, almost all the jobs subject to automation were low-skill jobs. That is no longer true. Now it is more accurate to say that the jobs that are most vulnerable are the jobs involving routine work. If someone can figure out the algorithm for a routine job, chances are that it is economical to automate it. Many good, well-paying, middle-class jobs involve routine work of this kind and are rapidly being automated.

In this environment, it makes sense to ask how American workers can possibly maintain, to say nothing of improve, their current standard of living. Today, Indian engineers make $7,500 a year against $45,000 for an American engineer with the same qualifications. If we succeed in matching the very high levels of mastery of mathematics and science of these Indian engineers — an enormous challenge for this country — why would the world's employers pay us more than they have to pay the Indians to do their work? They would be willing to do that only if we could offer something that the Chinese and Indians, and others, cannot.

Those countries that produce the most important new products and services can capture a premium in world markets that will enable them to pay high wages to their citizens. In many industries, producing the most important new products and services depends on maintaining the worldwide technological lead, year in and year out, in that industry and in the new industries that new technologies generate. But that kind of leadership does not depend on technology alone. It depends on a deep vein of creativity that is constantly renewing itself, and on a myriad of people who can imagine how people can use things that have never been available before, create ingenious marketing and sales campaigns, write books, build furniture, make movies, and imagine new kinds of software that will capture people's imagination and become indispensable to millions.

This is a world in which a very high level of preparation in reading, writing, speaking, mathematics, science, literature, history, and the arts will be an indispensable foundation for everything that comes after for most members of the workforce. It is a world in which comfort with ideas and abstractions is the passport to a good job, in which creativity and innovation are the key to the good life, in which high levels of education — a very different kind of education than most of us have had — are going to be the only security there is.

A world in which routine work is largely done by machines is a world in which mathematical reasoning will be no less important than math facts, in which line workers who cannot contribute to the design of the products they are fabricating may be as obsolete as the last model of that product, in which auto mechanics will have to figure out what to do when the many computers in the cars they are working on do not function as they were designed to function, in which software engineers who are also musicians and artists will have an edge over those who are not as the entertainment industry evolves, in which it will pay architects to know something about nanotechnology, and small businesspeople who build custom yachts and fishing boats will be able to survive only if they quickly learn a lot about the scientific foundations of carbon fiber composites.

It is a world in which the rewards will go to the marketing director who sees the opportunity to build a global business in cars selling for $2,000 each, where others see only poor people who can't afford cars; the clothing designer whose grasp of the direction of fashion is uniquely matched to her understanding of the new fabrics that the new technologies are making possible, and creates the perfect match of fabric and taste and . . .

The best employers the world over will be looking for the most competent, most creative, and most innovative people on the face of the earth and will be willing to pay them top dollar for their services. This will be true not just for the top professionals and managers, but up and down the length and breadth of the workforce.

Strong skills in English, mathematics, technology, and science, as well as literature, history, and the arts will be essential for many; beyond this, candidates will have to be comfortable with ideas and abstractions, good at both analysis and synthesis, creative and innovative, self-disciplined and well organized, able to learn very quickly and work well as a member of a team and have the flexibility to adapt quickly to frequent changes in the labor market as the shifts in the economy become ever faster and more dramatic.

If we continue on our current course, and the number of nations outpacing us in the education race continues to grow at its current rate, the American standard of living will steadily fall relative to those nations, rich and poor, that are doing a better job. If the gap gets to a certain — but unknowable — point, the world's investors will conclude that they can get a greater return on their funds elsewhere, and it will be almost impossible to reverse course. Although it is possible to construct a scenario for improving our standard of living, the clear and present danger is that it will fall for most Americans.

The core problem is that our education and training systems were built for another era, an era in which most workers needed only a rudimentary education. It is not possible to get where we have to go by patching that system. There is not enough money available at any level of our intergovernmental system to fix this problem by spending more on the system we have. We can get where we must go only by changing the system itself.

To do that, we must face a few facts. The first is that we recruit a disproportionate share of our teachers from among the less able of the high school students who go to college. The second is that we tolerate an

This is a world in which a very high level of preparation in reading, writing, speaking, mathematics, science, literature, history, and the arts will be an indispensable foundation for everything that comes after for most members of the workforce.

★ ★ ★ ★

The best employers the world over will be looking for the most competent, most creative, and most innovative people on the face of the earth and will be willing to pay them top dollar for their services. This will be true not just for the top professionals and managers, but up and down the length and breadth of the workforce. Those countries that produce the most important new products and services can capture a premium in world markets that will enable them to pay high wages to their citizens.

That kind of leadership does not depend on technology alone. It depends on a deep vein of creativity that is constantly renewing itself. Now many students just slide through high school, because they know that all they have to do is get passes in their courses or a satisfactory score on an 8th- or 9th-grade-level literacy test to go to college. With this system, they will know that they have to work hard in school to get anywhere, and, the evidence shows, that is exactly what they will do.

★ ★ ★ ★

The core problem is that our education and training systems were built for another era. We can get where we must go only by changing the system itself.

enormous amount of waste in the system, failing our students in the early years when the cost of doing the job right would be relatively low, and trying to remediate it later at much higher cost. The third is that this inherently inefficient system has gotten progressively more inefficient over time. While the standards movement has produced real gains, especially for minority students, in recent years, those gains have been leveling off, and the gains have been modest in relation to the increase in per-pupil expenditures over the last thirty years. The fourth is that the growing inequality in family incomes is contributing heavily to the growing disparities in student achievement. The fifth is that we have failed to motivate most of our students to take tough courses and work hard, thus missing one of the most important drivers of success in the best-performing nations. The sixth is that our teacher compensation system is designed to reward time in service, rather than to attract the best and brightest of our college students and reward the best of our teachers. The seventh is that, too often, our testing system rewards students who will be good at routine work, while not providing opportunities for students to display creative and innovative thinking and analysis. The eighth is that, too often, we have built a bureaucracy in our schools in which, apart from the superintendent of schools, the people who have the responsibility do not have the power, and the people who have the power do not have the responsibility. The ninth is that most of the people who will be in our workforce are already in it, and if they cannot master the new literacy at high levels, it will not matter what we do in our schools. And the tenth is that although we have an elaborate funding mechanism to provide funds to send young people to college and university to launch them in the careers of their choice, we have done a very poor job of making it possible for adults who have full-time jobs and family responsibilities to get the continuing education and training they need to survive in the world that is coming.

But the most important truth is none of these. It is that we do not need new programs, and we need less money than one might think. The one thing that is indispensable is a new system. The problem is not with our educators. It is with the system in which they work. That is what the new Commission focused on. And it is the implementation of this system that will take courage and leadership.

Our recommendations follow. As you read them, bear in mind that our aim here is to stimulate the creative energies of our states, where most of the responsibility for these core functions in American life resides. We will not be disappointed if one state chooses to do it one way and another chooses a different path. We did not write legislative specifications. Our aim is to stimulate many variations of these ideas. But that does not mean that we encourage cherry-picking only those ideas that cost the least and offend the fewest. Without the pain inflicted by the proposals we make for saving money, there will be no gain from the ways we propose to spend it. If legislatures pocket the gains from the savings we propose and fail to make the investments we recommend, then that will simply lead to lower performance all

around. We do not propose a collection of initiatives. We propose a system that has its own integrity, though it can be implemented in many ways.

STEP 1:
Assume that we will do the job right the first time

A number of other countries assume that their students are ready for college — really ready for college — when they are 16 years old. So let's start out assuming that we can match or even exceed their performance if we are doing everything right. Further assume for the moment that we want to send everyone, or almost everyone, to college. Now set up a system to do it. Our first step is creating a set of Board Examinations. States will have their own Board Examinations, and some national and even international organizations will offer their own. A Board Exam is an exam in a set of core subjects that is based on a syllabus provided by the Board. So the point of the exam is to find out whether the student has learned from the course what he or she was supposed to learn.

For most students, the first Board Exam will come at the end of 10th grade. A few might take it earlier — some might not succeed on their first try, so they might take another year to two to succeed. The standards will be set at the expectations incorporated in the exams given by the countries that do the best job educating their students. But it will in any case be set no lower than the standard for entering community colleges in the state without

We propose a system that has its own integrity, though it can be implemented in many ways.

★ ★ ★ ★

These changes would enable the nation to pay beginning teachers about $45,000 per year, which is now the median teachers' pay, and to pay about $95,000 per year to the typical teachers working at the top of new career ladders for a regular teaching year and as much as $110,000 per year to teachers willing to work the same hours per year as other professionals typically do.

remediation. We believe that when all of our recommendations are implemented, 95 percent of our students will meet this standard.

Students who score well enough will be guaranteed the right to go to their community college to begin a program leading to a two-year technical degree or a two-year program designed to enable the student to transfer later into a four-year state college. The students who get a good enough score can stay in high school to prepare for a second Board Exam, like the ones given by the International Baccalaureate program, or the Advanced Placement exams, or another state or private equivalent. When those students are finished with their program, assuming they do well enough on their second set of Board Exams, they can go off to a selective college or university and might or might not be given college credit for the courses they took in high school. These students and the ones who went the community college route will have the option when they finish their programs of taking a second set of state Board Exams, and if they hit certain scores, they will be guaranteed the right to go to their state colleges and some state universities as juniors.

Our full report provides a lot more detail, but that is the essence of the idea. Students could challenge these Board Exams as soon as they were ready, and they could keep challenging them all their lives, if necessary. No one would fail. If they did not succeed, they would just try again.

Now many students just slide through high school, because they know that all they have to do is get passes in their courses or a satisfactory score on an 8th- or 9th-grade-level literacy test to go to college. With this system, they will know that they have to work hard in school to get anywhere, and, the evidence shows, that is exactly what they will do.

But they will have a lot of help along the way, as you will see in the next section.

STEP 2:
Make much more efficient use of the available resources

The changes just described, plus a couple we will describe in a moment, will save $67 billion nationally. Some of this will be offset by the fact that many, many fewer students will become dropouts, and we will have to pay for the students to complete school who would otherwise have dropped out. We asked ourselves what would happen if we took the savings and deployed it in roughly equal amounts against three buckets of expenditure: (1) recruiting, training, and deploying a teaching force for the nation's schools recruited from the top third of the high school students going on to college; (2) building a high-quality full-service early childhood education system for every 3- and 4-year-old student in the United States, and (3) giving the nation's disadvantaged students the resources they need to succeed against internationally benchmarked education standards. If we do not do these things, there is not a prayer that we will be able to get our 10th graders to do college-level work. But if we actually do these things, along with the other things

we recommend here, there is every reason to believe that we can send almost everyone to college and have them do well there. This redeployment of resources is a key feature of the plan to do just that.

STEP 3:
Recruit from the top third of the high school graduates going on to college for the next generation of school teachers

It is simply not possible for our students to graduate from our schools by the millions with very strong mathematical reasoning skills, a sound conceptual grasp of science, strong writing skills, world-beating capacity for creativity and innovation, and everything else we talk about in this report unless their teachers have the knowledge and skills we want our children to have.

Many of our teachers are superb. But we have for a long time gotten better teachers then we deserved because of the limited opportunities for women and minorities in our workforce. Those opportunities are far wider now, and we are left with the reality that we are now recruiting more of our teachers from the bottom third of the high school students going to college than is wise. To succeed, we must recruit many more from the top third.

To get this group requires us, first, to change the shape of teacher compensation, which is currently back-loaded, in the sense that it is weak on cash compensation, especially up front, and heavy on pensions and health benefits for the retired teacher. This is what one would want if the idea were to retain the teachers with the most years of service, but it makes no sense if what we are after is to attract young people who are thinking most about how they are going to get the cash they need to enjoy themselves, buy a home, support a family, and pay for college for their children. The first step in our plan is to make retirement benefits comparable to those of the better firms in the private sector and use the money that is saved from this measure to increase teachers' cash compensation. We would add to this a substantial amount from what is saved by changing the progression of students through the system. These changes would enable the nation to pay beginning teachers about $45,000 per year, which is now the median teachers' pay, and to pay about $95,000 per year to the typical teachers working at the top of new career ladders for a regular teaching year and as much as $110,000 per year to teachers willing to work the same hours per year as other professionals typically do.

These figures are on average for the nation as a whole. Higher-cost states would have higher salary scales, and lower-cost states would pay less. And within many states, adjustments would be made to take account of differences within the state in the cost of living. But salaries would rise substantially everywhere.

We would have teachers be employed by the state, not the local districts, on a statewide salary schedule. There would be salary increments for especially effective teachers, teachers at higher points on a new career ladder, those willing to teach in remote or especially tough urban areas, and teachers in shortage fields like mathematics and special education. Those teachers would be licensed by the state and put on a list of available teachers, but none would actually be paid until they were hired by schools (see below).

In the new system, it would be relatively easy for teachers to reach out to other teachers and form organizations to operate schools themselves, much like doctors, attorneys, and architects form partnerships to offer their services to the public.

The current policies regarding teacher education would be scrapped. The state would create a new Teacher Development Agency charged with recruiting, training, and certifying teachers. The state would launch national recruiting campaigns, allocate slots for training the needed number of teachers, and write performance contracts with schools of education, but also teachers' collaboratives, school districts, and others interested in training teachers. Those providers that meet the state's performance requirements would get a larger number of slots than providers whose graduates perform less well. To get listed by the state on its register of available teachers, candidates would have to show that they had at least a bachelor's degree in the subject they propose to teach and would have to pass a rigorous teaching performance assessment.

In states with collective bargaining laws, legislatures would need to work closely with the organizations that represent teachers to effect the kinds of changes we have in mind, for it is obviously easier to implement such changes with strong union support.

STEP 4:
Develop standards, assessments, and curriculum that reflect today's needs and tomorrow's requirements

Many states have tests that students must pass to graduate from high school. But few require more than an 8th-grade-level of literacy in international terms. While many states have increased the proportion of the test that enables students to construct their own answers to questions rather than select an answer from a preselected list, these tests still have a way to go to provide the kinds of information that the world's best high school exit examinations provide. On balance, they are designed to measure the acquisition of discipline-based knowledge in the core subjects in the curriculum, but, more often than not, little or nothing is done to measure many of the other qualities that we have suggested may spell the difference between success and failure for the students who will grow up to be the workers of 21st century America: creativity and innovation, facility with the use of ideas and abstractions, the self-discipline and organization needed to manage one's work and drive it through to a successful conclusion, the ability to function well as a member of a team, and so on.

Moving from America's tests to the kinds of examinations and assessments that will capture these and other qualities at the level of accomplishment required will entail a major overhaul of the American testing industry. If that is not done, then nothing else will matter, because the old saw that what gets measured is what gets taught is essentially true. A system that pursues the

The changes just described, plus a couple we will describe in a moment, will save $67 billion nationally.

★ ★ ★ ★

We asked ourselves what would happen if we took the savings and deployed it in roughly equal amounts against three buckets of expenditure: (1) recruiting, training, and deploying a teaching force for the nation's schools recruited from the top third of the high school students going on to college; (2) building a high-quality full-service early childhood education system for every 3- and 4-year-old student in the United States, and (3) giving the nation's disadvantaged students the resources they need to succeed against internationally benchmarked education standards.

★ ★ ★ ★

Moving from America's tests to the kinds of examinations and assessments that will capture these and other qualities at the level of accomplishment required will entail a major overhaul of the American testing industry.

wrong goals more efficiently is not a system this nation needs.

When we have the right assessments, and they are connected to the right syllabi, then the task will be to create instructional materials fashioned in the same spirit and train our teachers to use the standards, assessments, syllabi, and materials as well as possible, just as we train our physicians to use the techniques, tools, and pharmaceuticals at their command as well as possible. But it all starts with the standards and assessments.

STEP 5:
Create high performance schools and districts everywhere — how the system should be governed, financed, organized, and managed

The governance, organizational, and management scheme of American schools was created in the early years of the 20th century to match the industrial organization of the time. It was no doubt appropriate for an era when most work required relatively low literacy levels, most teachers had little more education than their students, and efficiency of a rather mechanical sort was the highest value of the system.

In recent years, American industry has shed this management model in favor of high-performance management models designed to produce high-quality products and services with highly educated workers. Some school districts are moving in this direction. That movement needs to be accelerated, formalized, and brought to scale. We share here one way to make that work. No doubt there are others that would work as well.

Schools would have complete discretion over the way their funds are spent, their staffing schedule, their organization and management of the school, their schedule, and their program, as long as they provided the curriculum and met the testing and other accountability requirements imposed by the state.

First, the role of school boards would change. Schools would no longer be owned by local school districts. Instead, schools would be operated by independent contractors, many of them limited-liability corporations owned and run by teachers. The primary role of school district central offices would be to write performance contracts with the operators of these schools, monitor their operations, cancel or decide not to renew the contracts of those providers that did not perform well, and find others that could do better. The local boards would also be responsible for collecting a wide range of data from the operators specified by the state, verifying these data, forwarding them to the state, and sharing them with the public and with parents of children in the schools. They would also be responsible for connecting the schools to a wide range of social services in the community, a function made easier in those cases in which the mayor is responsible for both those services and the schools.

The contract schools would be public schools, subject to all of the safety, curriculum, testing, and other accountability requirements of public schools. The teachers in these schools would be employees of the state, as previously noted.

The schools would be funded directly by the state, according to a pupil-weighting formula as described above. The schools would have complete discretion over the way their funds are spent, the staffing schedule, their organization and management, their schedule, and their program, as long as they provided the curriculum and met the testing

and other accountability requirements imposed by the state.

Both the state and the district could create a wide range of performance incentives for the schools to improve the performance of their students. Schools would be encouraged to reach out to the community and parents and would have strong incentives to do so. Districts could provide support services to the schools, but the schools would be free to obtain the services they needed wherever they wished.

No organization could operate a school that was not affiliated with a helping organization approved by the state, unless the school was itself such an organization. These helping organizations — which could range from schools of education to teachers' collaboratives to for-profit and nonprofit organizations — would have to have the capacity to provide technical assistance and training to the schools in their network on a wide range of matters ranging from management and accounting to curriculum and pedagogy.

Parents and students could choose among all the available contract schools, taking advantage of the performance data these schools would be obligated to produce. Oversubscribed schools would not be permitted to discriminate in admissions. Districts would be obligated to make sure that there were sufficient places for all the students who needed places. The competitive, data-based market, combined with the performance contracts themselves, would create schools that were constantly seeking to improve their performance year in and year out. The fact that schools

High-quality early childhood education is one of the best investments a nation can make in its young people.

★ ★ ★ ★

The Commission's proposals, taken together, should transform the prospects of disadvantaged children.

serving students from low-income families and other categories of disadvantaged students would get substantially more money than schools with more advantaged student bodies would ensure that these students would be served by high-quality school operators. It would be very hard for low-quality school operators to survive in this environment.

STEP 6:
Provide high-quality, universal early childhood education

For decades, researchers have almost universally concluded that high-quality early childhood education is one of the best investments a nation can make in its young people. But this country has never committed the funds necessary to provide high-quality early childhood education to its 3- and 4-year-olds. The funds freed up by the Commission's proposals for altering the student progression through the system will, for the first time, make it possible for the whole nation to do what should have been done many years ago.

STEP 7:
Give strong support to the students who need it the most

The Commission's proposals, taken together, should transform the prospects of disadvantaged children. The proposal to abandon local funding of schools in favor of state funding using a uniform pupil-weighting funding formula, combined with the addition of $19 billion to the system as a whole, will make it possible, for the first time in the history of the United States, to have an equitable means of funding our schools, while at the same time leveling up the funding of the system as a whole, so that relatively well-to-do districts will not have the incentive to defeat the system that they would have if the existing funds were simply redistributed.

The additional funds for schools serving high concentrations of disadvantaged students will make it possible for those schools to stay open from early in the morning until late at night, offering a wide range of supportive services to the students and their families. They will have the funds needed to screen and diagnose their students, and to make sure that they get the eyeglasses they need or the hearing aids or the therapy for dyslexia or any of the many other things that have prevented these children from learning as well as their wealthier peers. These schools will be able to afford the tutors they need, the counselors and mentors that are the birthright of richer children elsewhere. And they will have the staff needed to reach out to the community and to find the community leaders in the private sector who will develop campaigns to raise the aspirations of these young people, so they come to believe that they too can reach the top if they work hard enough.

In this scheme, schools serving poor students will no longer be routinely outbid for the services of our best teachers by wealthier communities. Nor will our experienced teachers be able to avoid teaching the students who need them the most by virtue of their seniority in the system. In fact, our teachers will be offered additional financial incentives to teach in remote areas and our toughest urban neighborhoods. And the state Teacher Development Agencies will be charged with making a special effort to recruit first-rate teachers for our minority children who look like them and can connect with these children. In all these ways and more, this plan will give the students who need our help the most a much better chance than they have now.

STEP 8:
Enable every member of the adult workforce to get the new literacy skills

As we pointed out above, most of the people we will have in our workforce in 20 years are in the workforce now. The Commission proposes that the federal government pass legislation entitling every adult and young adult worker — at no charge — to the education required to meet the standard set by the new Board Exam standards that most young people will meet by age 16. This is the standard that the state determines will entitle the holder to enter college without remediation.

Not all young adults and older members of the workforce will choose to take advantage of this opportunity, but many will. And, as some do, others will be encouraged to try. In this way, millions of people whose prospects can only be described as grim will get a new lease on life, and the economy as a whole will become much more productive. High schools all over the country and many other institutions as well will find that they have a new clientele of people who will be very grateful for a second chance at the opportunities that life affords those with an education.

STEP 9:
Create personal competitiveness accounts — a GI Bill for our times

The intention of Step 8 is to provide a foundation of high literacy among our entire workforce. But foundation literacy is not enough. Our economic analysis suggests that the next few decades will be a time of increasing turbulence in the job market as outsourcing increases, product cycles get shorter, and technological change destroys not just firms but entire industries with increasing frequency. In this environment, it will be extremely important that workers everywhere be able to get the training they need to move quickly to other jobs, other professions, and other industries over and over again. As we noted above, the higher education finance system was set up to serve the needs of full-time students, not full-time workers with family obligations, the very people we are talking about here. So we propose that the government of the United States create Personal Competitiveness Accounts enabling everyone to get the continuing education and training they will need throughout their work lives. The government would create these accounts for every baby when born, with an initial deposit of $500, and continue to contribute at a lower level until that young person is 16, and later if the account holder was earning very little. The account would earn tax-protected interest as long as there was

principal in it. Employers could contribute to it tax free. So could the individual, through salary reductions, and even states might want to contribute as well. The account holder could use the money to pay for tuition at any accredited institution for any work-related program of study, as well as books and fees.

The cost of getting our adults to the new standards of literacy, combined with the cost of this new GI Bill, comes to about $31 billion per year. This is a lot of money for a country deeply in debt. But it is probably the single most important investment we can make in our economic future. No other step the nation could take would have a higher payoff in economic agility and competitiveness, for both the individual and the society as a whole.

STEP 10:
Create regional competitiveness authorities to make America competitive

Government-funded job training programs in the United States were mostly created to provide relatively unskilled people the skills needed to get a job — any job — as quickly as possible. So it is not surprising that government-funded job training has not, on the whole, been connected to the government's efforts to stimulate economic development. That being so, the jobs that people who go through this system get are all too often short term and dead end. It is now clear that the most effective strategies for economic development are technology based and regionally focused. It is also clear that the most effective way to provide a real future for people who need jobs is to provide training that is related to the economic future of the region those people live in, for jobs in growth industries.

So the Commission recommends that the federal government develop legislation to encourage the states to create regional economic development authorities involving the key leaders from many sectors in those regions in the development of economic development strategies that make sense to them. These authorities would not only be responsible for coming up with development goals and strategies for their regions, but also for coordinating the work of the region's education and training institutions to make sure that each region's workers develop the skills and knowledge needed to be successful in that labor market.

We settled on the word "authorities" to describe these new bodies because we wanted to convey the idea that they need to be more than debating societies. They need to be able to raise and spend the money needed to develop their regions over time. If these new bodies are as successful as we think they will be, the federal government should consider lifting many of the restrictions on the separate programs they will administer and permitting them to combine the funds from these programs in ways that are more likely to lead to both strong economic growth and strong job growth, especially for the most vulnerable people in the country.

We propose that the government of the United States create Personal Competitiveness Accounts enabling everyone to get the continuing education and training they will need throughout their work lives.

★ ★ ★ ★

Encourage the states to create regional economic development authorities responsible not only for coming up with development goals and strategies for their regions, but also for coordinating the work of the region's education and training institutions.

★ ★ ★ ★

Millions of people whose prospects can be described only as grim will get a new lease on life, and the economy as a whole will become much more productive.

PREFACE

The report of NCEE's first Commission on the Skills of the American Workforce, *America's Choice: high skills or low wages!,* was released 16 years ago in New York City. Its message was that, in a globalized world, there would be no place for the low-skilled to hide. We had to educate everyone to the standards that the world's highest performers had set.

Over the next few years, almost all of the Commission's recommendations were transmuted into national and state legislation, and it was clear that the idea of a standards-based education system — one of the driving ideas in the report — had taken hold of the popular imagination.

Last year, however, Marc Tucker, President of the National Center, persuaded NCEE's Board of Trustees that it was time to create a new Commission. The advent of China and India as major world players on the world's economic stage had made it clear that it was now possible for large nations to offer high skills at low wages, a possibility that we had not dreamed of in 1990. The education and training reforms the nation had launched in the 1990s, partly in response to our first report, were clearly inadequate to meet the new challenge.

What the Commission has produced is no less than a framework for a major reorganization of the states' education and training systems. Few of the Commissioners began this task as revolutionaries, but the data and analysis have convinced us that the alternative to dealing with the tough issues described in this report will be the steady erosion of the American standard of living.

Generous gifts from the Annie E. Casey Foundation, the Bill and Melinda Gates Foundation, the William and Flora Hewlett Foundation, and the Lumina Foundation for Education made our work possible. We are deeply grateful for that, but we need to note that none of our benefactors are in any other way responsible for what we have written here.

The Commissioners also wish to express a deep debt of gratitude to the entire staff who worked so hard and well on this report.

We would be remiss if we did not single out the central contributions of Marc Tucker to this report. Marc has a unique and extraordinary grasp of the issues considered in this report. It was his leadership that brought the Commission to understand both the scale of the current threat and the dramatic nature of the policy changes that were necessary.

CHARLES B. KNAPP
Chairman

PROLOGUE

This book portrays a great nation which, even in the pride of apparent world power, was already rotting towards its fall. It portrays a nation blinded by that very pride to the signs of decay at the technological roots of its strength. It analyzes the poignant contrast between this waning strength and a national illusion of continuing greatness, a national dream of an ideal society where all should enjoy opportunity and none should be poor. It demonstrates how a nation will cling to the political and economic faiths of its past era of creativity and expansionism even after fundamental change in the operating environment has rendered these faiths suspect as strategies for survival.

The nation in question is Great Britain, original engine room of the industrial revolution. . . . The historical focus of this study lies in the Second World War. . . . For the Second World War subjected Great Britain to a ruthless audit of her resources . . . , an audit concealed from the nation at the time by patriotic myth and propaganda and by the outward facade of victory.

The "audit of war" demonstrates that Britain was failing exactly where she believed herself most successful — as an advanced technological society. She had neglected to adapt and modernize the traditional industries in which she had once been the world leader, and so had been surpassed by newly industrialized nations, where industries and mindset were "green-field." The War demonstrates that in the most advanced technologies Britain had allowed her competition to outstrip her, except in the specialized field of defense Research and Development, so leading to immense imports of foreign technology, with devastating consequences for the balance of payments.

The analysis probes deeper still, into social conditions and the quality of national education. It documents how Britain failed to match the education and training efforts at all levels being made by her challengers to supply the highly skilled and motivated workforce and professional management essential for continued industrial success. It reveals how [the] factors of poor education and training and "them and us" industrial relations compounded with appalling urban living conditions to produce a workforce in no way a match for competition in terms of developed intelligence and capability or effective team effort.

And finally the book analyzes how and why this outwardly still great nation and world power failed to embark on the necessary profound adaptation of itself as an industrial society — and so by default left the way clear to the fall that was to come after the pride. Although this history concerns itself with a particular nation in a particular time, other nations in other times might profit from the moral.

CORELLI BARNETT, military historian, quoted from the Preface to the American edition of *The Pride and the Fall: The Dream and Illusion of Britain as a Great Nation* (NEW YORK: FREE PRESS, 1987, pp. xi–xii)

TIME LINE

1989 BERLIN WALL COMES DOWN
    U.S. TRADE DEFICIT WITH CHINA IS $6.2 BILLION

1990 *America's Choice* REPORT RELEASED

1991 GORBACHEV RESIGNS AS LAST PRESIDENT OF U.S.S.R.

1992 BILL CLINTON ELECTED PRESIDENT
    NAFTA TRADE PACT SIGNED

1993 51-DAY SIEGE OF WACO

1994 NELSON MANDELA BECOMES PRESIDENT OF SOUTH AFRICA

1995 THE INTERNET IS TURNED OVER TO COMMERCIAL PROVIDERS

1996 BILL CLINTON REELECTED PRESIDENT
    74% OF AMERICANS WORK IN SERVICE INDUSTRIES
    INTERNET USE INCREASES ONE-HUNDREDFOLD FROM PREVIOUS YEAR

1997 CHINA RESUMES CONTROL OF HONG KONG

1998 DOLLY, A SCOTTISH SHEEP, CLONED

1999 INFOSYS BECOMES FIRST INDIAN-REGISTERED COMPANY TO LIST ON
    THE NASDAQ

2000 GEORGE W. BUSH ELECTED PRESIDENT
    NUMBER OF ADULTS USING THE INTERNET EXCEEDS 100 MILLION IN U.S.

2001 WORLD TRADE CENTER DESTROYED
    UNITED STATES INVADES AFGHANISTAN

2002 ENRON AND ARTHUR ANDERSEN COLLAPSE IN SCANDAL
    PASSAGE OF NO CHILD LEFT BEHIND ACT

2003 UNITED STATES INVADES IRAQ

2004 RED SOX WIN THE WORLD SERIES
    GEORGE W. BUSH REELECTED PRESIDENT
    GOOGLE'S IPO

2005 HURRICANE KATRINA DEVASTATES NEW ORLEANS
    U.S. TRADE DEFICIT WITH CHINA BALLOONS TO $201.5 BILLION

2006 *Tough Choices* OR *Tough Times* REPORT RELEASED

Part

THE NATURE OF THE CHALLENGE NOW

In the spring of 1990, in the Grand Hyatt Hotel in New York City, the Commission on the Skills of the American Workforce released its report, *America's Choice: high skills or low wages!* Looking back over the two preceding decades, the Commission observed that real average weekly wages had dropped more than 12 percent. A few Americans had become richer but a far larger number had lost ground. More than ever before, this earnings gap reflected differences in education. What we earned was increasingly a function of what we had learned.

That first Commission had worked hard to understand the forces at work on the American economy and had concluded that globalization, only then really gathering force, was creating a new world, a world in which there would be less and less room in the advanced industrial nations for people with relatively low skills, because the plummeting costs of transportation and telecommunications were putting low-skilled workers in high-cost countries in direct competition with low-skilled workers in low-cost countries, and that was a competition that our low-skilled workers could only lose.

The alternative, the first Commission said, was to go after the worldwide market for high-value-added products and services, and the only way we could successfully compete in that market was through a form of work organization that demanded high skills on the part of virtually everyone, from the boardroom to the hourly workers on the factory floor.

The solution put forward in the 1990 report was to provide to the vast majority

AMERICA HAS BEEN DIVIDED INTO COLLEGE HAVES AND HAVE-NOTS

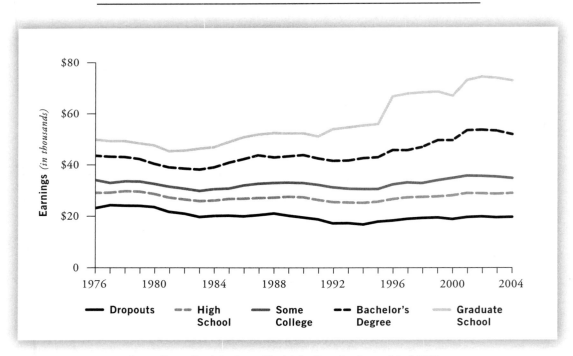

Source: *Current Population Survey*, March Labor Force Supplement (March 2005).

of American elementary and secondary students a kind and quality of education that had heretofore been afforded only to a privileged few, and to create a job training system designed to provide higher skills to many employed adults. Based on its extensive review of the countries with the best education and training systems, the report proposed that the United States create a strongly standards-based approach to education and training at every level.

That was 16 years ago. It turns out that the first Commission was right. People with no high school diploma have seen their earnings continue to erode. Those with a high school diploma or some college have seen their incomes increase very modestly in the intervening years. In fact, only those with bachelor's and graduate degrees have seen a significant increase in their real wages since we issued our previous report.

But the first Commission, as it turns out, had significantly underestimated the threat as well as the extent of the reforms that would be required to respond to it.

The first Commission had summed up both the nature of the threat and the nature of the needed response in the subtitle to their report: high skills or low wages. The proposition was that high skills would lead to high wages, as night does to day.

None of the people involved in producing the first report had imagined that any country could or would produce large numbers of highly educated people willing to work for very low wages. But that, of course, is exactly what China and India have done; they have in effect adopted a marketing slogan that reads: "high skills and low wages!"

"Earnings for workers with four-year degrees fell 5.2% from 2000 to 2004 when adjusted for inflation, according to White House economists. Not since the 1970s have workers with bachelor's degrees seen a prolonged slump in earnings during a time of economic growth. The White House economists did not lay out wage trends for people with master's and other advanced degrees. But other studies have found that their inflation-adjusted wages were essentially flat between 2000 and 2004, and the studies have confirmed a decline for people with four-year degrees."

MOLLY HENNESSY-FISKE, "THAT RAISE MIGHT TAKE FOUR YEARS TO EARN AS WELL: THOSE WITH BACHELOR'S DEGREES ARE FINDING THEIR INCOMES STAGNATE DESPITE A GROWING ECONOMY."
Los Angeles Times, JULY 24, 2006.

It turns out that the United States largely embraced the standards-based agenda put forward by the first Commission, but it failed to ask what it would take, beyond standards and accountability measures, to radically improve student performance without radically increasing what it was willing to spend. This is different, by the way, from saying that the nation was stingy when it came to public spending on elementary and secondary education. Quite the contrary.

Over the past 30 years, public spending on elementary and secondary education has increased by a factor of 2.4 in inflation-adjusted dollars. But student performance on the 4th-grade national reading test has improved only modestly (though we have done better in mathematics). It is to say that while we had underestimated the nature of the challenge, we had grossly underestimated the kinds of changes in our system that would be needed to meet those challenges.

COST OF SCHOOLING SPIRALS UPWARD, BUT ACHIEVEMENT DOES NOT

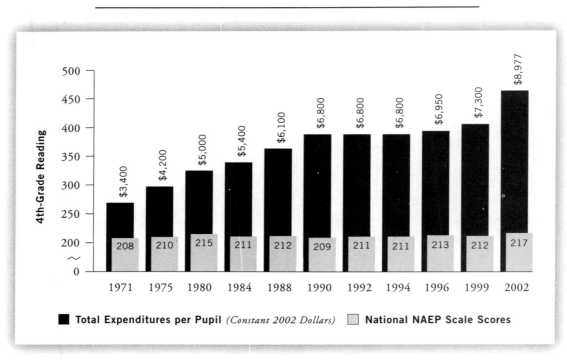

Sources: NCES NAEP Trends in Academic Progress Through 1999; NCES Digest of Education Statistics 2003.

These were the facts on the ground that led the Board of Trustees of the National Center on Education and the Economy (NCEE) to revive the Commission on the Skills of the American Workforce in 2005. The realities had invalidated some of the most important premises of the first report and introduced new competitive factors that the first Commission had not considered at all. The challenge to the new Commission was to try to understand the nature of the new dynamics of the global economy and the implications for American education and training.

We began by asking where we are now with respect to the indicators that led NCEE to assemble the first Commission.

In the 1990s, decades of American investment in the application of new information technologies in virtually every sector of the economy paid off in a burst of productivity improvement that lifted all boats.

AVERAGE WEEKLY EARNINGS
from 1969 to 2005 (in 1982 dollars)

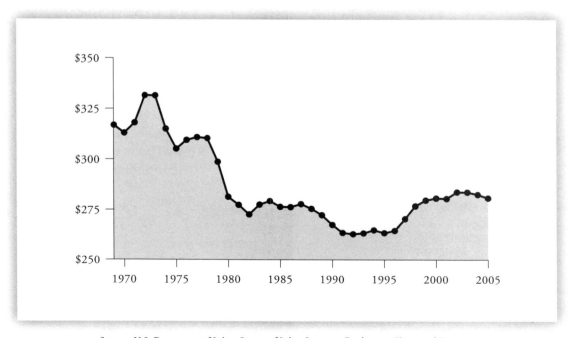

Sources: U.S. Department of Labor, Bureau of Labor Statistics, *Employment, Hours, and Earnings*, from the Current Employment Statistics Survey (2006).

DISPERSAL OF THE MIDDLE CLASS
by Level of Education

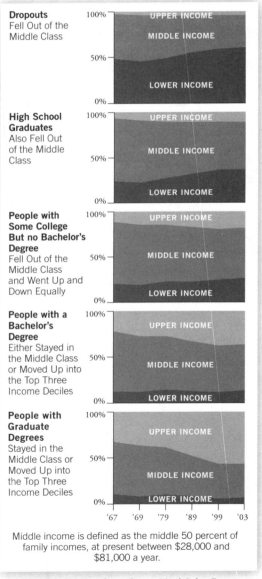

Dropouts
Fell Out of the Middle Class

High School Graduates
Also Fell Out of the Middle Class

People with Some College But no Bachelor's Degree
Fell Out of the Middle Class and Went Up and Down Equally

People with a Bachelor's Degree
Either Stayed in the Middle Class or Moved Up into the Top Three Income Deciles

People with Graduate Degrees
Stayed in the Middle Class or Moved Up into the Top Three Income Deciles

Middle income is defined as the middle 50 percent of family incomes, at present between $28,000 and $81,000 a year.

Source: Current Population Survey, March Labor Force Supplement (March 2004).

Even at its height, though, the weekly wages of workers fell well short of their earlier highs, and beginning about three years ago, the long decline in average weekly wages resumed its downward trend. There are fewer people in the middle class. In fact, the middle class appears to be dispersing into two groups: the upwardly mobile who have been to college and the downwardly mobile who have not. If these trends continue unabated, more and more Americans will see themselves frozen out of the American dream forever, and the social contract that has kept the peace in this country will come undone.

The question is, Why is this happening, and what can be done about it?

THE CHALLENGE FROM CHINA AND INDIA: HIGH SKILLS AND LOW WAGES!

"Why the world's biggest democracy is the next great economic superpower," screams the headlines of the cover of one our biggest newsweeklies, capturing the fevered projection of China and India as the 800-pound gorillas of the modern world, dominating or about to dominate everything in their paths. Authoritative journals tell us that these two countries are producing in the neighborhood of 950,000 engineers a year, compared to our 60,000. American engineers are reported to be telling their children to go into any career except engineering.

The truth is that the majority of engineers being produced by China and India are graduates of two- and three-year college programs and cannot reasonably be compared to what America calls engineers. Many with four-year engineering degrees are not skilled enough to be hired as engineers by American firms. Our own research and the best authorities in the United States agree that China and India between them are probably producing not more than 135,000 engineers a year who could compete with the engineers that our universities are turning out.

But 135,000 is more than twice 60,000. And the rate at which these countries are turning out competent engineers is rapidly increasing, whereas the rate at which we are turning out engineers is stagnant. Moreover, a substantial fraction of the engineers who we are turning out are from China and India. They used to stay in this country in overwhelming numbers and, in doing so, have made a mighty contribution to our economy. Some statistics indicate that as many as one-third of the senior staff in the Silicon Valley companies that led the dot-com revolution were of Chinese and — mainly — Indian origin. But, increasingly, these highly competent people are now returning to their native countries rather than staying here.

One might reasonably ask why we should be so concerned about engineers. After all, engineers represent a very small proportion of the workforce. Surely, in an age in which services are coming to dominate the economy, a problem with the supply of engineers is hardly a body blow to the nation's economy!

That argument is plausible — and will lead us to a very dangerous conclusion. For a long time, economists believed that economic growth was mainly a function of how much of what we made was saved and invested in the machinery and plant required to expand production. Now, though, they have come to believe that, more than ever before, growth now depends on advances in technology that capture advances in new knowledge.

But why should we be so concerned with growth? We are, after all, the champion consumer among nations. Perhaps we already have enough. The problem is that the baby boom generation is about to retire, to be replaced by a workforce that is much smaller in relation to the retired population than any workforce we have ever had. Put another way, many fewer of us will have to support many more of us than has ever been the case before. If each of us produces only as much as each member of the baby boom generation, then each of us will be poorer than we have been, because there will be more nonproductive mouths to feed. In that sense, we have to grow — a lot —to stay even.

So we must have three objectives: to increase the earning power of individual wage earners, to employ everyone of a working age who wants to be employed, and to grow the economy as a whole. High wages and growth are both associated with firms and industries that are on the leading edge of exploiting new technological breakthroughs. As soon as other firms and industries start to exploit those breakthroughs, the profits that can be made by the leaders greatly diminish. When firms located in countries whose workers charge relatively little for their labor learn how to

According to the American Electronics Association, one out of five U.S. scientists and engineers are foreign-born. Yet the number of skilled workers immigrating to the United States declined by 27% between 2001 and 2003. India's National Association of Software and Service Companies (NASSCOM) reports that, whereas in 1993, 84% of Indian computer science graduates headed for jobs or advanced study in the United States, only 60% do so now.

★ ★ ★ ★

"The number of engineering degrees awarded in the United States is down 20% from the peak year of 1985. More than 50% of all engineering doctoral degrees awarded by U.S. engineering colleges are to foreign nationals. Some 34% of doctoral degrees in natural sciences (including the physical, biological, earth, ocean, and atmospheric sciences) and 56% of engineering Ph.D.s in the United States are awarded to foreign-born students."

Tapping America's Potential,
Business Roundtable,
July 2005.

produce these new goods and services, they can sell them at much lower cost than the companies that first offered them.

So countries like ours that pay their workers very well have to be constantly coming up with new technologies and new ways to exploit those technologies. Researchers have shown that the time a firm has to exploit a new technology before someone else figures out how to do it more cheaply is getting shorter and shorter. And that means that the leading-edge firms have less and less time to come up with the next big new thing.

The result is that the United States will have to be number one or two in technology leadership in every industry in which it expects to be a major competitor if we expect to maintain our current wage levels and grow our economy enough to maintain the standard of living of the society as a whole. This is not an argument about engineers. Engineers in this context are just a stand-in for the large body of people we will need with very high skills in mathematics, science, and technology, of whom our engineers are only a small part. Given the need to be among the world's top technological leaders in industry after industry if we want to continue to maintain our current standard of living, we simply must have a large and growing supply of world-class scientists, mathematicians, and engineers. We will return below to the issue of the demands of technological leadership, but, the point here is that while people who specialize in these disciplines alone are hardly sufficient, without them, nothing else will matter.

Now let us return to the challenge from China and India. As we do so, we can see that the challenge is by no means limited to engineers. To see why this is so, it is useful to focus for a moment on the sources of India's mathematics and engineering talent.

The story goes back to 1949, when India gained its independence. Jawaharlal Nehru, India's first prime minister, looked to the Soviet Union as his model for promoting rapid industrialization in a very poor country. The Soviet model was driven by massive investment in domestic heavy industry. Nehru knew that, to make this model work, he would need very good engineers. He turned to Western governments, among them the United States, to help India build a small set of elite technological institutions, the Indian Institutes of Technology (IITs), which could produce the engineers the country would need.

The Communist economic model would prove to be a disaster for India, but the IITs were an unqualified success. From the beginning, there was great demand for places in these institutions because they were an instant ticket to elite status in India. Because that was so, the IITs created their own entrance examinations. They examined only in English, math, and science. Because the best students wanted to go to these new institutions, the makers of the exams were forced to create exams set to a level far above what was actually required to succeed at the IITs. This was particularly true in mathematics.

In the 1950s and 1960s, the United States offered very generous graduate fellowships to foreign nationals in American universities. Graduates of the IITs discovered that their level of preparation, especially in mathematics, made it very easy for them to gain admission to the engineering programs at our very best universities and to earn these government fellowships. The fellowships paid so well that they could send half of their fellowship earnings home, an amount that often doubled the income of their families.

Few went home when they graduated, because the Indian economy was a persistent basket case. So they stayed in the United States, going on to teach mathematics, science, and engineering in our leading universities and entering the business world here. In time, according to some reports, they would constitute between one-quarter and one-third of all of the top officers and engineers in the Silicon Valley at the time of the dot-com revolution in the 1990s.

Thus, the IITs became a tiny keyhole through the door to the very pinnacle of success for ambitious, able Indian young people. In time, more than 300,000 young Indians would take the examinations for the IITs every year, competing for not more than 3,500 positions in the freshman classes. The level of mathematics competence of these students is astonishingly high. Behind them are hundreds of thousands whose mathematical competence is only slightly less.

In time, enterprising individuals saw an opportunity to get rich running for-profit tutoring operations to prepare secondary students for the IIT exams. Bent on success, they determined to hire as tutors only people who could pass the exams themselves. Unable to find

"At present, about 25,000 IIT graduates are working in the U.S. Over the years, Cisco Systems Inc., in San Jose, California, says it has hired more than 1,000 for its operations, and the director of a major U.S. research firm says the IITs are one of its most important sources of research talent, both in the U.S. and in Asia. It's not uncommon for Indian applicants to fail to get into the IITs, but win admission to top U.S. engineering colleges. IIT Kanpur has a particularly impressive record. Rated top IIT by the domestic news magazine *India Today* for the past three years, the institute, like all the IITs, emphasizes technical creativity and innovation. 'The importance is not in just getting the right answer, it is how you get the right answer,' says Sanjay Dhande, Kanpur's director. 'Problem solving is the crux of training. We teach [students] to think creatively, independently, aggressively and provocatively.' He adds that it is these qualities that make IIT graduates successful not just as engineers, but also as bankers and corporate executives."

SHAILAJA NEELAKANTAN, "WHY HAVE SO MANY INDIAN
ENGINEERS SUCCEEDED AROUND THE WORLD? THE INDIAN
INSTITUTES OF TECHNOLOGY MAY BE ONE ANSWER,"
Wall Street Journal, SEPTEMBER 27, 2004.

★ ★ ★ ★

"An Indian engineer costs only 20% of an American. The difference between Bangalore and many East Asian cities is that it has prospered through cheap brains rather than cheap hands. Although India produces two million graduates, it trains fewer than 50,000 computer science engineers. With demand growing so rapidly, wages have been climbing 20% a year and companies routinely lose a quarter of their workforce every year. The pressure is accelerated by the foreign companies, who transfer their best Indian engineers to the United States or to their other foreign operations. Many Indians are also lured to Silicon Valley, where one-third of the high-tech companies are today run by Chinese and Indian engineers, according to London's *Financial Times*. "

GURCHARAN DAS, *India Unbound: The Social and Economic
Revolution from Independence to the Global Information Age*
(NEW YORK: ANCHOR BOOKS, 2002).

secondary school teachers who could do so, they ended up hiring IIT graduate engineers for the purpose.

In recent years, new tutoring institutions have opened that specialize in preparing students to take the exams that now must be taken in order to compete for admission to the best tutoring programs for the IIT exams. Teachers at the best secondary schools in India now expect those of their students who are preparing for the IIT exams to be absent from school not less than a quarter of their regular classes, in their last year, in order to prepare for the exams. Parents of students studying for their IIT exams often stop going to social and sporting events for 6 to 12 months in order to help their children prepare for the exams.

Only a fraction of these superbly prepared students actually went to the United States for their graduate studies. Many stayed in India, forming the core of one of the world's most highly skilled workforces, and they are now powering a 10 percent annual growth rate, one of the highest in the world, much of which is accounted for by business process outsourcing, including and especially software development. And they are now being joined by a swiftly rising number of the Indians who, until recently, stayed in the United States to teach in our graduate institutions and drive our high-tech firms to success, but who are now flooding back to India to participate in the boom.

It would be a mistake to think of these Indians simply as very good at mathematics. That skill, and the way it

was learned, have given India the gift of a top-level workforce with very impressive broad analytical skills. Recently, the top-level Indian universities have not been able to keep up with the demand for software engineers. No problem, say the top firms. They are simply hiring engineers trained in other fields and retraining them in six months as software engineers. They can do that because of the very high-quality educational foundation that was laid when these students were in secondary school.

The story in China is very different — but the result is much the same. For a very long time, China has maintained a system of "key schools," schools mostly for the children of party officials that receive far more and better resources than the regular government schools. These schools are easily on a par with the better schools in the West. While the Chinese government claims to have abolished the system of key schools at the compulsory schooling level, the Commission staff saw much evidence that they are alive and well, the key element in the Chinese elite schools strategy.

When Deng Xiaoping became premier after the death of Mao Zedong, he saw clearly that China's future depended heavily on excellence in research and teaching at its leading universities, particularly in engineering. Shortly after coming to power, he set a goal of creating 100 research universities and 20 world-class research parks. The system of key schools was to be the feeder system for these internationally competitive research universities. As in India, admission to university is determined entirely by scores

"Standing amid the rolling lawns outside his four-bedroom villa, Ajay Kela pondered his street in the community of Palm Meadows. One of his neighbors recently returned to India, from Cupertino, Calif., to run a technology start-up funded by the venture capital firm Kleiner, Perkins, Caufield & Byers. Mr. Kela's neighborhood is just a small sample of a reverse brain drain benefiting India. Nasscom, a trade group of Indian outsourcing companies, estimates that 30,000 technology professionals have moved back in the last 18 months. Bangalore, Hyderabad and the suburbs of Delhi are becoming magnets for an influx of Indians, who are the top-earning ethnic group in the United States. Homes have tripled in value in Palm Meadows over the last 12 months, and rents have quadrupled. "Expatriates are returning because India is hot. There is an increasing feeling that significant action in the technology industry is moving to India," said the CEO of Infosys Technologies, India's second-largest outsourcing firm. While most returnees are first-generation expatriates, second-generation Indians living in the United States are also returning. Even as lifestyle gaps between India and the West have narrowed rapidly, salary differences at top executive levels have virtually disappeared. Annual pay packages of a half-million dollars are common in Bangalore, but even for those taking a pay cut to return home, the lower cost of living balances smaller paychecks."

SARITHA RAI, "INDIANS FIND THEY CAN GO HOME AGAIN,"
New York Times, DECEMBER 26, 2005.

★ ★ ★ ★

"During the period 1993–2002, government spending for universities totaled 619.3 billion yuan, with an average annual growth of 28.5%. In 2002, 16 million students were attending college across the land, with 2.12 million more enrolled than in 1998, raising the university enrollment rate (percentage of students taking entrance exams) to 59% from 36%, and the university attendance rate (percentage of total college-age population) from 9.8% to 15%. Entering the 21st century the nation's higher education picture looked significantly different than it had just one decade before."

LI LANQING, SENIOR OFFICIAL IN THE CHINESE GOVERNMENT RESPONSIBLE
FOR EDUCATION REFORMS, IN HIS BOOK, *Education for 1.3 Billion*
(BEIJING: FOREIGN LANGUAGE AND TEACHING PRESS, OCTOBER 2004).

on examinations. And, as in India, the desire to get into the top universities on the part of young people is enormous.

In India, the elite secondary schools are private schools, whereas in China, they are operated by the government. In China, there is an explicit strategy to create an elite level of research universities to drive the economy. The Indian government has failed to adequately finance its premier technological institutions, whereas the Chinese have continued to place a very high priority on spending to improve their best institutions. But in both countries, the public at every level sees education as the way to a better life, and both parents and students show a hunger for education that has no parallel in the United States. In very different ways, from the slums to the top of society, the institutional structure of education is accommodating that hunger in both countries. The inescapable conclusion is that both countries will continue to see intense demand for more and better education for the foreseeable future, and supply will surely follow.

Though the proportion of people in both countries that is highly educated is small relative to the United States, the absolute number, which is what really matters, is very large. Add to that the fact that the number of highly educated people in both China and India is growing rapidly, while the number in this country has been stagnant for years, and there is cause for deep concern with respect to our ability to compete on the world stage. Beginning high-quality engineers in India are being paid the equivalent of $7,500 per year. A new graduate with the same qualifications in

the United States can expect about $45,000 per year. As we will see in a moment, these two people are actually competing in the same market, and we will ask why anyone in the market for engineers would pay $45,000 when they could pay far less for the same skills. If we go beyond engineers in particular to include in our analysis people with strong mathematical and analytical skills, then the scale of the problem starts to come into focus.

QUANTITY MATTERS: THE ISSUE OF EDUCATIONAL ATTAINMENT

China and India, however, are only the visible tip of the iceberg. In the chart on page 14, we see, decade by decade, the changes in national education attainment over the past half century for a large number of advanced industrial nations and many less developed ones. What is measured is the proportion of the population that has completed what we call high school. Throughout the first half of the 20th century, and well into the second half, the United States led the world by a comfortable margin. Then things began to change as one nation after another focused on educating its population, and, one by one, many overtook the attainment levels of the United States. It is very important to look at this chart not as a snapshot, but as a motion picture. One can see that the rate of change in the attainment in the United States is glacial, whereas it is very fast in a growing number of other nations, some of which have already overtaken us, with others on the verge of doing so.

Thus, the enormous surge in skills we described in China and India is not

THE U.S. ATTAINMENT LEAD DISAPPEARS

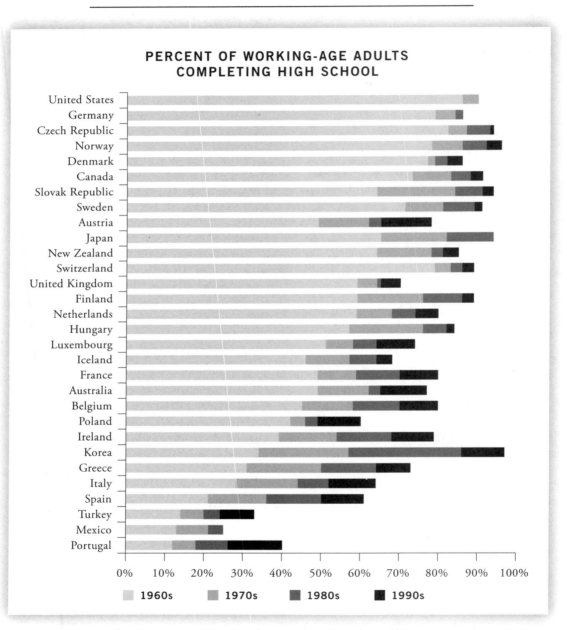

**PERCENT OF WORKING-AGE ADULTS
COMPLETING HIGH SCHOOL**

Source: Organization for Economic Cooperation and Development, *Education at a Glance*, Table A1.2a. (Paris: Author, 2006).

"China's pool of potential talent is enormous. In 2003 China had roughly 8.5 million young professional graduates with up to seven years' work experience, and an additional 97 million people that would qualify for support-staff positions. Despite this apparently vast supply, multinational companies are finding that few graduates have the necessary skills for service occupations. Consider engineers. China has 1.6 million young ones, more than any other country we examined. Indeed, 33% of the university students in China study engineering. But the main drawback of Chinese applicants for engineering jobs, our interviewees said, is the educational system's bias toward theory. Compared with engineering graduates in Europe and North America, who work in teams to achieve practical solutions, Chinese students get little practical experience in projects or teamwork. The result of these differences is that China's pool of young engineers, considered suitable for work in multinationals, is just 160,000, no larger than the United Kingdom's."

DIANA FARRELL AND ANDREW GRANT,
"CHINA'S LOOMING TALENT SHORTAGE,"
McKinsey Quarterly, NO. 4 (2005).

★ ★ ★ ★

"In the late 1980s, between 500 and 1,000 scientists a year returned to Taiwan including some Nobel Prize winners. They were hired as senior faculty and as directors of laboratories, particularly at their national centers of scientific excellence."

NATIONAL SCIENCE BOARD,
Science and Engineering Indicators—1998
(ARLINGTON, VA: NATIONAL SCIENCE FOUNDATION, 1998).

an isolated instance but is rather is typical of what is happening in a large number of other less-developed nations. There can be no doubt that a large share of the economic dominance this country now enjoys is a result of the very large lead we had for virtually the whole first half of the 20th century in educational attainment. This attainment lead combined with a brain drain from the Fascist countries in the years leading up to the Second World War and the other brain drain we have just described from the Asian countries to confer on the United States a decisive edge in education and skills over the rest of the world through the entire century.

Now, all the arrows are running in the other direction. The brilliant people who fled Hitler for the United States are retired or dead. The immensely talented Asians who came here because their own countries could not compete with the opportunities we had to offer are still coming for their graduate education, but are then returning, along with many of their countrymen and women who stayed to teach in our universities but are now returning.

But overwhelming all of these numbers is the effect of the rise of educational attainment in many other parts of the world. In a few decades, the U.S. share of the global college-educated workforce has fallen from 30 percent to 14 percent, notwithstanding a very large increase during the same period in the fraction of Americans entering college. To the extent that our skills are the foundation of our economic dominance, that foundation is eroding in front of our eyes, but we have been very slow to see it.

QUALITY MATTERS — A LOT!

It obviously matters how much education a national workforce has. We now know, though, that the quality of education a workforce has matters even more than the quantity. Recent research by Eric Hanushek, a Senior Fellow at the Hoover Institution at Stanford University, shows that one standard deviation difference in math and science scores is related to a 1 percent difference in annual per capita gross domestic product (GDP) growth rates. Hanushek points out that "one percentage point higher growth — say, 2 percent versus 1 percent a year — will over a 50-year period yield incomes that are 64 percent higher."

That is a very large difference in income. But as most Americans now know, the performance of American students on many measures of mathematics and science has been essentially flat for a long time, and well below the performance of students in other countries with whom we compete economically. As we have just seen, we are now in competition with other relatively poor countries that have managed to produce large and growing student bodies whose math and science performance is world class.

The inescapable conclusion is that we are losing the race on both quantity and quality relative to our competitors.

THE GLOBAL HIGH-SKILLS WORKFORCE IS ONLY A CLICK AWAY: THE ADVENT OF DIGITIZED WORK

One could argue, of course, that the rise of high skills on the other side of the globe is no affair of ours, that, while the making of toys and shirts can easily migrate to poor countries, it is harder to export highly skilled work, especially work in the services arena. Services, after all, need to be rendered where the customers for those services are, and, as the richest nation on earth, it should be relatively easy for us to attract people with those skills.

That is an appealing argument, but it does not square with the facts. Thomas Friedman has famously described in *The World Is Flat* how more and more of the work product of people engaged in the production of both products and services is in digital form and that work product is increasingly the digital input for someone else's work. Friedman also described how, in the 1990s, hundreds of thousands of miles of glass cable were laid and satellite capacity created that made it possible to ship these digital signals around the globe almost free of charge. And,

ECONOMIC GROWTH DRIVEN MORE BY EDUCATION QUALITY THAN QUANTITY

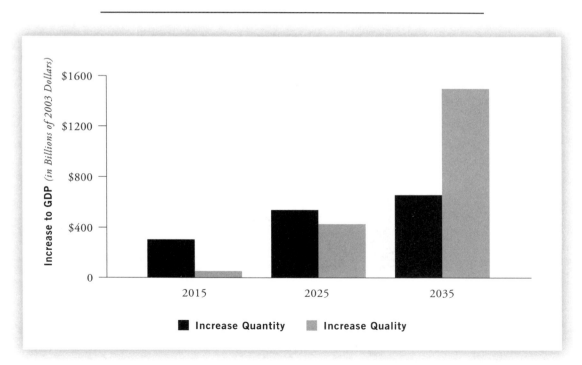

Sources: Erik Hanushek, Hoover Institution (2004) and Anthony Carnevale, Wissam Harake, and Jeff Strohl (2006, unpublished research).

"When officials of Florida-based United Group Programs, a company administering employer health insurance plans for 39 years, heard that hospitals in developing countries such as Thailand and India were offering high-quality services at cut-rate prices, they decided to look into it. 'What we found was that Americans can go overseas and get health care for about 80% less than in the U.S., and actually get better care in nicer hospitals,' says United Group Programs Vice President Jonathan Edelheit. 'And more amazingly, there are doctors over at these hospitals that actually went to school and practiced here in the U.S., so it's almost as if you're not going to a foreign country and a foreign doctor, you're going to see an American doctor overseas.' Using only a hospital in Thailand, the company has found that the savings can be dramatic. A heart bypass that would cost $80,000 in the United States costs about $16,000, according to Edelheit. He says the quality is equal, and in some cases superior, to what's available in the United States."

JULIE ROVNER, "EMPLOYERS MAY SPONSOR OVERSEAS SURGERIES," NATIONAL PUBLIC RADIO, SEPTEMBER 14, 2006.

★ ★ ★ ★

"A job that depends on routines — that can be reduced to a set of rules, or broken down into a set of repeatable steps — is at risk. If a $500-a-month Indian chartered accountant doesn't swipe your comfortable accounting job, *TurboTax* will. The routine functions are increasingly being turned over to machines. Indeed, a small British company, called Appligenics, has created software that can write software. . . . Automation is also changing the work of many doctors. Much medical diagnosis amounts to following a series of decision trees. . . . So an array of software and online programs has emerged that allow patients to answer a series of questions on their computer screens and arrive at a preliminary diagnosis without the assistance of a physician. . . . A similar pattern is unfolding in the legal profession. Dozens of inexpensive information and advice services are reshaping law practice. For instance *CompleteCase.com* which calls itself 'the premier online uncontested divorce service center,' will handle your divorce for a mere $239. . . . The attorneys who remain will be those who can tackle far more complex problems and those who can provide something that databases and software cannot — counseling, mediation, courtroom storytelling, and other services."

DANIEL H. PINK, *A Whole New Mind: Moving from the Information Age to the Conceptual Age* (NEW YORK: RIVERHEAD BOOKS, 2005).

finally, he described the process by which it became possible for people to communicate with each other over these channels using very different software packages. The result, as he pointed out, is a world in which it is just as easy to create work teams composed of people on four continents as it is to create work teams composed of people from four divisions of the same firm located in the same city.

So, now, the market for highly educated people is even more integrated than the market for people with low skills. Which means that highly skilled people with roughly the same qualifications are competing directly with each other, no matter where they are located on the globe. Again, India is the best illustration, though there are many others that could be used. Indian radiologists read American X-rays, analyze bond markets for Wall Street firms, do taxes for American taxpayers, and create animated sequences for Hollywood studios.

OUTSOURCING AS THE NEW STANDARD PRACTICE: THE MODULARIZATION OF INDUSTRY

But, surely, this picture is a little exaggerated. The notion of international work teams has a certain cachet, but is it not more likely that American firms will compete with firms from some other countries rather than with individuals from other countries? After all, the United States invented the vertically integrated firm at the turn of the last century. The Ford Motor Company mined and refined the iron ore at one end and sold the finished automobile at the other. Almost every single operation

in between was done by a Ford Motor Company employee.

Actually, American firms, like other firms all over the world, are now running away from that model of vertical integration as fast as they can. Now, analysts in the firm are carving the work up into small pieces and asking whether any or all of those pieces can be done at higher quality or at less cost — or both — by some other company anywhere in the world. If my company is engaged in 100 separate processes and the analysts show me that we are actually best at only 4 of those processes, in today's world I am likely to contract with others for the other 96. And given the digitalization of work, I am likely to contract with individuals and organizations anywhere on the face of the globe.

This process of modularization will create firms that are ever more efficient and ever more productive, but it will also create a situation in which every highly educated individual in all the nations of the world will be in direct competition with all the other individuals in his or her field, worldwide.

ROUTINE WORK DISAPPEARS AS IT IS INCREASINGLY AUTOMATED

Americans gather around their television sets in the evening to watch CNN's Lou Dobbs sound the alarm about the way offshoring is causing Americans to lose jobs. And they shake their heads. But the fact is that many more jobs are being lost because they are now being done by machines than are lost due to offshoring.

Consider the grocery store and big box hardware store checkout lines, where the customer is now increasingly expected to run his or her own groceries or electrical components hardware through the bar code reader and then bag them. In many cases now, that customer pays with a debit card rather than a credit card. Gone are the jobs of the check-out clerk, the inventory taker, the bagger, and the people who used to physically transfer the information from the credit card slip to the data files of the credit card company. Almost all of us now pump our own gas and pay for it with a credit or debit card, which initiates a billing process that requires not a single human hand or eye. Gone are the typists of yore. We do our own typing now and our own filing and our own corrections, and we send and receive our own mail, and it is all digital. And with those changes, hundreds of thousands of typists, clerks, mail carriers, truck drivers, mail handlers, wood cutters, paper mill workers, envelope makers, and many others lost their jobs.

In our first report, when we noted these changes, we described what was going on as the loss of low-skilled jobs. And, in fact, millions of low-skilled jobs were lost in this way. But it is clear now that we were a little off the mark. What is really going on is the loss of routine work, not just at the low-skill level, but at every level.

It turns out that many middle managers were paid in the past for collecting data, analyzing them in fairly routine ways, and passing the results up to senior management. Not any more. Now those data are collected automatically, as the business processes unfold, by the same digital machines that enable those processes themselves, at almost zero cost. And software is written to store, analyze, retrieve, and display that information much faster and more accurately than the middle managers ever could, and the same machinery that performs these tasks then distributes the information not just to top management, but to everyone who needs it up and down the line, in a twinkling. And, in that way, hundreds of thousands, perhaps millions, of good, solid, middle management jobs are lost.

Insurance staffers in the home offices of insurance companies who used to take the order forms from sales reps and figure out the premiums don't do that anymore because software programs literally held in the hands of the sales reps can do it much faster and more accurately. Software programs can actually design sails for sailboats, calculating the stresses on each part of the sail faster and more accurately than the highly paid human sail designers used to. Other software programs can do the mathematics needed to figure out how an airline can maximize its revenues from the unsold seats on an airplane much more cheaply than a human being can.

If the work is routine, no matter how complex it is, chances are it can be automated. And if it can be automated, it probably will be sooner or later, because the costs of automation are swiftly declining and the costs of human labor are rising, so, inevitably, simple economics dictates the progressive automation of more and more jobs.

And the most important point here is that even the highly skilled are not immune to this process. Sail design is skilled work. Airline seat pricing is skilled work. So is the pricing of insurance. But, as we have seen, that is not proof against the disappearance of these jobs. What counts now is not whether the job involves real skills, but rather whether the work involved can be done by a machine that can learn a few algorithms, or routines, for doing the work involved. If the answer is yes, then that job is probably a prime candidate for replacement by a machine. This is especially true in high-cost countries like our own, because the economic incentives to automate are stronger in such countries than elsewhere.

TECHNOLOGICAL CHANGE AS THE UNIVERSAL DRIVER

We explained above why it is that the United States must be number one or two in each of the industries in which it hopes to be competitive if we want to maintain our current standard of living. In the 1990s, we led the world economically largely because of our dominance in information technologies, which had reached a point such that simultaneous advances in the application of those technologies in a wide variety of industries greatly increased the rate of productivity in the economy as a whole.

The application of information technologies has by no means run its course, but there is every reason to believe that several other technologies are poised to make a similar impact on the same scale. Among them are nanotechnology, biotechnology, and a group of technologies that may hold the key to energy independence. Through history, new sources of energy, particularly steam and electricity, have powered decades-long economic growth, destroying entire collections of old industries and giving rise to new ones. There is every reason to believe that the widespread use of fuel cells or of hydrogen as a basic energy source would have much the same effect. Nanotechnologies have the same potential for the destruction of old industries and the creation of new ones. Consider the use of new nanotechnology-based fabrics for construction, for use as both structural elements in buildings and their skins, replacing structural steel, bricks, and mortar all at once. Consider too the use of devices that can be implanted in your body, powered by your body heat, that can monitor your blood pressure and cholesterol and release medicines automatically when you need them. Indeed, we appear to be on the cusp of developing computing power that can rival the human brain; of being able to develop custom metals, fabrics, tissues, and membranes with properties not yet dreamed of; of affordable power sources that are cheap, readily available, and nonpolluting; of disease treatments that will seek out and destroy the bad cells and leave the good ones in peace, enabling us to conquer scourges like HIV/AIDS.

Much has been written about these and similar developments elsewhere. The point in the context of this report is that these technologies have the potential to destroy not just existing products and services but entire industries. If those new industries are first developed in the United States, then Americans will reap the enormous rewards that come with being a leader in a new field. If they are not first developed here, we will

"Our economic future is inextricably linked to our ability to come up with more technological breakthroughs that equal the Internet in magnitude. Such large-scale innovations drive growth, create new jobs and industries, push up living standards for both rich and poor, and open up whole new vistas of possibilities."

MICHAEL J. MANDEL,
Rational Exuberance: Silencing the Enemies of Growth and Why the Future Is Better Than You Think
(NEW YORK: HARPERCOLLINS, 2004).

have to settle for a lot less in terms of our standard of living.

When China and India first caught the world's attention as important new economic players, it was widely assumed in the West that though they might become the world's workshop, the West would remain the brains of that workshop and would reap all the rewards that go with being the world's center for research, development, innovation, design, finance, and marketing.

It is now clear that neither the Chinese nor the Indians accept that vision of the future, and why should they? These countries and others like them know that there is a strict limit to the growth that they can get just by offering low wages on the world market. As their economies do better, wages go up, and other countries become more attractive to investors looking for low-wage producers. This is exactly what is happening in China and India as this report is being written.

If the story stopped there, the boom in these countries would slow down and peter out. But it will not stop there. The leaders of these countries know that the richest rewards go to those countries that become home to the workers who can add the most value in the industries they are involved in, not simply offer the lowest wages. And so they too have set out to become world leaders in research, development, design, and all the other disciplines involved where advancing technology has become the driver of economic growth.

Successfully running a national economy based on technological growth depends on assured strength in many arenas, including strong research universities, sustained national investment in basic research, good protections for intellectual property, the availability of plentiful risk-oriented investment capital, cushions for those who fail — and a bountiful supply of highly talented, highly educated, and highly creative people at every level of the workforce, from the lab to the factory floor, who can do the research, create the new ideas, and take them to scale.

All of these supporting arenas are important, and the United States should take some comfort in knowing that we are stronger on balance with respect to these requirements than any other nation on the globe. But there is good reason to worry about the direction of public policy in several of these arenas, and that is nowhere truer than with respect to the quality of our workforce. And that is where we will focus in this report, on the quality of our workforce, considered against the requirements of an economy driven by technological change operating at a furious pace.

THE CHALLENGE IN A NUTSHELL

Try the following thought experiment. Imagine for a moment that the United States was able to match the high school performance of the best-performing countries in the world in mathematics and science. As you do this, bear in mind that we are not competing with all of China and India, but only with their best, because they are so much bigger than we are.

We would have a very long way to go to meet the standard just posited. It would take years and a great deal of treasure and determination.

And now ask yourself what we would have achieved when we hit the target. In a world in which employers can get their talent anywhere around the globe, our young people — the ones who are now as well educated in math and science as the best Chinese and Indians — would be eligible to earn what they earn. Why should an employer pay more?

Assume that some years have gone by, and Chinese and Indian wages have gone up relative to ours. Be generous, and assume that their engineers, mathematicians, scientists, and others will at that point make fully half of what ours do now. Since there is no reason for our hypothetical employer to pay more for our professionals than theirs, if they have the same skills, ours would be making half of what they do now. And that is after we had worked so hard to create a much larger pool of qualified people than we have now.

But we are not interested in earning half of what we earn now. So what would we have to do to maintain our standard of living? Clearly, our workers — not just the engineers, but most of us — would have to at least match the skills of our leading competitors in the core curriculum — math, science, and command of our native language — but we would have to offer something else, something our competitors could not offer. What could that be?

WHAT IT WILL TAKE TO HANG ON TO OUR STANDARD OF LIVING:

High Skills Combine with Creativity and a Hunger for Education to Become the Key to Success

If the routine work is largely going to be done by machines and by people who charge much less for their labor than we do, it follows that what is left is the nonroutine work.

How we think about what is routine and not routine is important. Engineering can be routine work, or it can be highly creative. If we are successful, the routine engineering work will migrate to other countries, and Americans will be known for their creative abilities. The same is true of laboratory research. To be creative is not to do one more time what has been done countless times before but rather to combine things — some new and some old — in new ways, hopefully in useful ways.

Seeing new patterns and possibilities is the essence of creativity. Acting on them — turning these new patterns and possibilities into products and services that can be sold at scale — is the essence of innovation. Creativity without innovation benefits few, if any. Innovation without real creativity will put one in second place.

We have already hinted at the crucial importance of creativity and innovation. If we are merely competent — even if our competence is world class — we will not be able to produce the new services or products that are path breaking and highly desired. Those are precisely the products and services that people the world over are willing to pay dearly for. Once others routinize their production, the high margins disappear, and so do the high wages and rapid growth that typically come in their train.

The reason — and the only reason — that the rest of the world would be willing to pay us twice as much as equally competent people is if we can add creativity and innovation on a grand scale to sheer competence.

It is certainly true that the people who are designing the technologies of the future and discovering the principles from which those technologies emerge are highly creative people. But they are only the tip of the iceberg.

Consider the American entertainment industry, one of our biggest export industries. That industry depends on a large army of creative people in jobs ranging from lighting director to digital animator, from producer to agent, from the costumers to the cameramen and -women, from the mathematicians who specialize in the esoteric discipline of fractals to the rock stars and entertainment industry attorneys.

It is the boundless creativity of this extraordinary assemblage of people that has centered the world entertainment industry on Hollywood. Some of these people are superb technologists, but most are not.

For an entire industry to succeed in the world that is coming, it will have to sense where the markets are going before its competitors do, be more creative with its marketing strategies than the competition, make more creative use of contractors and partners, innovate its production processes ceaselessly, organize and manage in very innovative ways — in short, be on the creative edge in every single business function.

Firms that succeed in this will constantly be looking for ways to shed their routine work, either by automating it or outsourcing it. They will be constantly preoccupied with the search for competent and highly creative people and for management and organizational methods that will provide the best support to those people. And the staff themselves will be constantly organizing and reorganizing in a never-ending array of teams, like a turning kaleidoscope, some of whose members are regular employees of the firm and many who are brought in from the four corners of the world for particular projects.

Because markets and technologies will be so volatile, firms will want to keep their permanent staffs down and their temporary staffs up, so they can maximize their flexibility. This will provide enormous opportunities for individual entrepreneurs and small firms, but their only security will be their expertise, their own flexibility, and their ability to learn very, very quickly. They will have to turn on a dime, over and over and over.

Creative people often thrive in chaos, are constant learners, value excellence, and prefer to be in stimulating environments with others like themselves.

Creativity, innovation, and flexibility will not be the special province of an elite. It will be demanded of virtually everyone who is making a decent living, from graphic artists to assembly line workers, from insurance brokers to home builders. The Japanese, in the 1980s, taught American firms the importance of involving front-line workers in the search for new and better ways of meeting customers' needs, as well as improving production methods. They also taught American firms the value of organizing work in teams and multi-skilling all the members of those teams. And those same firms are learning now how important it is to make sure that those workers have a very solid education foundation, of the sort that will make it possible for them to learn new skills quickly as technologies and consumer tastes change.

"For the past 25 years, we have optimized our organizations for efficiency and quality. Over the next quarter century, we must optimize our entire society for innovation."

NATIONAL INNOVATION INITIATIVE, COUNCIL ON COMPETITIVENESS, *Final Report, Executive Summary* (DECEMBER 2004).

A SUCCESSFUL AMERICAN ECONOMY: THE "PICTURE"

The graphic below was designed to capture in visual form many of the points we have been making.

The first and most obvious point is that large firms and industries, regardless of where their headquarters is located, will be organized on a global scale. They will not simply be collections of national entities nor will they manufacture or generate services in one place to be sold in many others. They will be truly integrated at the same time that they will be completely modularized. They will source in the high-cost countries the labor they cannot get more cheaply elsewhere, but that labor will have to add more value than the cheaper labor they can get elsewhere. They will add

PROTOTYPICAL U.S. INDUSTRY
in 10 years if all goes well

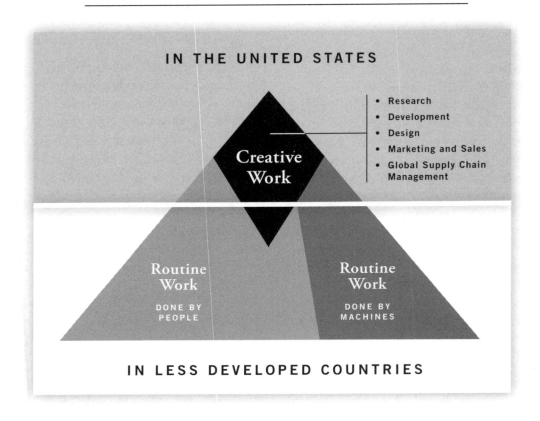

IN THE UNITED STATES

Creative Work

- Research
- Development
- Design
- Marketing and Sales
- Global Supply Chain Management

Routine Work
DONE BY PEOPLE

Routine Work
DONE BY MACHINES

IN LESS DEVELOPED COUNTRIES

more value as a result of more and better core skills and the potential to contribute more creative and innovative solutions than their competitors in other countries.

Most, but not all, of the routine work will be done in low-cost countries and by machines, in both those countries and the high-cost countries. Most, but not all, of the creative, high-value-added work will be done in the countries with the best education and training systems and the highest-cost structures. Companies will choose to locate research and development facilities in poor countries in order to be close to their markets, just as companies will choose to spend their money on high-cost people to do routine work in high-cost countries in order to be close to those customers. But, on the whole, countries like the United States, if they are successful, will see the continued erosion of low-skill, routine work and an enormous surge in demand for people with a very high level of foundation skills and great creativity.

The fact that the graphic shows an entire industry, and, in many cases, individual firms, as a single triangle encompassing work done in both high-cost and low-cost countries is also meant to suggest that firms and industries will organize work so that much of it is done by teams that work across the divide represented by the horizontal white line, that is, in teams that cut across countries and general income levels, just as is happening now at a rapidly increasing rate with respect to firms being organized with Indian and American team members.

This suggests, among other things, that Americans are not likely to succeed unless many more of us than at present understand a good deal about the other peoples of the world: how they think, why they think that way, what they like and do not like, and how they operate. This kind of international empathy and knowledge will, we think, be no less important than language literacy, mathematical literacy, and scientific literacy.

It is important to note that this graphic is not about what it will take for firms headquartered in the United States to succeed. The most successful of our firms will site their operations anywhere in the world where the cost and quality factors are most favorable. They will, in other words, find the competent people they need wherever they are and locate their research, development, production, and service operations where it is most advantageous for them to do so. That is what we would want them to do.

But it is entirely possible for firms headquartered in the United States to generate handsome returns for their stockholders at the very same time that the American people get poorer and poorer. For our people to be successful, they need to be employed at high wages. The point of this chart is that that will happen only if we can produce a remarkable increase in the proportion of our population that is educated to world-class levels and is creative and prepared to learn continuously.

One last point about this graphic: for the United States to succeed, we do not need others to fail. In fact, the contrary is true. For the economy behind this graphic to work, there must be a steady increase in the worldwide customer base for the kinds of goods and services we hope to produce for world consumption. We will succeed only if China and India and many other relatively poor countries grow and prosper. Nor do we have to make the Europeans or the Africans or the South Americans poorer to succeed.

But we do have to hold our own in a world in which most of the forces at work will tend to drive our wages down. To do that, we must be as good as our best competitors, and to do that, we will have to be as well educated as any and better educated than most rather than, as at present, watching one competitor after another surge past us.

HOW VULNERABLE ARE AMERICAN WORKERS TO OFFSHORING AND AUTOMATION?

Of course, not all jobs involving routine work or low skills are at risk of being offshored or automated. We will still need people to make beds in hotels, wait on tables in restaurants, and drive taxis. Even some high-skill jobs are not at risk, like firefighter, dentist, and school teacher, because they cannot be done at a distance from the fire, teeth, or student. However, we find that some people are beginning to take vacations in other countries like India and combining them with complex surgeries, which can be done there in luxury surroundings for a fraction of what the same operation would cost in the United States. And Indian tutoring companies are beginning to offer very high-quality tutoring services to American students using the Internet.

But in general, jobs revolving around routine work, where standard procedures are the rule, are very much at risk. So too

are jobs with minimal face-to-face contact with the customer or requiring little originality or creativity. And they can be found across the skills spectrum. Computer programmers, accountants, auditors, financial analysts, and telemarketers are, for example, very much at risk.

The Commission has used these sorts of distinctions to query a U.S. Department of Labor database called O*NET in order to get an idea of the numbers of people whose jobs are at risk of being offshored or automated. This database comprises a highly detailed inventory of skills, knowledge, competencies, attitudes, and job tasks that are required to perform thousands of jobs in the American economy. By this analysis, 16 percent of workers are currently vulnerable to losing their jobs through offshoring. Although we have not gone further and estimated the percentage of workers vulnerable to losing their jobs through automation, it is likely to be a somewhat larger figure that overlaps the outsourcing estimate.

We are not predicting that these jobs will disappear, only indicating that they are particularly vulnerable. But these numbers are large, and they represent an enormous risk for this country, as well as for the individuals who occupy those jobs. This list is the canary in the coal mine. It is also a measure of the scale of the task ahead of us.

WHAT WILL IT TAKE TO SUCCEED IN THIS NEW ENVIRONMENT?

And then there is the other side of the picture: the qualities that individuals will have to have to get and keep jobs that will enable them and their families to live decent, middle-class lives in the future.

What follows is based on our analysis of the O*NET data concerning the qualities associated with jobs that pay well and are in demand now, combined with the analysis we shared about the trends in the global economy and the nature of the economy that is most likely to enable the United States to provide a high-employment, high-wage economy in the future.

First, we begin with our observation that there will be no success for the country unless we are among the top two in technology in every industry in which we hope to be a major player. That requires us to be among the very best performers in international comparisons of mathematics and science achievement. Not all students will need to be first rate in these fields, but many more will have to be than are now, and the numbers of students who have that competence at high levels will have to rival the numbers of those countries with the highest performance, beginning with the Indians and the Chinese. Being good at math will entail not just being able to do math well but being very good at mathematical reasoning, which is not the same. Furthermore, we will have to do a much better job of making many more of our high school students comfortable with technology and the principles of engineering than is the case now. And it is just as clear that we will have to be among the world's best performers with respect to our command of English. The skills of reading, writing, and careful listening at relatively high levels will be more important than ever.

The O*NET data show that high earnings are not just associated with people who have high technical skills. In fact, mastery of the arts and humanities is just as closely correlated with high earnings, and, according to our analysis, that will continue to be true. History, music, drawing and painting, and economics will give our students an edge just as surely as math and science will.

But that is only the beginning, because, as we said earlier, if all we can do is match our low-cost competitors in these core subjects in the traditional curriculum, then, in time, all we will qualify for is their wages.

The crucial new factor, the one that alone can justify higher wages in this country than in other countries with similar levels of cognitive skills, is creativity and innovation. Our firms will not win unless they can produce not merely an incremental improvement on the lower-cost competition, but with ideas that will lead to a quantum leap in value to the customer. They will have to ask themselves not how they can improve a bit on the product and service line they already offer, but what they would do if they were starting fresh. They will have to look at the world from the customer's point of view and ask what they can offer that meets all of those needs in a unique and new way, even if that means building whole new competencies and ditching existing ones.

This capacity for out-of-the-box and breakthrough thinking will be decisive for large firms and small, for individuals as well as organizations, for not just a few, but the vast majority — and therefore for the nation.

There is a substantial body of research on the sources of creativity in individuals. Creativity requires both deep knowledge and technical expertise with one area and very broad knowledge of many, apparently unrelated, areas. It depends on being able to combine disparate elements in new ways that are appropriate for the task or challenge at hand. Thus, it relies heavily on synthesis, the ability to see patterns where others see only chaos. It will happen only in circumstances in which the creator is allowed to fail many times in order to succeed only once. Those who are most successful respond very poorly to extrinsic motivation. They are turned on by the chase for the new conception, the new idea, the uniquely valuable solution. They march to their own drummer, choosing the unconventional over the conventional. This is not surprising, because their aim is to produce the unexpected, the wholly new, the unconventional.

Robert Sternberg, one of the leading researchers in this area, points out that most instruction in our schools emphasizes memory and analytical abilities and therefore may not benefit creative students.

This is not true in the best of our suburban and independent schools. But it is emphatically true of most of our schools. That is not least because many of our accountability tests ask students to identify the one right answer from a list of possible answers to the test question. That is, literally, the answer in the box. But what we need is the out-of-the-box answer, the one that did not occur to the framer of the test.

Because our tests frame what our teachers actually teach, they cannot be blamed for teaching the "right" answers and the ways to find them. Thus, the typical curriculum as experienced by the student is inimical to the development of strong, creative abilities. Researchers agree that the best way to assess creativity in students is to make judgments about the products of their creative work. But because there is not much room for such assessments in many of our accountability testing systems, too few students are asked to produce such work.

But it is also more broadly true, as Sternberg suggests, that our curricula and our pedagogy heavily emphasize analysis over synthesis, the distinguishing feature of the creative impulse. We categorize and dissect and compare and contrast. But we do not often ask our students to create something new. The quintessential act of creating something new is the act of design. Design is a very large field. It ranges from the design of graphical images to the design of a new toaster, from the design of a new inventory system to the design of a new home. For some design challenges, aesthetics is the most important consideration. In others, it is sound engineering or a sound system sense. Designers can be creative and innovative, or derivative and uninspired. The American economy will not succeed in the circumstances we foresee unless people at every level of our society are accomplished, original designers. And that will not happen until design — good design — plays a much larger role in the American curriculum.

No less important than creativity and innovation, the ability to deal easily with ideas will be far more important for far more students than ever before, not least because a firm grasp of the main ideas and concepts from a variety of disciplines is the best asset one could have for learning new things quickly. Much more of the work of the future will be dealing with abstractions than has been true in the past (think of the auto mechanic who must now analyze what is going on inside a computer chip instead of taking a carburetor apart). But it is also true, as we just saw, that creativity often springs from combining ideas from many different fields. As the Commission staff examined educational systems around the world, they noticed that the project- and problem-based curricula that they found in some of the countries most concerned about creativity failed most often for lack of real intellectual substance — that is, when the teachers and students had only a shallow grasp of the core concepts and ideas underlying the knowledge they needed — and were most likely to succeed when those intellectual foundations were firmest. Similarly, curricula that cut across the disciplines are most likely to foster creativity, but they will produce little of value unless the students have a firm grasp of the central ideas and concepts in the underlying disciplines.

We have known for some time that processing skills that contribute to the more rapid acquisition of knowledge and skills are ever more important, among them critical thinking, explicit learning strategies, and the ability to monitor one's own learning.

Complexity of many different kinds will be a hallmark of the future workplace, as will swift change, driven by rapid advances in technology and changes in consumer tastes. So workers will need to be flexible, constantly drawing on different knowledge and skills to solve different problems, moving in a supple way between occupations and employers, the range and depth of their skills their only security.

People who prefer conventional work environments are likely to see their jobs disappear. But those who are comfortable working in artistic, investigative, highly social, or entrepreneurial environments are more likely to succeed if the country succeeds. Schools will have to learn how to simulate these environments in many ways if our students are to develop the abilities that will be so important to them.

We said earlier that there will be many more opportunities for individual entrepreneurs and small firms than ever before, so people who flourish in autonomous situations will do well, among them writers, researchers, trainers, consultants, and service technicians of various kinds. But many of these people, though self-employed or employed by a small firm, will work on ever-changing teams with people from other organizations or working solo, teams built to do particular projects before that team dissolves and another is assembled. So workers will have to have all the skills needed to work solo (for example, to frame the problem, set a goal, take responsibility for achieving it on time and within budget, be self-disciplined and well organized, find out what he or she needs to know to get the job done, and so on) and all the skills needed to work as a strong member of a team.

What is striking about this whole list is that our schools, up to now, have only been expected to do the very first part of it, the part dealing with the cognitive skills and knowledge associated with the core subjects in the curriculum. And we are far behind our major competitors in those areas. If we are correct in our analysis of what will be needed, it will be necessary for the states to reconsider both their standards and their assessment regimes at a fundamental level.

The universal complaint of employers and colleges is that our students cannot write well. Our students seem to have no trouble solving an arithmetic problem when they have seen one just like it before, but they come up short on mathematical reasoning. Our schools, on the whole, are hostile to ideas. Too often, our tests ask students to come up with the one right answer, and the curriculum, pegged to the tests, penalizes the creative student rather than rewarding him or her for the unexpected but thoughtful — or even brilliant — response. Too many schools reward only individual effort — not good teamwork (except on the playing field) — but don't seem to be able to produce many students who can frame a problem on their own, and have the self-discipline to see a complex undertaking through to a successful conclusion.

No doubt there are countless exceptions to these statements, but as we see it, they are exceptions that prove the rule.

Our schools, in every important respect, are very much as we created them at the beginning of the 20th century, when the aim was to build a mass education system that could provide basic literacy for a nation of factory workers, shopkeepers, and (low-technology) farmers. That was an age in which math skills were far more important

than math reasoning; when only the elite were expected to deal with ideas well and engage in abstract thought; when factory owners definitely did not want workers coming up with their own ideas about how to make a product or render a service; when great profits were to be made not by coming up with the wholly new and exciting and customized thing, but by stamping out millions of copies of one thing at the lowest possible cost.

The United States dominated the world economically for decade after decade using the business model just described. And our low-cost competitors are using it now to beat us at our own game. While we know a lot more now than we did only a few years ago about the business model that we need to provide a high standard of living to our people, we continue to use the education model that was invented to support the old business model. Nothing could be more dangerous. It is time now to leave that model to those developing countries for which it represents real progress and for us to create the model that we need to prosper in the future.

SQUARING THE CIRCLE: WHY REDESIGNING THE EDUCATION AND TRAINING SYSTEM IS THE ONLY ALTERNATIVE

Redesigning the whole system seems rather ambitious, maybe a little scary. Is it really necessary?

Consider the standards that the states have set in recent years. After the most recent round of standard setting, few states have set a high school graduation standard

Dundalk, MD — "At first, Michael Walton, starting at community college here, was sure that there was some mistake. Having done so well in high school in West Virginia that he graduated a year and a half early, how could he need remedial math? Because he had no trouble balancing his checkbook, he took himself for a math wiz. But he could barely remember the Pythagorean theorem and had trouble applying sine, cosine and tangent to figure out angles on the geometry questions. Mr. Walton is not unusual. As the new school year begins, the nation's 1,200 community colleges are being deluged with hundreds of thousands of students unprepared for college-level work. Instead, the colleges have clustered those students in community colleges, where their chances of succeeding are low and where taxpayers pay a second time to bring them up to college level. Nearly half the 14.7 million undergraduates at two- and four-year institutions never receive degrees. The deficiencies turn up not just in math, science and engineering, areas in which a growing chorus warns of difficulties in the face of global competition, but also in the basics of reading and writing. According to scores on the 2006 ACT college entrance exam, 21% of students applying to four-year institutions are ready for college-level work in all four areas tested: reading, writing, math and biology. For many students, the outlook does not improve after college. The Pew Charitable Trusts recently found that three-quarters of community college graduates were not literate enough to handle everyday tasks like comparing viewpoints in newspaper editorials or calculating the cost of food items per ounce. The unyielding statistics showcase a deep disconnection between what high school teachers think that their students need to know and what professors, even at two-year colleges, expect them to know. 'Students are still shocked when they're told they need developmental courses,' said Donna McKusi, the senior director of developmental or remedial education at the Community College of Baltimore County. 'They think they graduated from a high school, they should be ready for college.'"

Diana Jean Schemo,
"At Two-Year Colleges, Students Eager But Unready,"
New York Times, September 2, 2006.

AMERICA'S LEAKY EDUCATION PIPELINE

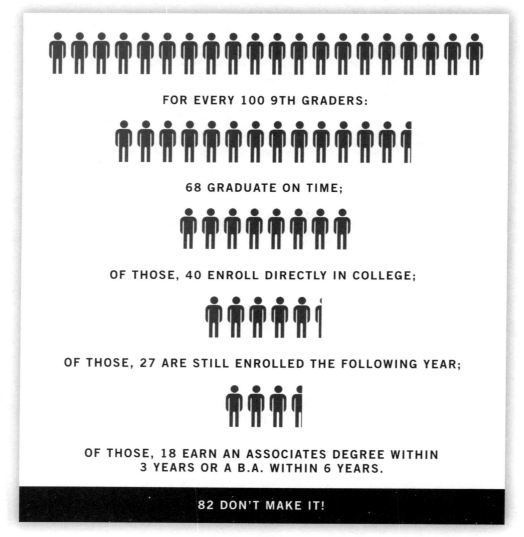

Source: James Hunt, Jr. and Thomas Tierney, *American Higher Education: How Does It Measure Up for the 21st Century?* (San Jose, Calif.: National Center for Public Policy and Higher Education, May 2006).

above the 8th-grade level of English and mathematical literacy in international terms. This level of literacy was approximately the level that our high schools were shooting for in the first half of the 20th century! Yet the states have struggled with countless critics of the new graduation standards, as if they were unreasonably high. The truth is that they are tragically low.

Consider the dropout rate. About two-thirds of those who enter high school graduate. About two-thirds of those who do go on to some form of higher education. About two-thirds of those who go on to higher education take remedial courses in college (so they are not doing college-level work; they are really in high school). Fewer than half of those who go to college get a degree of any sort. Yet virtually all analysts agree that those who do not have at least two years of real college-level work will be in real trouble as adults. They are talking about more than *three-quarters* of those young people who originally entered high school with such high hopes.

Look for a moment at the progression we just described. We fail to teach very large numbers of our young people how to read well enough or develop mathematical reasoning skills in elementary school. We send them to middle school, where they struggle with the material. Many drop out as a result of their frustration. But a large number of those who do not drop out struggle through their courses in high school and get very little out of it. Then some of them go to community college, where some are taught the skills they should have gained years earlier, and some just drop out because it is too hard.

At each stage of this sad tale, we spend more per student than we spent at each preceding stage. The cost of this waste is staggering, yet we do not do what American industry learned to do in the 1980s: get it right the first time. Instead, we operate a stunningly inefficient system year after year after year in the vain hope that somehow it will get better.

Consider our teachers. Imagine for a moment a dimension line of all the people who graduate from our four-year colleges in any given year. At the left end of the dimension line are the young people who entered college with the lowest measured ability. At the right end are those who entered with the highest. One hundred years ago, we thought it reasonable to set policy in such a way that we were most likely to recruit our teachers from the left end of the line. That was a reasonable thing to do, given our aim of providing most of the students they would teach with a fairly low level of literacy. In those days, though, the situation was very different. Many fewer people were going to college, so even though we were recruiting from the left end of the line, we were probably getting the middle of the ability group. Much more important, women and minority groups had few alternatives to teaching if they wanted to enter the professions, so we got far better than the policy entitled us to. And that continued for a long time, until very recently. We still have much better teachers than we deserve, but that situation will not last.

Now we need students who leave school being good readers, able to write well and engage in mathematical reasoning. We told you above that when the new Indian tutoring firms wanted to offer top-notch tutoring

"High school graduates in Nevada with at least a B average can win $10,000 college scholarships — enough to guarantee them free rides at any public university in the state. But that ride has proven rough for many. Nearly one-third of the kids who get the scholarships, created to keep the state's most promising students in Nevada, have to take remedial classes when they start college. They are not alone. Around the country, students, even those with stellar high school records, have discovered they don't have all the skills to survive in college. In Georgia, for instance, 4 out of 10 students who earn the popular Hope Scholarships to the state's university system lose the scholarship after they earn about 30 credits — roughly one year's worth of work — because they can't keep their grades up. Student performance on college-admissions tests also point to possible grade inflation. 'Fifteen years ago, students with A averages accounted for 28% of SAT test takers,' said Wayne Camara, who oversees research for the College Board. Today a whopping 42% of college-bound seniors have A averages, but they score no better on the college admissions tests than did 'A' students a decade earlier. Only one in three 18-year-olds is even minimally prepared for college according to a recent report by the Manhattan Insitute. The picture was even bleaker for minority students. Only 20% of blacks in the class of 2001 were college-ready."

Fredreka Schouten, "Students Unprepared for Rigors of College. Grade Inflation May Be Culprit as Even Top Grads Struggle to Keep Up," Gannett News Service, October 30, 2003.

services that would get their students into the Indian Institutes of Technology, they had to hire graduates of the IITs, because they could find no school teachers who could pass the exams. If we want students graduating from our high schools with the skills we have described, we will have to have teachers who can write well, who read a lot and well, and who are themselves good at mathematical reasoning. And we will need teachers who are very comfortable with ideas. And teachers who have the kind of creative skills and abilities that we want their students to have. Companies that want such people know that they have to recruit from the right half of the imaginary dimension line to get such people. And that is exactly what the schools will have to do. We have kidded ourselves into believing that we can do that by offering small signing bonuses. That does not come within a country mile of what we will have to do to attract these young people in great numbers. We will have to offer compensation and working conditions on a par with what the better employers in the country are now offering, because that is what the competition is. And that will cost a great deal of money.

Consider our students. First, the United States, almost unique among the advanced industrial nations, has managed to construct a system that could not be better designed to deprive the vast majority of our students of a reason to take tough courses or to study hard. We described how the Indian system works to produce an enormous hunger for education and achievement among Indian students. It is hardly clear that it is the quality of instruction that has produced very high mathematical literacy among so many young

Indians. It is very clear that a very high level of student motivation has played a crucial role in their achievement. Many of the advanced industrial countries have education system designs that produce much the same result. But in our system, the message has gone out to all except the students aiming at selective colleges (a very small proportion of all students) that all they need to do is achieve an 8th- or 9th-grade-level of literacy to go to college in their state. And in many states, even that minimum has been waived. So why make the effort to do more?

But that is not all. Study after study has shown that high-quality early childhood education can make a very large difference in the ability of students to succeed in elementary school, where the basis for all later success is laid. But a very large proportion of our students are denied that crucial assist at the starting gate, and they never catch up. It has not happened because that, too, will cost a lot of money.

And we have also known for a long time that there are enormous differences among children in terms of the incomes of their parents, much greater differences than can be found in most other industrialized countries. These differences translate into lower school budgets, less capable teachers, more medical problems that interfere with learning, more trauma that they carry with them into the classroom, and less support for learning from their peers, all very important factors in their ability to get the kind of education they will need to succeed in the world we have described. But fixing this too will take a great deal of money.

The nation, however, is burdened with unprecedented personal, business, and governmental debt at every level, and money is in short supply.

Actually, it would be a mistake to try to solve our problems that way. Over the past 40 or so years, we have tried every conceivable programmatic solution, and none have made a difference in the achievement of our students anywhere close to the improvements we must now produce. We have tried innovations in teacher training, professional development, curriculum, team teaching, school choice, school finance, school organization, school governance, pedagogy, and much, much more. The reason that nothing has made much difference is that every time we tried to change something, we did not change much of anything else. When we invested hundreds of millions in producing curriculum materials that captured the key ideas in the disciplines, we failed to invest in attracting teachers who were well enough educated (not trained — educated) to teach it well. When we found a way to attract some of our most able college graduates to teaching, they stayed only a year or two, because we did not change the compensation and working conditions to enable us to keep them. When we added extra money for low-income children, we failed to change the underlying financing system, which overwhelmed the effect of the add-on funding. When we introduced strong accountability systems, we did very little to help our teachers learn how to improve their teaching, and so we behaved as if the teachers had always known what to do but had been holding back because they were not being held accountable. When we finally got concerned about the students who were falling through the cracks in high school, we decided we had a high school problem, and

failed to think through how we could give the high schools a fighting chance by fixing the overwhelming problems that many students face when they first arrive at high school.

Over and over again, we have leaped from one partial solution to another. When they did not work, we declared their advocates to be wrong and went on to the next. Most were not wrong; their solutions were simply insufficient.

And they were also too much. To visit the typical American school is to practice a certain kind of archaeology. We do not throw anything away. Policies are not discontinued; we simply add new ones. Professional development programs go on long after their rationale has withered, as do curriculum initiatives and approaches to school organization. The worst of our schools are not short of initiatives and programs. They typically have too many, most of them in conflict with one another, a discordant symphony of barely controlled chaos. Much the same can be said of state policies and programs.

There is another reason we cannot solve this problem with money. There are schools in the United States that are as good as any others in the world. Disproportionately, they are our best independent and suburban schools. Those schools are as good as they are partly because the spending levels in those schools are high, but mainly because they are home to the most advantaged students in the United States. We cannot spend our way into a condition in which all schools have that kind of student body. To get the results in all of our schools anywhere close to the results we get in our elite schools, we

"If there is one thing we know from research and common sense, it is that if you take a kid from a disorganized home in a stressful neighborhood, where nobody is reading bedtime stories and where the vocabulary in daily use is small, and you put that kid in a quality preschool with books, stability and conversation, the results can be impressive. That kid is more likely to be able to recognize numbers and letters, more likely to be able to predict events in a storybook, more likely to do better on vocabulary tests. Moreover, because the kid will be in a structured environment, he or she is more likely to develop social skills and self-control. Experts disagree over how long these preschool effects last, but the bulk of the evidence suggests that disadvantaged kids enrolled in quality preschools have a better shot at graduating from high school and avoiding prison. As a result, many scholars have concluded that money spent on preschool more than pays for itself over time."

DAVID BROOKS, "GOOD INTENTIONS, BAD POLICY,"
New York Times, JUNE 4, 2006.

★ ★ ★ ★

"Classroom enrollment is up in most parts of the country and so is the demand for public school teachers. But many states report that fewer people are choosing to become teachers. Increases in college tuition and new pressures to up student test scores have made low-paying teaching jobs less appealing. The shortfall is hitting schools hardest in the core subjects of math and science and in traditionally hard-to-staff areas such as special education and language training for non-English speakers. According to the Iowa Department of Education, the state has seen a 21% drop in student teachers from its three largest public universities in the past two years and a 23% drop in new teacher licenses since 2000."

KAVAN PETERSON, "FEWER CHOOSING TEACHING JOBS,"
STATELINE.ORG, MARCH 28, 2006.

will have to change the system from one that was designed a century ago to meet the needs of our emerging mass production economy to one that will sustain the knowledge-based, technology-powered, globally interconnected economy we described above.

In the years since the first Commission produced its report in 1990, the National Center on Education and the Economy has benchmarked the education systems of two dozen countries around the world. The overwhelming conclusion is that it is the system that counts, the ways all these factors and many more are joined together to create a coherent and powerful system, all the parts and pieces of which reinforce each other to produce consistently fine results.

The research that the NCEE staff has conducted for the Commission shows that most of the countries with the most effective education systems are themselves redesigning their systems. In the process, they are adopting many of the practices being used by the most successful firms in the kind of economy that is now emerging. In the second section of this report, we describe what such a system might look like. While we have drawn on our international research, trying to learn as much as possible from the countries the staff has studied, the plan we offer is copied from no one. It is intended to produce not a shadow of what others are doing, but a model for others to follow. The system we describe is a state system any state could adopt, not a national system, because our Constitution reserved the education function to the states, and did not vest it in the national government.

THE END OF AN ERA: WHY WE MUST HAVE BOTH EQUITY AND QUALITY

Through much of the 20th century, education policy debates have alternated between a focus on quality and a focus on equity, between improving the education of our elites and improving the education of our average students, between the needs of future professionals and managers and the needs of working people.

The plan we offer rejects these choices. We have no choice now but to do both. A glance at the chart on page 26 shows why that is so. If we succeed in creating a high-wage, high-employment economy that can sustain us over the coming decades, it will be because we have succeeded in educating and training the vast majority of our citizens to a very high level, in all the ways that we described.

There will be no net growth in our workforce for a long time coming from native-born Americans. All the net growth will come from immigrants. And most of our immigrants are coming from populations who are very poorly educated. Even with the children of our immigrants, the proportion of working people to people they must support will decline. So, to maintain our standard of living, every working person must be much more productive than our generation has been, and the children of our immigrants will have to be vastly more productive than their parents.

If we do not do a far better job of educating the children of these immigrants and our other low-income minority populations than we have done up to now, we can confidently expect the knowledge and skill of our workforce to decline precipitously at the very time that we desperately need the opposite to happen. And this has to happen at the same time we are doing a much better job of educating the native born. Our proposals are designed to do exactly that.

AND...WHAT ABOUT THE ADULT WORKER?

The report of our first Commission addressed the education and training needs not just of our school-age children, but also of our workers. The reason for that still holds. The vast majority of the workers in our workforce 20 years from now will be the people who are already in our workforce. Assume for the moment that it takes five years to implement the kinds of changes we recommend. Then the first child to enter 1st grade under the new systems would do so five years from now. The earliest that that student would enter the workforce, having completed a two-year college program, would be 12 years later, 17 years from now. We cannot wait that long to make a major improvement in the skills of our workforce. If we do, investors may well decide to move many more of their investments offshore, and employers will do the same with their operations. The country may not be able to recover.

WHAT WILL ADULT WORKERS NEED TO KNOW AND BE ABLE TO DO?

If the conclusions we reached as to how the global economy is evolving are correct, a very large fraction of our workforce —

much higher than at present — will need to have a foundation level of literacy much deeper and broader than we have thought necessary in the past, at a very minimum the level needed to do college level work. In principle, everything we have said about the kind of education young people should be getting in school applies as well to the adult worker — from the high school dropout to the 30-year-old mother of four who immigrated to this country in her teens, speaks very poor English, and knows very little math, to the 45-year-old shipyard worker with only a high school diploma and an 8th-grade-level of literacy whose yard was shut down three years ago and has been unable to find a job paying more than a quarter of what he was earning. For the same reasons that our young people will have to be highly competent in the core subjects in the curriculum and, at the same time, creative and innovative in the ways they apply what they know to the challenges of the workplace, our adult workers will need the same foundational skills and knowledge.

Beyond the need to provide the same kind of foundation education to our workers that we want for our children, we must make sure that they have access to a continuing, if intermittent, stream of technical education programs that will enable them to adapt to the demands of the dynamically evolving economic environment we have described. They will clearly have to do this without taking years or even months off for full-time study on a college campus. This almost constant infusion of new skills and abilities will have

"December saw the release of the important, once-a-decade National Assessment of Adult Literacy (NAAL). Fewer than one-in-three college graduates can successfully perform tasks such as understanding and comparing the viewpoints of two newspaper editorials, interpreting a table with data about blood pressure and physical activity, or computing and comparing the cost per ounce of different food items. Perhaps more disturbing, nearly one in five college graduates score at only the Basic literacy levels, which means they have trouble with tasks like consulting reference materials and calculating the total cost of items ordered from a catalogue."

"New Adult Literacy Data Puts College Credential in Questions," Education Sector, *2*(1), January 10, 2006.

★ ★ ★ ★

"Each year, approximately 1.2 million students fail to graduate from high school. That means that every school day, 7,000 American high school students become dropouts. While, on average, approximately 70% of students graduate from high school with a regular diploma, students from historically disadvantaged minority groups have little more than a 50% chance of finishing high school."

Lyndsay Pinkus, *Who's Counted? Who's Counting? Understanding High School Graduation Rates* (Washington, D.C.: Alliance for Excellent Education, June 2006).

★ ★ ★ ★

"In the most recent OECD study of education expenditures around the world, the United States ranked second only to Korea in expenditures on educational institutions — both public and private, primary, secondary and higher education — as represented by percentage of our nation's GDP."

Data from *Education at a Glance: OECD Indicators 2005* (Paris: OECD, 2005).

to take place in a flexible, accessible way to be practical for people with families and full-time jobs.

Dealing effectively with this challenge will involve rethinking our whole approach to the education and job training of the people in our workforce.

THE ADULT EDUCATION AND JOB TRAINING SYSTEM WE HAVE NOW

The system we have now was never designed to produce the outcomes we have described. It is very complex, but at its roots, it is founded on two main premises.

The first is that a primary purpose of adult basic education and publicly funded job training is to get poor people a job as soon as possible. In this sense, the adult basic education system has been an extension of the social services system — not very well funded, set to minimum standards, and intended not mainly for the middle class but for the more vulnerable workers at the bottom of the job food chain. Because this has been so, the adult basic education and job training system has been largely disconnected from public policies and institutions designed to promote local and regional economic development.

The second premise is that the highest priority for access to higher education should go to helping young people pay for full-time study in degree programs. They work well for young people leaving high school and acquiring one or more degrees before they ever enter the full-time paid

workforce. But that, of course, describes an ever smaller proportion of the people who need some form of education beyond high school.

These characteristics of the American system are not uniquely American, but many of our competitors have systems that are conceived very differently. We learned earlier that the United States is falling behind its competitors in terms of the quality and quantity of education it provides to our young people entering the workforce. It is also true that, in many highly industrialized countries, the adult basic education system is intended to enable a much larger fraction of the adult population to achieve much higher education standards. It is also true that most of those countries have national occupational skills standards and curricula designed in a modular form so that people can accumulate modules as they need them to achieve their personal goals or adjust to changes in the patterns of job availability as the economy changes. And their financial aid systems are designed to help workers take advantage of these modular programs. In fact, some of our competitors provide these modular programs to their workers free of charge.

WHAT DO WE KNOW ABOUT HOW OUR WORKERS' LITERACY SKILLS COMPARE TO THOSE OF WORKERS IN OTHER COUNTRIES?

If our educational attainment rates are slipping compared to those of our competitors, if the quality of our schooling has also slipped

mpetitors, if we
mmigration from
do a good job of
... own people, if our job
training system is set to education
standards below those of our competitors,
and if other countries provide better access
to specialized training then we do — and
all of these things are true — then we
should not be surprised to find out that
the foundational skills and knowledge of
our workers are well below those of our
competitors.

In fact, about 12 percent of those not
in school or prison do not have a high
school diploma or a general equivalency
diploma (GED). Twenty-five percent have
a high school diploma but no college. So
we can safely say that on the order of 37
percent have what amounts to an 8th-
grade-level of literacy or less. It is helpful
to know that, but it would be even more
helpful to know how the basic skills of
our workforce compare to the basic skills
of the workforces in the countries that
are our major competitors. Fortunately
the International Adult Literacy Survey
(IALS) provides very good measures of
the literacy of our workers compared to the
literacy of workers in other countries with
which we compete. The authors of the
IALS report characterize the literacy levels
of American workers compared to the
levels of the workers in the other countries
as "mediocre." More precisely, three kinds
of literacy were surveyed: prose literacy,
document literacy, and quantitative literacy.
Of the 20 countries and language groups
surveyed, the U.S. ranked 9th in prose

literacy, 14th in document literacy, and
13th in quantitative literacy.

Lest the reader think that the IALS
was measuring skills that few people really
need, it might be useful to quote the study
document on the definition of quantitative
skills: "The knowledge and skills required
to apply arithmetic operations, either alone
or sequentially, using numbers embedded
in printed materials; for example, balancing
a checkbook, figuring out a tip, completing
an order form, or determining the amount
of interest from a loan advertisement."

The problem does not end with our
low median performance relative to our
competitors: the range of scores in the
United States was among the greatest of
all nations studied. Workers at the top of
the range score well compared to workers
elsewhere. That is the good news. The bad
news is that the proportion of the workers
at the bottom of the literacy range is among
the highest for all countries studied.

We have said that we have no choice
but to set a goal of getting all of our
students ready to the level of literacy
required to do college-level work. If that
is true for the young people in school, it
is no less true for those who are out of
school and in the workforce. It is, arguably,
the highest priority in our whole basket
of urgent priorities for education and
training, because all specialized training
and the ability to turn on a dime as the
world changes depend on the solidity of
the general education foundation we have
built for every member of the workforce.
The workers for whom the new literacy
is an urgent matter are in very different

circumstances. Some are school dropouts between the ages of 16 and 25. Some of them are very poor readers, and some are very bright young people who were simply unchallenged and bored, and some are both. Some are immigrants whose English is poor. Of these, many are uneducated according to any reasonable meaning of that term, but some just need good language training. Some will be eager to go back to school, and many will need to be convinced that they should do so. Some are working three minimum-wage jobs, and some are unemployed. Many have a high school diploma or a GED, but only a 7th- or 8th-grade level of literacy, which served their parents well but is no longer enough for the work that will enable them to stay afloat. Many have tried community college more than once but have never been able to acquire the literacy levels required to stick it out.

ADULT EDUCATION, PUBLIC JOB TRAINING AND ECONOMIC GROWTH

Earlier, we pointed out that this country needs economic growth, and the kind of growth we need is the kind that is driven by leading-edge technologies. Over the past 20 years, researchers have learned a lot about that kind of growth, and one of the things they have learned is that it tends to have a strong regional focus. It works best when a kind of ecological balance occurs among key researchers and research facilities, innovators who can apply what the researchers learn in creative ways, suppliers of risk capital who

"... The global integration of production cuts costs and taps new sources of skills and knowledge. ... As shared business practices spread, along with shared modes of connecting business activity, companies can hand over more and more of the work they had previously performed in-house ... to outside specialists. ... The corporation is emerging as a combination of various functions and skills—some tightly bound and some loosely coupled—and it integrates these components of business activity and production on a global basis to produce goods and services for its customers. ... The single, most important challenge in shifting to globally integrated enterprises—and the consideration driving most business decisions today—will be securing a supply of high-value skills."

FROM SAMUEL J. PALMISANO, CHAIR OF THE BOARD, PRESIDENT AND CHIEF EXECUTIVE OFFICER OF IBM, IN "THE GLOBALLY INTEGRATED ENTERPRISE," FOREIGN AFFAIRS, MAY/JUNE 2006.

understand the industry in which these developments are taking place and the players and who therefore are in a position to place well-informed bets, specialized suppliers who can deliver high quality on time — and a strong supply of well-educated and highly trained people capable of doing the work at every level from technicians to engineers. Actually, all industries, not just those at the leading edge, are likely to produce the best economic results for their shareholders, their workers, and their communities if they too exist in this sort of ecological balance.

Because the adult education and public job training community has been largely isolated from the people responsible in their communities for economic development and growth, and because those responsible for adult education and public job training have typically worked in agencies with a very small geographical reach, they have rarely been in a position to contribute effectively to that growth and have therefore not been seen as useful players in the discussion. This is no small matter. It results in underinvestment in a large number of people who could be making a much stronger contribution to the economic well-being not only of themselves but of the community as a whole. It is time to change the organization of the adult education and public job training functions in our society to better align them with the forces and institutions of economic development.

GIVING OUR WORKERS ACCESS TO THE RESOURCES THEY NEED TO ADAPT TO THE CHANGING ECONOMY

Whereas American schools, according to the Organization for Economic Cooperation and Development (OECD), are well funded relative to the schools in other advanced industrial nations, this country's public job training system is not, relative to the job training systems in the countries with which we compete. We have, for that reason, allowed ourselves a little more latitude to recommend budget increases here. There are few investments this nation can make that are likely to have a greater payoff in improved productivity and economic growth.

THE CHALLENGE AHEAD

So now we can see the full scope of the challenge ahead. If we do not prepare to succeed in a highly competitive, knowledge-based, technology-driven global economy, we can expect the long-term decline in the earning power of our workers to continue and accelerate until we join the ranks of the second-rate powers. To avoid that outcome, our whole population needs to be much better educated and very differently educated. We need to figure out how to accomplish that without greatly increasing our budget for education, because we do not have the money and it would not work anyway. So we must redesign our system to get vastly more from the money we do spend.

We do not have a choice.

Part

II

THE SCENARIO

THE RECOMMENDATIONS AS THEY MIGHT LOOK FROM THE VANTAGE POINT OF AN OBSERVER IN 2021

What follows is a story, a scenario drafted from the point of view of someone writing 15 years after this report was released.

What we offer is a concrete vision of what we think it will be possible to achieve if we act boldly. The concreteness is important because there would be a very strong disposition almost everywhere to implement generally stated principles within the framework of the system we already have, a system that has been in place a very long time and no longer serves us well. So it is vitally necessary to sketch the dimensions of quite a different system and to describe how it might work.

The members of the Commission are both experienced and realistic. That being so, we are aware that many will look at this scenario with some amazement. We are very much aware that the document gores many sacred cows and in many places says things that many have felt but few have said out loud. It is time, we think, to say those things out loud and, much more to the point, to do something about them before it is too late.

Over the years, many vested interests have grown up around the system. This is the case with any social system as it develops over time. It is precisely this growth of interests from powerful sectors of the community that makes needed changes so difficult. As a Commission, we worked hard to set these differences aside as we worked together to craft a better system. We hope that the country as a whole will be able to do the same thing.

Not every member of this Commission agrees with every aspect of this plan. But we do not think that matters very much, which is why we agreed — enthusiastically — to sign it. What matters is that the proposals put forward here are, we feel, exactly the kind of plan that this country needs to focus on, talk about, and wrestle with. It is the only plan we know of that is couched in terms that are equal to the magnitude of the problems we face.

The report is intended to inspire creativity. It is not intended to be a detailed recipe but rather a framework. The nation will be well served if the states go at it differently, so that we can see what works best under which conditions. The states in our federal system were once described as the laboratory of democracy. That conception fits our stance very well.

That said, we do not intend to encourage cherry picking only those ideas that cost the least and offend the fewest. Without the pain inflicted by the proposals we make for saving money, there will be no gain from the ways we propose to spend it. If legislatures pocket the gains from the savings we propose and fail to make the investments we recommend, then that will simply lead to lower performance all around. We do not propose a collection of initiatives. We propose a system that has its own integrity, though it can be implemented in many ways.

A comment is in order about getting from where we are to the vantage point of this scenario, 15 years hence. As a general matter, if we knew exactly how to get from here to there, neither this Commission nor this report would have been necessary. This will be a collective act of invention, calling on the commitment, creativity, and skill of leaders at every level of our rather complex society for years to come.

It will not happen at all unless key stakeholders are involved in appropriate ways. A few examples will suffice. In states that have collective bargaining statutes for the schools, the state would become the successor employer for possibly hundreds of existing contracts, and the changes we have in mind for employment and compensation of teachers can be achieved only through agreement between the governors' office and the unions. We are confident that the legislative and collective bargaining processes will bring the best result because they will engage the frontline education professionals. This may also be the best way to make sure that the savings the Commission proposes to effect will get ploughed back into the education reforms we propose.

The sea changes we propose in higher education will not happen unless the higher education community is deeply involved in the discussion. The equally profound changes we propose in the rules governing school finance will be shaped in part by discussions with the representatives of various groups of disadvantaged students, as well as those more fortunate. The list is much longer, but the point is made. No constituency should be allowed to stonewall the changes on which so much depends, but nothing will happen unless many are involved in shaping the new system.

And so we turn to the scenario.

The Scenario

The year is 2021, 15 years after the *New* Commission on the Skills of the American Workforce made its report calling for sweeping changes in the American education and training system.

Fifteen years ago, when the report was issued, American graduate schools were the best in the world. But American grade schools fared poorly in international comparisons of student achievement. Dropout rates in American high schools were in the neighborhood of 30 percent. Fewer than half of the cohort went on to any kind of postsecondary education. But even that number was a mirage, because one-third of the students going on to "higher" education were taking one or more remedial courses, trying to master material that their peers in other countries had mastered in grade school.

Once they got into two-year and four-year colleges, fewer than half had gotten a degree four years after entering a two-year degree program or six years after entering a four-year degree program. But many who would never get a degree carried mountains of debt that they would take years to pay off. America's education system was among the more expensive in the world, but it was also among the world's most inefficient, failing large numbers of students at every stage of the education progression.

During virtually the entire preceding century, the United States could take pride in having the highest proportion of its population with 12 years of postkindergarten education and the highest proportion with college degrees in the world, but it had lost that advantage two decades earlier, and many other countries had already surpassed it or were about to do so. Even China and India, two very poor countries, had succeeded in outstripping the United States in production of young people whose command of mathematics — surely one of the keys to world economic leadership in a high-technology age — was world class. As the 21st century began, it looked to many keen observers that the United States' days as the world's leading economy were numbered, because no serious analyst could imagine how any nation could lead the world economically that was not also a world education leader. There was no shortage of education reform — there never had been — but it all seemed modest and incremental, tinkering at the edges, never getting to the fundamental problems with the system.

The Commission meetings had been preceded by a year and a half of intensive research on, among other things, the dynamics of the global economy. The researchers had come to the conclusion that the workers in the United States could look forward to a steadily declining standard of living unless the vast majority of American workers not only had world-class academic skills and knowledge, but were among the most creative and innovative in the world. World economic leadership would belong to the nations that were technological leaders in field after field and were able to translate that technological prowess into an endless stream of products and services that were the most creative, distinctive, and irresistible products and services available from anyone anywhere. From the boardroom to the factory floor, workers would have to be among the best educated, flexible, most creative, and most innovative in the world. In a nutshell, that seemed to mean that the United States would have to learn how to build schools for all of its children that provided a kind and quality of education that only the very best public and independent schools had ever provided before.

The Commission, in its report, had wondered out loud whether our country had the will required. They wondered whether what had happened to the United States was what had happened to all the great nations sooner or later as they passed into "the dustbin of history," whether, in other words, America had become the victim of its own success and, taking its success for granted, had become lazy. It had noted in its report that students in many other countries seemed to be much hungrier for education, and willing to work much harder to get it, than students in the United States. And it had noted too that while Americans thought schools in general needed reform, they thought schools in their own community were just fine. On the whole, it looked to the Commissioners as though the United States might not have the stomach for the kind of changes in the American education system that the Commissioners were quite certain would be needed to keep the United States competitive.

Winston Churchill, dryly observing half a century earlier the same American tendency to teeter on the brink before doing what was obviously necessary, once said that America always did the right thing — after it had exhausted all the alternatives. It seems he had it right. Down on its knees 15 years ago, it is once again a world leader in education and training and its economic prospects are as bright as ever.

1. A PERFORMANCE-BASED SYSTEM

The Commission began by recognizing that something had to be done about the colossal inefficiency of the American education system. It noticed that one of the striking contrasts between the American system and those of the most successful countries was that American students thought of themselves as putting in time in the successive stages of the system (elementary school, middle school, high school, college, and so on), whereas students in the most successful systems thought of themselves as studying for examinations that opened the doors to the things that they really wanted for themselves. The result was that most American students avoided taking tough courses and studying hard, while most students in these other countries rose to meet the expectations set by the examinations, because they understood that that was the only way they could achieve their aims. American educators prided themselves on a system that offered second, third, and fourth chances to students who had failed at earlier stages, letting them rise

up through the system as they did so, while the systems in other countries took pride in offering students repeated chances to master the material, but never letting anyone move on in the system until the standard for doing so had been met.

The Commission had taken its cue from American business in the 1970s and 1980s, when leading corporations were forced by foreign competitors to redesign their businesses so that all the products and services they produced were very high quality from the beginning. In this case, the aim was to make sure that American students would be educated to high standards from the day they first showed up for school, rather than being passed up through the system with poor educations until they finally got a triage at very high cost in the higher education system.

The key was designing a set of State Board Qualifying Examinations. Passing them became a requirement for moving on to the next stage of one's education. They were called examinations rather than tests because they were intended to measure the extent to which the students had mastered a particular curriculum. These State Board Qualifying Examinations were conceived of as performance examinations. That is, a student would be able to take them whenever he or she was ready and would be able to move on in the system as soon as they were passed. Unlike the systems in many other nations, students could take the tests repeatedly. In a sense, no one fails these exams. They might succeed and go on to the next stage of their education. They might succeed in part and not meet the standard in part and that would tell them what they had to study to succeed on the next try. Not passing does not consign a student to a life of struggle. In fact, the idea was to organize the system with the aim of sending every student to college and, at the same time, making sure that every student had the skills to succeed in college once there.

For most students, the State Board Qualifying Examination came at the end of the first 10 years of education beyond kindergarten. For those 10 years, the curriculum would be pretty much the same for all students, with some choices along the way. However quickly or slowly they might proceed, all would be expected to master this core curriculum.

Students get scaled scores on this first State Board Qualifying Examination, but there are passing scores set for two possible destinations, and no one can go on to those destinations unless they achieve that score. The first passing score is set to the level at which the community and technical colleges and certain designated state colleges are required to admit students as freshmen for credit, without remediation, in every program they offer. There is also a passing score at which students should be able to read, write, and do mathematics well enough to succeed in College Board Advanced Placement (AP) courses, International Baccalaureate (IB) programs, and other similar demanding academic upper-secondary programs. In rare cases, a student might be ready to take this first State Board Exam earlier than the end of the sophomore year. No student below the compulsory education age, of course,

could leave unless that student was going on to full-time study at a higher level. In fact, though, most students who, before these reforms, would have dropped out, stayed in school to prepare for another shot (sometimes several shots) at the State Board Qualifying Examinations. They did that because, as we will see below, they had much more support than such students had ever had before. Most important, the vast majority were working harder in school and therefore succeeding, because they knew that they would not be allowed to go to any kind of college without meeting the standards set by this examination.

Many students who wanted a demanding technical program leading to a career in anything from specialty welding to software engineering went right to their community or technical college, because those were the only institutions that had the resources to pay for the teachers and equipment. Many others went who wanted other kinds of occupational programs and still others who wanted to enroll in two-year programs that would enable them to transfer into the junior year of four-year college programs.

Many of those who wanted to go on to demanding college prep programs typically offered by high schools, like AP and IB programs and many state equivalents, stayed in their high schools for those programs. But, over time, some community and technical colleges began to offer AP and IB and other similar programs too, and some high schools began to offer some of the more popular technical preparation programs. The state realized that the students and their

New Commission on the Skills of the American Workforce

SCHEMA FOR STUDENT PROGRESSION THROUGH THE SYSTEM

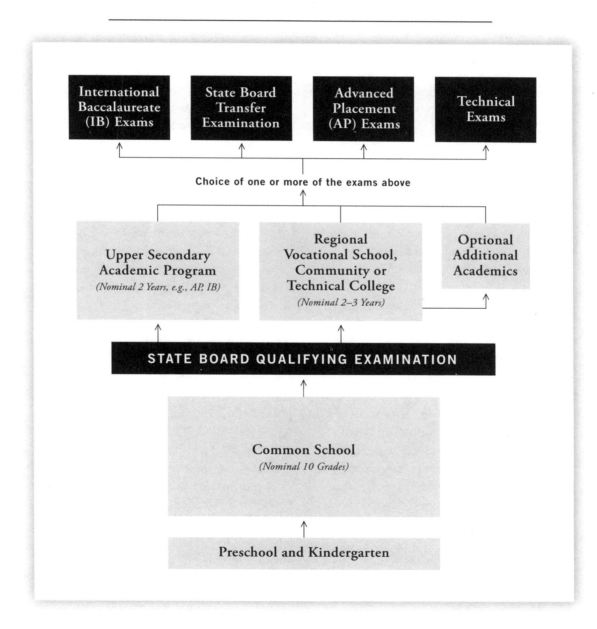

parents would be better off if they had lots of choices of institutions that could offer these programs, so they said that the students could take their state money with them to any accredited institution that offered any of these programs.

But it was not a free-for-all. The state would pay only for programs leading to examinations that it approved. In most states now, this includes the program of AP courses that the College Board put together, a similar set of examinations created by the American College Testing organization, the International Baccalaureate, the Cambridge University International General Certificate of Secondary Education exams, other national board exams that have been developed over the years since the Commission report was released, a series of state-approved technical and trade qualifications, and a state board examination similar to the New York State Regents Examinations.

Students who entered the community and technical colleges after passing their first State Board Exam had the option of participating in a front-end program that allowed them to sample a range of technical and occupational programs to get a sense for what they might like to do. The length of this front-end program could be tailored to the needs of the student. During the front-end experience, the student was guided by a counselor whose job was to make sure that the student fully understood the options and was not rushed into a decision on which program to pursue.

But there were no dead ends in the new system. Students opting for the community and technical college route could always go on to four-year colleges and polytechnics in any program for which they chose to take the necessary prerequisite courses. Students who chose the academic board exam route could always detour back to a community or technical college to pick up technical courses, certificates, or degrees, and an increasing number of students did exactly that, though many chose to do so after they had joined the full-time workforce.

When students completed their national and State Board Exam programs, they could take the appropriate examinations. If they had been studying for their second State Board examinations, called the State Board Transfer Examinations, that is what they could take. A passing score on this examination in English and math entitled the student to enter many designated state colleges as a junior. The state had to specify which parts of these exams had to be passed with which scores to meet the entrance standards. Of course, students who wanted to go on to some other institution would take whatever tests those institutions require. Over time, what has happened is that states with similar standards for their college transfer examinations have agreed to honor each other's exams, and all public institutions have specified what scores on the AP, IB, ACT, and other exams they will accept for automatic entrance into their institutions as sophomores and juniors. One of the unexpected consequences of these policies is that students from states that set their standards low compared to other states found that they could not transfer on the same terms to colleges in those states, and the public outcry over this has led to a steady ratcheting up of standards in those states.

These measures have transformed the grade schools over the past 15 years. Students all over the country now realize that they can no longer get into college — any college — by just coasting through secondary school. So they are working much harder than students did before, to succeed on their State Board Qualifying Exams. This, of course, makes it easier for teachers, who find their students more motivated to learn.

Students who had been bored to tears in high school realized that they could get out earlier and get on with their lives if they put in the effort required to pass their State Board Qualifying Exams earlier. Students who wanted the relative freedom and responsibility of a community or technical college and whose parents agreed could get what they wanted, and most thrived in it. But high schools that saw their students leaving early worked harder to make their courses more engaging for the students, and many who might otherwise have left chose instead to stay, some because they were attracted by the improvements in the academic program, some because they wanted to stay with their friends in high school, and some because their parents thought they were not yet mature enough for the relative freedom and responsibility of a community or technical high school.

Some community colleges, realizing that they had learned a lot over the years about how to provide high-quality remediation in very innovative ways, decided to offer special noncredit-bearing programs to high school students who were having trouble passing their state qualifying examinations. Because the money in the new system followed the students, the students could use state money to pay for these programs. When high schools realized that this was happening, they came up with their own nontraditional — and much more effective — ways to get their students to the new standards. And so many students who might have gone to the community colleges to prepare themselves to take the qualifying exam again chose instead to stay where they were.

And that illustrates a larger point. High schools, community colleges, and technical colleges, when they realized that they were competing for the same students did what competitors always do: they trimmed fat, improved quality, and worked harder to figure out what their customers wanted and gave it to them.

One of the consequences of letting students go to college earlier than they would have otherwise was to raise a lot of questions about high school athletics and other extracurricular activities. So, in most places, communities decided to continue to organize their competitive sports programs, school plays, school bands, and many kinds of clubs for young people around their high schools, and to encourage students to continue to participate in those programs, even when they had gone off to the local community college for their academics. A lot of issues around eligibility rules had to get ironed out to make this possible and "protect the mascots" but eventually, everyone calmed down, high school athletics resumed the role they had always played in welding and keeping communities together, and the high school plays were still the big draw they had always been.

"Five years ago, spurred by the creation of a new high-stakes state test, Framingham High School began an experiment. The goal was not simply to get students to pass a test, but also to prepare more students for college. Teachers teamed up to help struggling students. They coaxed high achievers to take tougher classes and recruited upperclassmen to tutor freshmen and sophomores. So far, the experiment has paid off. Compared with the class of 2000, the first group to take the MCAS as sophomores, many more students in the class of 2005 passed the tests. About 90% in the class of 2005 passed both tests on their first try, while only 58% of the class of 2000 passed the math exam and 78% passed the English. More than 90% of its sophomores passed the English and math tests taken in the spring, and the majority scored at the highest levels. Statewide, 81% of sophomores passed the exams. Students need a passing grade in order to graduate. More students from the class of 2005 took Advanced Placement math classes and passed them. They scored higher on the SATs, they were less likely to drop out, and more went on to four-year universities. Framingham's successes, educators say, are a sign that education reform is working at the school, whose students reflect state demographics: Roughly a quarter are Hispanic, African-American, or Asian, while the majority are white. A fifth come from low-income families. 'Education reformers hoped the high-stakes tests would motivate high schools to transform themselves, starting with what and how teachers teach,' said state Education Commissioner David Driscoll. But after the tests became a graduation requirement, he said too many schools made superficial changes, such as adding tutoring centered around test questions. Their sole focus was on getting students to pass, he said. 'Just passing the MCAS does not greatly prepare kids for college. I don't want to hear how many kids pass. That thing [passing the MCAS] was a minimal standard.' Framingham, he said, took the right tack. 'Those are the things that will make kids high achievers, not just test takers,' he said. The school is pushing all of its students to aim higher than passing the MCAS exams. It has added Advanced Placement courses in three subjects in recent years, but also has started classes to prepare freshmen and sophomores so they are ready to handle AP work as upperclassmen. The classes are small, with roughly 15 students each. Teachers treat the classes like a discussion section of a college course, allowing them to delve deeper into concepts that students have trouble grasping. Math classes across the board also became more rigorous. Teachers encouraged sophomores to double up on math, taking Geometry and Algebra II simultaneously so they not only had a better shot at doing well on the MCAS but could handle AP calculus their senior year. As a result of the changes, students who never before thought about attending college began to see it as a possibility. For the last five years, the school has taken many of its African-American students on a tour of historically black colleges in the South over spring break. The school brings Hispanic business leaders and academics from the Framingham community to talk to Hispanic students about college. Students get adult mentors to keep them on track."

Tracy Jan, "On MCAS and Beyond, School Gets Results," *Boston Globe*, September 29, 2005.

One of the biggest challenges was raising the aspirations of young people from poor and minority families and communities, places where there was very little history of young people going on to college and entering the professions, places where children were often counted on to help support the family from an early age, or places where the youth culture viewed students with academic ambitions as having gone over to the other side.

The Commission, concerned about this issue, had strongly urged local philanthropies and businesses to create campaigns to raise the aspirations of these young people. In some cases, this meant new or expanded mentor programs. In others, it meant filmed or taped ads featuring personalities that these students could identify with. And other things were tried too. The Commission ended up being rather surprised at the extent to which communities were willing and able to mount effective campaigns of this sort.

The Commission's plan for restructuring the way students progress through the education system had enormous financial implications.

The financial analysts working with the Commission's staff had calculated the savings from the plan at close to $70 billion when the plan was fully implemented. They assumed that a handful of students would successfully challenge the State Board Examinations at the end of the 9th grade, most would do so at the end of the 10th grade, and some would do so at the end of the 11th and 12th grades. A majority, they thought, would then choose to go on to their local community and technical colleges, but

a substantial minority would choose to stay in high school to study for examinations that would then prepare them for highly selective colleges as freshmen or less selective or non-selective colleges as sophomores or juniors. All those who chose to go immediately to community colleges would no longer be in high school and would therefore represent a savings against what would otherwise have been spent on them in high school. Similarly, more money would be saved by students who went on to their community and technical colleges after the 9th, 10th, or 11th grades and then entered four-year colleges as sophomores or juniors, since the sums that would have been spent on their freshman or sophomore years would not have to be spent at all. Furthermore, because students would be admitted to community or technical colleges as degree candidates only if they did not need remedial courses, all the money that had been spent on remedial courses in these institutions could be saved. It was all these changes that together produced the savings.

All of this, of course, assumed that most of the students who would otherwise have dropped out or been so poorly educated that they could not do college-level work by the time they had completed college — to say nothing of the time they finished 10th grade — could and would be educated to a college-ready standard by the end of 10th grade.

To do that would require a wholesale transformation of the system. That remarkable transformation is described below. Some of the most far-reaching aspects of that transformation cost little, if anything, in dollars (though a great deal in social and institutional change). But other aspects cost a great deal. Both are described below. What is important to note here is what the Commission chose to do with the funds released by the structural changes just described.

The amount saved was divided three ways. The first third — a little more than $18 billion a year — was used to produce far-reaching changes in teachers' compensation, a change so great as to transform the teaching force.

The second third of the fiscal dividend was combined with a basic transformation in the formulas used by the states to distribute funds to the schools to transform the way the nation would finance its schools, one key result of which was a vast increase in the funds available to educate disadvantaged children, especially those from low-income families, those from homes in which English was not spoken at home, and students with disabilities.

And the last third of the fiscal dividend was used to accomplish a goal that one group after another had long advocated but none had figured out how to fund: full funding for the provision of high-quality early childhood education for all the 3- and 4-year-olds in the United States.

It was these three measures, combined with the other far-reaching proposals made by the Commission, that made it possible to save the money spent in the later years. By redirecting these funds, the Commission had found a way to do the job right early rather than continue to fix much later the problems that had gone unaddressed early on.

The result was a system that produced a vastly better outcome for millions of American children and for the country they lived in — all for a net increase of about $8 billion, or less than 2 percent of what the country was spending on elementary and secondary education at the time the Commission's report came out.

We turn now to a description of these proposals and the story of what happened as they were adopted.

2. GETTING AND KEEPING WORLD-CLASS TEACHERS

Teachers are the heart of any education system, so it should surprise no one that the highest priority for the use of the money saved in the higher reaches of the system was to transform the prospects for recruiting and retaining a first-rate teaching force in the grade schools in the years ahead. The research done for the Commission had shown that maintaining the American standard of living, to say nothing of improving it, would require an enormous improvement in the mathematics, science, and language abilities of most members of the American workforce, and no less important, a comparable increase in the ability of ordinary Americans to be creative, innovative, and flexible. Americans, it seemed, would have to be not only much better educated, they would have to be differently educated. Key to success would be the ability of the developing American workforce to deal well with ideas.

The Commission had realized that it is simply not possible for students to acquire these characteristics if their teachers do not have them. When the 20th century was young and the nation did not need many people who could deal easily with ideas, use them creatively, produce a steady stream of innovations in a high-technology environment, or learn large volumes of highly abstract material easily and quickly, the nation could quite comfortably recruit a disproportionate share of its teachers from the ranks of the least able college graduates. That is not what happened, however. The Commission knew that America had gotten lucky many times. It had access to millions of female and minority college graduates, who had few choices other than teaching. And when women were expected to be home for their children after school anyway, teaching was the job of choice for very able women decade after decade. For able young people, teaching had also been a refuge from the draft and, in the 1930s, from the Great Depression. But the draft had been abolished. The Great Depression was long since over. Though there were still many college-educated women and minorities who had become teachers when there were few alternatives, they were retiring in great numbers. The country would need the best teachers it had ever had, if the new standards were to be met by all the students who would have to meet them, and it would get the worst teachers it had ever had if the rules were not changed drastically.

There was a whole host of problems that would have to be dealt with if disaster was going to be averted. The data presented to the Commission showed that the vast majority of countries with high math and science performance employed teachers in their elementary schools who specialized in math and science. Given the tough competition

"A report by the National Council on Teacher Quality in 2004 said that the profession attracts 'a disproportionately high number of candidates from the lower end of the distribution of academic ability.' And, college graduates whose SAT or ACT scores were in the bottom quartile were more than twice as likely as those in the top quartile to have majored in education."

U.S. DEPARTMENT OF EDUCATION, NATIONAL CENTER FOR EDUCATION STATISTICS, *The Condition of Education 2002* (WASHINGTON, D.C.: U.S. GOVERNMENT PRINTING OFFICE, 2002).

"Two in three teachers polled (66%)
described the value of the teacher
preparation coursework they received
before entering the classroom as simply
okay or not good. Only one in three (33%)
said the preparation was very good."

TEACHING COMMISSION,
*Teaching at Risk: A Call to
Action, 2004 (*NEW YORK: TEACHING
COMMISSION, 2004).

from industry for people who could teach
math and science in our secondary schools,
it seemed virtually impossible to even think
about how to get what we really needed in our
elementary schools.

Pay was part of the problem, because
starting pay was so low for new teachers,
relative to what very good college graduates
could get in other professions, and teachers'
pay topped out early in their careers, unlike
what happened in many other professions.
More and more, the brightest and most
able college graduates were not interested in
committing themselves to lifetime careers.
They saw themselves as doing something
that really interested them for a while and
then going on to something else no less
interesting. So pay for teachers turned out
to be very badly structured to get the people
who were most desirable.

And then there was the problem of
teacher education. The plain fact no one
had much wanted to talk about was that
teacher education was viewed by the best
and brightest young people as irrelevant at
best and intellectually vapid at worst. Many
of the most capable of our college graduates
said that, if they had to go to a teachers'
college to pick up the full complement of
teacher education courses required by the
state, they would do something else.

Interestingly, the Commission learned
that a surprisingly large fraction of the most
able college graduates were interested in
teaching and were willing to spend some time
engaged in it. But those who actually signed
up drifted away from it early because of the
pay, the quality of teacher education, and the
conditions under which they had to teach.

The best of the nation's independent schools had long ago learned all of this. They paid their teachers at the top of the public school range, did not require them to go to conventional teacher education, and provided a very different set of working conditions than all but a small handful of elite public schools could provide. The result was a teaching force in these leading independent schools that could compete with our better private liberal arts colleges.

The Commission was very much aware that these institutions did not face the problems of schools full of students who were not well prepared and not particularly interested in learning. And it knew that teaching under such conditions required very good professional training. Nevertheless, the Commission set out to see if it might be possible to attract to teaching in our public schools people with the same high level of academic preparation and the same range of possible career choices as could be found among the faculties of our best independent schools. Their aim was to fashion a set of policies designed to attract and retain teachers many of whom came from the top third of the entering college classes.

The states that implemented the Commission's recommendations made fundamental changes in state laws affecting the recruitment, licensing, employment, compensation, tenure, and retention of teachers.

Among the most important of these changes was a fundamental restructuring of teachers' compensation. The restructured pay package was offered to all teachers, and the old package denied to new teachers. Many younger, experienced teachers converted

to the new plan because the increased cash compensation was very attractive to them, and they were prepared to give up what they might otherwise have gotten in retirement benefits, though few who were close to retirement felt that way because the old package was so much more attractive to teachers approaching retirement.

The crux of the change in teacher compensation was a shift from what the Commission thought of as a rear-loaded system, in which much of the compensation came at the end of one's career and in retirement, to a front-loaded system, in which much more came earlier in one's career. Though the public believed that teachers were not paid very well, when benefits of all kinds were added to cash compensation, teachers were actually paid above the average for people with comparable amounts of education. That is because many teachers were getting 60 percent or more of their final salaries for life, sometimes adjusted for inflation, and some were getting lifetime health benefits, a benefit that was rapidly becoming untenable in the private sector. It was also true, the Commission learned, that teachers' salaries went up the scale for a few years and then stopped, so that teachers discovered that longevity was rewarded after retirement, but experience was not rewarded while working. None of this made sense if the aim was to attract very capable young people who were looking forward to many careers in their lifetime and wanted to feel that they would be paid as much for teaching — and especially teaching well — as they would be if they had gone into any other profession.

The Commission recommended that the states set up either defined contribution plans

The 2005 Condition of Education, U.S. Department of Education, stated, "The data show that the amount of turnover accounted for by retirement is relatively minor when compared to that associated with other factors, such as teacher job dissatisfaction and teachers pursuing other jobs."

★ ★ ★ ★

"The likelihood that a highly talented female (one ranked among the top 10% of all high schoolers) will become a teacher fell from roughly 20% in 1964 to just over 11% in 2000."

SEAN CORCORAN, WILLIAM N. EVANS, AND ROBERT M. SCHWAB, "CHANGING LABOR MARKET OPPORTUNITIES FOR WOMEN AND THE QUALITY OF TEACHERS 1957–1992," NATIONAL BUREAU OF ECONOMIC RESEARCH, WORKING PAPER NO. 9180, 2002.

for their teachers or cash-balance pension plans. One possible defined contribution plan, they noted, was the one offered by TIAA-CREF, which was set up to provide pension plans for college teachers many years ago. The advantage that plan offered was complete portability across the whole country. Under the defined contribution plan, the employer (in this case, the state) was obligated to deposit a certain amount of funds in the employee's retirement account every pay period, and the amount in the account was then invested in whatever investment vehicles were permitted by that state plan. In a cash-balance plan, the state was also obligated to deposit a certain amount in the employee's account every pay period, but the money in the account was invested at a fixed interest rate that was in the employee's contract, so, in that sense, both the contribution and the benefit were fixed at the outset. Both the pension benefits and the health benefits in the state plans were set at levels that were competitive with those of the better private employers.

These new retirement plans cost the states only a small fraction of what their previous retirement plans had cost. It took a while for the states to see the full extent of their savings, because they were still obligated to pay the costs of the old retirement plans to those experienced teachers who elected to stay on the old plan. But many unfunded state plans that might otherwise have gone bankrupt were saved by this new approach.

The savings were plowed back into increased cash compensation. Then the plans were topped up with some of the proceeds from the restructuring of the progression of students through the grade school and higher education system. The result, averaged across all the states, was a salary structure that started around $45,000 for beginning teachers (on par with a teacher's average salary before these changes were made) and paid teachers at the top of the new career ladders $95,000 or $109,000 for teachers who chose to work the same number of hours per year as typical professionals in the economy. High-paying states ended up paying substantially more than these figures and low-paying states less, but in time, all the states greatly increased their salaries. It was also true that many states, especially those that included both large cities and extensive rural areas, decided to adjust what they paid according to the cost of living in the area to which the teacher was assigned.

Different states, of course, structured the compensation of their teachers differently. But most of the plans had elements related to student performance, professional development targeted at the skills needed to improve school performance, and achievement of goals negotiated with the principal, with premiums for teachers willing to teach in schools in which the district has recruiting problems or in shortage subject areas. They also included different pay bands based on where the teacher was in a teaching service career ladder. These ladders vary among the states, but were typically designed to keep good teachers in teaching and enable them to earn more as their reputation grew and, as a result, their responsibilities increased. Among the responsibilities typically assigned to the outstanding teachers rising up the ladder were mentoring new teachers,

doing demonstration teaching, coaching experienced teachers, and leading school-based instructional teams. Virtually all of the states moved away from compensation plans based on years of service.

The next thing that happened was a complete restructuring of teacher recruitment and teacher education. The Commission proposed a sea change in the way money for initial teacher education flowed through the system. It suggested that states create a new unit of government, a Teacher Development Agency, and vest in that agency the sole authority to grant institutions in that state the right to award degrees and certificates in education.

The new agency, it said, should approach its task like a major corporation would, doing extensive public opinion research to find out why talented young people were not going into teaching and what it would take to change their minds. It should make that information available to the policymakers, who would use it to change the profession in ways that would appeal to the people they were going after and also use it to conduct sophisticated campaigns to attract these young people to teaching.

The new agency would draft a set of performance contracts to be made with teachers' colleges and other kinds of organizations — from school districts to collaboratives of teachers — that wanted the right to train teachers. Those organizations that succeeded in delivering teachers who could meet the new performance criteria would get the right to train many teachers using the Teacher Development Agency's authority to grant degrees and certificates.

Those that did less well would get little or none. Most Teacher Development Agencies worked hard at finding ways to attract to teaching young people with strong academic backgrounds with whom young people of color could identify. This task was made much easier by the restructuring of teacher compensation just described.

At the time the Commission issued its report, the newspapers reported that there was a teacher shortage of 200,000 and the quality of the teachers who were teaching was often far below the very minimal federal standards contained in the No Child Left Behind Act. Five years later, there were eight applicants for every available teaching position.

After the Commission embraced this proposal in its report, state after state adopted measures based on this proposal. Following other Commission recommendations, they abandoned the kinds of curricula and requirements for licensing teachers that had long shaped the programs of the teacher education institutions. They required that everyone major in the subject they were going to teach (including majoring in mathematics or science for the specialists in those subjects in the elementary schools, a new state requirement), and they placed particular emphasis on the skills needed to identify the needs of individual students and engage them in their studies, especially in the lower grades. Teacher licensure systems were changed so that licensure was based not on courses taken but rather on a candidate's ability to demonstrate superior teaching ability. Teacher education programs largely became one- to two-year programs following the award of a bachelor's degree in another

subject, a substantial part of which consisted of very good mentoring by master teachers in the field. The Commission, in its report, had set as a goal recruiting the top third of the students entering college as measured by the SAT or similar tests. Many states, as it turned out, had met that goal within five years of the report's release.

All of this cost money, especially the increases in teachers' salaries. Many states concluded that they were not going to get value for that money unless they could be sure that they could set market rates for teachers in shortage subjects, get rid of seniority as a principle of teacher assignment, compensate teachers based on their actual classroom performance, retrain teachers who were not able to do the job that was now expected of them, and fire those who still could not do it after retraining.

Most of these rights had been negotiated away by school boards who gave them up in collective bargaining in lean years when it was easier to give the teachers control over these matters than to give them money. From the state legislators' point of view, if they were going to increase teachers' salaries to the levels comparable to the better-paid professionals, it was time for teachers to work under the same conditions as most professionals in all of the respects just mentioned.

In many states, the legislators realized that they could not address these matters unless the state itself became the employer of the teachers, a change that happened much more quickly than many had predicted. Generally this did not entitle the teachers who had been added to the rolls to a job. For that to happen, the teacher had to be

"In 1999, the UK found itself in a teacher 'supply crisis' which was hitting the headlines in papers across the country. The following is from an article in *The Independent* in 2000: Schools are using growing numbers of unqualified teachers to try to fill vacancies created by the recruitment crisis, secondary heads warn today. In Essex alone, 67 teachers without a teaching qualification are in post in 61 secondary schools. When the TTA [Training and Development Agency for Schools] began its new strategy with the arrival of Ralph Tabberer as chief executive, the strategy showed immediate results. Within three months of the launch of the advertising campaign, the number of people calling the national teaching recruitment helpline tripled. It was not straightforward, and doubting voices persisted for some time, but there is no doubt that the teacher supply shortfall began to be reduced in 2000–2001, on the back of a highly effective recruitment strategy. By 2003–2004 the vacancy to employment rate fell to below 1% for all subjects, for the first time. In 2004, teaching won further recognition as the 'number one choice' of graduate leavers in a university poll and a record 41,000 people entered initial teacher training, up from 24,000 in 2000."

ADRIAN ELLIS, PA CONSULTING GROUP, FOR THE NATIONAL CENTER ON EDUCATION AND THE ECONOMY, *The Training and Development Agency for Schools: A Political History of the Challenges Faced by the Government in Improving Teacher Training Provision in England: 1990–2005*, APRIL 2006.

★ ★ ★ ★

According to the Massachusetts Department of Education, there are currently a dozen district-based teacher licensing programs in the state. One example is found in Boston. Boston Public Schools runs the Boston Teacher Residency (BTR), a 12-month program to recruit, prepare, and license teachers to work in the city's schools. BTR is modeled after a medical residency in which aspiring doctors receive practical training in hospitals in conjunction with rigorous course work. BTR combines the best of theory and research with the best of practical training by placing Teacher Residents with a Mentor Teacher for a full school year. Teacher Residents participate in rigorous master's-level course work centered around a set of core teaching competencies during two month-long summer components, and after school and all day on Fridays during the school year. Teacher Residents graduate from the program with a Massachusetts Initial Teacher License in their primary content area and a master's degree in education.

The Connecticut State Department of Education developed the BEST program in 1986. BEST is a two- or three-year induction program for new teachers that is both a support program and an assessment. Teacher must reach all BEST requirements to receive a provisional teaching certificate. All assessment is done by portfolio. BEST assesses foundation academic standards as well as professional standards.

hired by a school, as we will see below. But it did entitle the licensed teachers to the pay and benefits the legislature had voted, no matter where in the state they worked, when they were engaged by a school. This worked fairly well in most states, but there were wide disparities in the cost of living from place to place in some states, and so the legislatures in those states found ways of compensating for these variations as they set the compensation policies.

These changes produced a revolution in the teaching profession. A surprisingly large fraction of students from the best colleges in the country decided to make teaching their first career. Many stayed for only five or six years, but many others stayed much longer. And some who stayed only five or six years, and then went on to do something else, decided to return later. Many of the best retired teachers who had gone on to other careers decided to come back. These teachers worked whatever hours were required to get the job done. Schools became places where ideas counted, where teachers spent time with other teachers working hard to pinpoint problems and to develop and implement solutions. It seemed they were never satisfied with where they were but were always looking over their shoulders to figure out how they could improve their performance. The best teachers were often given cash incentives to teach the hardest-to-teach students. Because there were strong incentives operating on school faculties to continuously improve the performance of their students, the members of those faculties had strong incentives to improve the performance of their colleagues or, if they did not improve, ask them to leave. Teachers were helping states to develop tough performance-based pay plans.

The new state schedules for teachers were partly based on the new career ladders, which were based not on seniority but on the quality of the teacher's work. In these systems, teachers who were most successful at producing outstanding student performance were paid more and were asked to demonstrate their methods to other teachers, sharing the methods that accounted for their success. As the public became aware of how hard it was to get into school teaching, and schools enjoyed more and more success, even with the students who had been the hardest to teach, the status of teachers shot up. For the first time in anyone's memory, the number of people applying for teaching positions far outnumbered the available positions.

3. CREATING HIGH-PERFORMANCE SCHOOLS AND DISTRICTS EVERYWHERE

When the Commission staff talked with talented young people who did not want to become public school teachers and to talented teachers who got out, the answer most often given was "the bureaucracy." They described a system that did not respect their professionalism, a system in which teachers learned quickly that loyalty to those above them in the hierarchy was much more highly valued than improving student performance. They would go into teaching in public schools when the system rewarded superior performance for children, not superior loyalty to their superiors. But the Commission staff had found just as much frustration, if not more, among principals and central office staff. No one felt that they had the authority they needed to do the job they were being held accountable for. Teachers and principals were settling for much less than they knew it would take to do the job because it had always been this way. And so the best bailed out. It became very clear that recruiting the best college graduates to be teachers and completely changing their training would produce much less than any of the Commissioners hoped for unless the image and the reality of the school bureaucracy could be radically changed.

The Commission had thought long and hard about how to do this and decided to look to the experience of American business in the late 1970s and early 1980s for guidance. That was a period when business was fighting for its life against mostly Japanese firms that had figured out how to produce much higher-quality products for much lower prices. Much of the answer, it turned out, was what some of the management gurus called "high-performance management" or "high-performance organizations," which meant much the same thing. The idea really goes back to Peter Drucker and his prescient book, *The Age of Discontinuity*, in which he said that the future belonged to countries that understood the only way to succeed in the global economy and pay high wages would be to employ people engaged in knowledge work and provide the kind of work environment that knowledge workers need to be successful.

People like Tom Peters and many others had taken up the story and described a success strategy in which the firm had to be very clear about its goals, communicate them to every member of the firm (over and over again), find ways to accurately measure progress toward those goals, push decisions as to how to achieve those goals as far down toward those responsible for making the product or rendering the service as possible, change the role of middle management from micromanaging the decisions to monitoring and supporting the front line, and then, and only then, hold the empowered people on the front line accountable for meeting the organization's goals as gauged by the agreed measures.

Just like business in the late 1970s, the schools would now have to produce much higher quality with no increase in cost. Also just like business in the late 1970s, they would have to figure out how to do this with a front-line workforce made up of professional knowledge workers, not blue-collar workers. This meant wholesale changes in who makes which decisions at which level of the organization. In this new system, there was much more autonomy at the lower levels of the organization (in this case, the schools) but much more accountability for the results, much greater rewards for success, and much more meaningful consequences for failure. Tough competition in this system sharpens the performance of those organizations that succeed and thins the ranks of those that fail. Those that succeed in the long run are those that do the best job of figuring out what their customers need and meeting those needs. That is what it means to be a professional in this era.

The Commission staff had realized that countries in other parts of the world — from Belgium to Australia — were ahead of the United States on this issue of modernizing the governance, organization, and management of public education, and they set out to find out what these other countries were doing. Eventually the Commission's recommendations built on this research in the form of an overall approach that reflected both the best the staff had found elsewhere and the unique realities of the American scene.

The idea the Commission came up with revolves around the notion of having school districts composed entirely of contract schools. At first, when the Commission's report was first released, many people thought the phrase *contract schools* was synonymous with *charter schools*. But it was not. In many places, charter schools had been created in reaction to what was perceived as too much bureaucracy, and as a result were places with inexperienced managers, unqualified teachers, a weak curriculum, and leaky finances, essentially unaccountable to the state or anyone else for the quality of the schooling they provided.

In other places, of course, charter schools had turned out to be the homes of some of the most exciting education in the United States, the very sort of schools the Commission was interested in promoting. This being so, the Commission had proposed that all of these schools be subject to the state accountability systems and requirements. All would be required to offer the state curriculum and to employ teachers from the list approved by the state, as was described earlier. All of their students would

"Voters in Denver, Colo., in 2005 overwhelmingly approved a $25 million tax increase to fund a new, nine-year performance-based pay system for the city's teachers. ProComp, the new teacher pay system funded by the tax initiative, reflects a landmark agreement between the Denver Classroom Teachers Association (DCTA) and the Denver Board of Education to link teacher pay more closely to performance and market conditions—something that rarely happens in public education. Unlike traditional teacher pay schemes, in which salary is determined by experience and higher education coursework, ProComp will tie raises or bonuses for teachers to positive professional evaluations, meeting objectives for improving student learning, working in hard-to-staff schools or positions, and building professionally relevant knowledge and skills. Teachers who perform well on these measures will be able to earn much more money over the course of their careers than under traditional pay plans based on experience and education."

Sara Mead, "Teachers Unions as Agents of Reform," *Education Sector,* April 18, 2006.

★ ★ ★ ★

"In most of the countries that performed well in PISA [Program for International Student Assessment], local authorities and schools now have substantial autonomy with regard to adapting and implementing educational content and/or allocating and managing resources. The trend towards devolved responsibility has, however, not been uniform across the different areas of decision making. In some countries, the development and adaptation of educational content can be considered the main expression of school autonomy. Others, by contrast, have focused on strengthening the management and administration of individual schools through market-oriented governance instruments or collaboration between schools and other stakeholders in local communities while, in some cases, even moving towards centralized governance of curricula and standards."

Andreas Schleicher, Head of OECD Education Indicators and Analysis Division, keynote presentation at America's Choice Annual Conference, January 19, 2006.

have to take the examinations approved or offered by the state. All would be required to hold a lottery for admission in the event that they were oversubscribed. These were not to be private schools operated with public funds; they were to be public schools meeting high standards in every way.

The Commission had considered recommending that the states run systems of contract schools alongside regular public schools whose staffs were employed by the school district, and, in fact, some states actually did that. Evidently, the reason the Commission decided not to recommend that was that, in such an arrangement, the district has a strong incentive to see the conventional schools as its schools and the contract schools as belonging to the people who run them, and therefore to favor the regular schools. Despite that, the Commission thought that the contract schools were likely to draw parents who were more ambitious for their children, leaving the regular schools to become dumping grounds for children whose parents were less discriminating or who perhaps had neither the time nor the energy to research the available schools and make a considered choice.

So in most states, all of the contract schools were run by organizations that districts contracted with. Such an organization could run one school or many.

The Commission had been very much aware that no amount of change in governance and finance and organization was going to make very much difference if the quality of instruction in the schools was not greatly improved. So it suggested that every school be required to be affiliated with a network approved by the state. These networks would be responsible for helping to shape the program, providing training, supplying regular technical assistance, and providing many other forms of support to the schools affiliated with them. Initially, both the states and the federal government had to work hard to strengthen the capacity of the existing network organizations and help new ones come into being. In time, though, successful network organizations were put together by schools of education, successful schools, teacher associations, entrepreneurs, and others. Those that grew with time were particularly good at using the best educational research, benchmarking the best practices in the world, using the best training and professional development techniques, and supporting the schools in their networks continuously with high-quality technical assistance. They had high standards for the schools in their networks and terminated schools that could not or would not meet their standards.

Even so, these schools had much more autonomy than schools had had before the Commission report was released, the very kind of autonomy that had led to the development of the best of the charter schools. This was in part because the district no longer called the shots as to what happened in the schools and in part because the Commission had proposed that the schools be funded directly by the state, under a formula built on a pupil-weighted funding scheme. All students started out with the same base funding, but the formulas added a certain amount if the student came from a low-income family, spoke a language other than English at home, had a disabling condition, and so on. Schools serving students in these categories got more money than those that were not. Most of the state's budget for schools was distributed to the schools based on this formula, in one lump sum, and decisions about how the money was to be used were made by the principal and his or her leadership team. That same team decided what the staffing structure of the school would look like, what programs were offered (beyond those mandated by law and the network they had decided to affiliate with), the organizational and teaming structure, the school calendar, and much, much more.

These decisions were more important than ever before because the students and their parents could choose another school and take their state-provided money with them. Schools had to compete with one another in this system, and in many areas of the states, that competition proved to be fierce.

The new plan therefore proved to produce more real choice for parents and students than most charter plans had before it. Because the states, and not the localities, funded the schools, students were free to go to any contract school they wished to attend. Of course, in the past, good schools with choice plans had filled up quickly, leaving the parents of students in poor-quality schools with little effective choice at all. But as it turned out, in this system, that was not true partly because of the incentives offered to good schools to expand, and

partly because the performance contracts were written in such a way as to force poor schools to get better or cease operation.

This aggressive embrace of choice might have produced a flight of the rich and white from the poor and people of color, but that did not happen. The kind of racial and social class isolation that had characterized American schools at the end of the 20th century was greatly reduced by going to a pupil-weighted financing scheme combined with direct state funding and the requirement that schools with excess demand admit by lottery. And no one needed to be coerced into going to a school he or she did not want to attend.

Some states decided to take the Commission up on two more of its proposals. One was to add a certain amount to the formula behind each student, as long as that student was in a school in which the progress students made was considerably greater than it was for schools enrolling similar student bodies. The second proposal was to add a little more to the student funding formula for schools that met the criterion just mentioned, and, in addition, added 15 percent or more to its student body in the preceding school year.

The point of the first incentive payment was to give an added incentive to the faculty to improve on the previous year's performance, whatever that was. And the point of the second incentive payment was to make it worthwhile for schools that were particularly successful at educating their students to take on more students (at the expense, obviously, of schools that were less successful at educating their students).

"The shift in public and governmental concern, away from mere control over the resources and content of education toward a focus on outcomes, has, in many countries, driven the establishment of standards for the quality of the work of educational institutions. Many of the high-performing PISA countries provide clearly formulated educational goals and standards, but have become less prescriptive in terms of how teachers should translate these goals into practice. Rather, they put the emphasis on creating a 'knowledge-rich' education system, in which teachers and school principals act as partners and have the authority to act, the necessary information to do so, and access to effective support systems to assist them in implementing change."

ANDREAS SCHLEICHER,
HEAD OF OECD EDUCATION
INDICATORS AND ANALYSIS
DIVISION, KEYNOTE PRESENTATION
AT AMERICA'S CHOICE ANNUAL
CONFERENCE, JANUARY 19, 2006.

As it turned out, many of these schools were run by teams of teachers who believed in themselves enough to form a professional partnership organization to manage a school as a franchisee of a larger organization or on their own. As one Commission member, a former teacher, put it, "Years ago, early in my career, I had a dream. I dreamed that I could reach out to the best teachers in the district and form a group of us. We would go and buy a barn and start a school in it. I knew for sure that we could make it the best school in our district. I've always wished I could have done that."

This dream, of course, is not very different from that of countless engineers, accountants, doctors, and many other professionals who had been forming such professional partnerships for a century or more to offer their expertise to the public. Over the years since the new legislation had been passed, the best of these partnerships have grown and swallowed up some of the less successful ones.

Because the schools were operating under lump-sum budgeting schemes, they could decide to use some of their funds to increase teachers' salaries or provide them with bonuses if they wanted to. Interestingly, many of the schools operated by partnerships of professional teachers decided to take on bigger classes, realizing that they could earn more money if they could do a better job with larger classes than small ones. The Commission had pointed out in its report that something very like this had happened in other countries with similar schemes, but few had believed that it would happen in the United States, where teachers had been campaigning for smaller class sizes as long as anyone could remember.

Virtually all districts included in their contracting rules provisions related to the involvement of parents and other community members in governing and providing input into their operation. These provisions varied greatly, but contract school operators quickly discovered in any case that, if they were going to have customers, they would have to know how they felt and what they wanted and they would have to keep them happy. Since, under the state rules, the districts had to publish all the school's relevant performance statistics and the results of its parent satisfaction surveys, they all worked very hard to improve performance as much as possible and keep parents happy.

School districts under this new regime no longer were in the business of running schools. Instead, their job became contracting with new schools, providing support to the schools they contracted with, monitoring the performance of the students in those schools, providing extra control over and support to the schools whose performance was slipping (whether they wanted it or not), and terminating the contracts of those schools whose performance was poor and not improving.

Thus, the districts had turned into performance contract managers, not operators, of schools. Some proved more aggressive than others in this role. A few large city systems and even a few states had taken a page out of Jack Welch's book and decided to terminate the contracts of the lowest-performing schools in their district or

state every year, turning over those schools to the best-performing operators or new applicants.

Some states, responding to one of the Commission's recommendations, decided to conduct special elections under which the citizens of each locality would choose between districts to be run by their mayors or districts run by their school boards. But the same legislation changed the roles and responsibilities of school boards substantially. They could appoint only the superintendent of schools, who would appoint all the other members of the central office staff without review by the board. And the board would no longer have the power to intervene in school affairs or approve expenditures after it had approved the annual budget. Of course, the budget was now the budget only for the central office and the centrally provided services, since the schools had their budget authority independent of the board, unless the school's performance was faltering, in which case the laws in some states provided some limited authority by the district over the school budget. A few states had even restricted the number of times a local board could meet in order to drive home the point that the role of the local board had changed and was henceforth to concentrate on policy, much as the role of a corporate board is concentrated on policy and leaves operations to its chief executive.

Over time, more and more city districts came under the control of their mayors, a natural consequence of the fact that the mayors often controlled many services of vital importance to the students, such

"External accountability is important, but alone it is not enough. If you look at the countries that do well today, you find that they place the emphasis on building various ways in which networks of schools stimulate and spread innovation as well as collaborate to provide curriculum diversity, extended services, and professional support. That is where you find countries like Finland today, countries that have moved from 'hit and miss' policies to establishing universal high standards, from uniformity in the system to embracing diversity, from a focus of provision to a focus on choice, from managing inputs and a bureaucratic approach to education towards devolving responsibilities and enabling outcomes, from talking about equity to delivering equity. Where schools no longer receive wisdom but take initiatives on the basis of data and best practice and where teachers and schools collaborate in a knowledge-rich environment, where schools do not look up but outwards."

ANDREAS SCHLEICHER,
HEAD OF OECD EDUCATION
INDICATORS AND ANALYSIS
DIVISION, KEYNOTE PRESENTATION
AT AMERICA'S CHOICE ANNUAL
CONFERENCE, JANUARY 19, 2006.

as public health services, juvenile justice services, foster care services, and family social services. The districts turned out to be the agencies in the best position to coordinate these services with the work of the schools, which was particularly important in communities and cities serving low-income families. In the countryside, the mayors and school board chairs often got together to work out regional arrangements for the coordination of these services and, in fact, for the responsibilities assigned directly to school boards.

Most of the new state laws provided that the schools would be free to get most of their supplies and services (like school maintenance) wherever they wished. This meant that the district central offices had to prove to the schools that they could provide those supplies and services in a more timely way and cheaper than the competition if they wanted to continue to provide them. Some decided to collaborate with others to offer these services, making those services less expensive than they would otherwise have been. So it turned out that most of these services did continue to be provided by "central," although as we just noted, "central" often turned out to be a regional authority, but the people who provided them started treating schools for the first time as customers who had other choices, and the bureaucratic behavior they used to display waned very quickly.

One of the key responsibilities of school districts under the new regime was the collection and analysis of a wide range of data, which were shipped to the state and made public locally along with a lot

of other information about the schools'
programs, network operators, and staff,
which parents and their children used to
made decisions as to which school to attend.
The data they collected included not just
student performance data but also parent
satisfaction data and, where appropriate,
teacher and student satisfaction data, all of
which turned out to be very useful both to
guide potential customers and manage the
system. Both the state and the local districts
worked hard to help parents and others
understand the school performance data and
use this information appropriately to make
good choices for their children.

Many school districts decided to take
advantage of the authority provided in the
new state legislation to use the state bonding
authority to float bonds to build facilities for
the schools in their districts, which the schools
then leased back from the state at market
rates. In other cases, the school operators built
or leased their own facilities. Either way, the
state funding formula took into account the
cost of leasing facilities or amortizing the cost
of facilities bought for the purpose.

Over time, it turned out that many
of the small entrepreneurial organizations
formed to operate schools found it hard
to develop the management capacity or
capital resources to operate their schools
effectively within the budget limits imposed
by the school funding formula. It was more
efficient for large organizations to franchise
successful operations and achieve economies
of scale as they did so, or simply develop their
organizations organically with the capital
generated by their cash flow. Sometimes
the network operators evolved from helping

organizations into owners or franchisers.
Sometimes they provided their services to
groups of schools owned and operated by
separate companies, both for profit and
nonprofit. Despite all this, because the most
important resource in the whole system
was capable teachers who could easily get a
good job doing something else, these new
organizations were far indeed from the
bureaucratic districts of old. The organizations
that succeeded had learned their lessons
not from 20th-century school districts but
from Apple Computer, Microsoft, Hewlett
Packard, Google, and Accenture.

In fact, this new organization of
the schools transformed them. Like the
organizations just mentioned, they became
beehives of innovation and creativity, places
where people with ideas who loved children
could flourish, good destinations for bright
and able people with drive and ambition.
The whole system had been changed from
one that ran on keeping trouble under control
and the adults happy to one that thrived on
continuous advances in student achievement.

None of this could have happened
without an equally important transformation
in the role of the state department of
education. Over the 10 years prior to the
release of the Commission's report, the
staff of the average state department of
education had declined in size by 50 percent.
The Commission had made the point
that vast improvements in state education
performance required a high quality of
state leadership and that was unlikely to be
forthcoming if the legislatures and governors
continued to starve that leadership of the
resources it needed to do the job.

The Commission began a continuing study of the way the best-performing countries were organized at the national level to lead and support their education systems. That work was continued by the Commission's sponsor, the National Center on Education and the Economy, in a series of studies. Eventually the states rebuilt their state education agencies on the model of the best ministries of education, did what was necessary to attract and retain top-quality leadership and staff for them, and staffed up to make sure that there were enough of these people to lead the statewide effort to a successful conclusion. The states created new agencies to recruit and train teachers. They built standards, curriculum, and assessment agencies to produce and implement curriculum-based standards and assessments that were much better than those they had before. They created new arms to investigate, review, and approve — and terminate, if necessary — the right of organizations that wanted to operate networks to support public contract schools in the state. They contracted with third parties to provide extra assistance to districts that were unable to perform their responsibilities under the law. And they developed special statewide schools to serve gifted children.

This last responsibility turned out to be particularly important. The Commission had noted that the No Child Left Behind Act, while clearly lifting up the performance of students who had been performing especially poorly, did not provide incentives to raise the performance of children performing at higher levels. Over time, the Congress changed the legislation so that it matched the measures described above that the legislatures had passed earlier, creating incentives for schools and districts to continuously improve student performance across the board, with an emphasis, but not an exclusive emphasis, on the least fortunate.

Still, the society stood in great need of the services of those students with the greatest potential. These students, as the Commission had noted, were not just those in the wealthiest communities. Shrewd inner-city principals had observed years earlier that some of the very brightest students they had ever encountered were inner-city gang leaders, utterly alienated from formal schooling. Harness that potential, and a society would have a tiger by the tail. So many states passed legislation setting up state schools for the gifted and allocating a set proportion of the slots in those schools for students from low-income, minority backgrounds, heavily recruiting in very unconventional ways in the communities where those students lived. They also offered special incentives to districts where those young people were concentrated to identify those students, support them, and get them into special schools and programs that would develop their talents. This program had proven a surprising success in many states.

In retrospect, it is clear that the success of the Commission's proposals in the area of the governance, organization, and management of the system depended more than anything else on building the capacity that was needed at every level of the system to get the job done. The prior experience with charter schools showed that lack of attention to this issue could be fatal to any reform plan. In this case, both the states and the federal government needed to work hard over a period of years to stimulate the development of a growing number of high-quality helping organizations and contract school operators of many different kinds. Sound criteria had to be developed. Training, consulting, and technical assistance were offered. Research was done on successful helping organizations and contract schools that enabled others to learn the ropes and improve their work much more efficiently than if they were completely on their own. The federal government and private foundations provided funds competitively to start-ups to help them get on their feet and created small regional versions of the cooperative extension service to offer information and help. States played a critically important role in defining their own standards for approving applications of helping organizations to work in their state and in providing technical assistance to the applicants so they could do what was needed to meet the state standards. Some of the centers established by the federal government also provided help to the states as they built their own capacity to play these new roles. Key in all of these were the school districts, which had to build their own capacity to play their roles in the new system. They, of course, had been tasked with making sure that there was an adequate supply of high-quality contract schools to serve their district, which meant not only that they had to develop and administer a complex and demanding contracting process, but also that they had to recruit school operators, sort through their qualifications, evaluate their proposals and

"Extending preschool programs to all students could yield $2–$4 in net present-value benefits for every dollar invested. Preschool investments for just one age cohort of students could generate as much as $150 billion in net present-value benefits to the United States. Of the fiscal benefits expected from new state investments in preschool, more than 70% are attributable to cost savings in crime and K–12 education. For every dollar spent on preschool, states are projected to recoup 50 to 85 cents in reduced crime costs and 36–77 cents in school savings. Preschool programs would boost long-term economic growth; by 2080, gross domestic product could be higher by 3.5%, or more than $2 trillion in today's dollars. Preschool also increases the long-run employment level of states by more than twice as much as traditional economic development programs."

COMMITTEE FOR ECONOMIC DEVELOPMENT, *The Economic Promise of Investing in High-Quality Preschool: Using Early Education to Improve Economic Growth and the Fiscal Sustainability of States and the Nation* (WASHINGTON, D.C.: COMMITTEE FOR ECONOMIC DEVELOPMENT, JULY 2006).

their records, monitor their performance, and sort out those that would be continued from those that would not, but they also had to work hard to create the largest and best pool of applicants possible. At the same time, the districts needed to figure out how to organize the coordination of a wide range of social, recreational, and other services with the new schools. And they needed to build effective tools for helping parents and students understand the system and navigate their way through it. Not least, they had to figure out how competitive sports would be organized in this new world and provide for all kinds of club activities that had always gone on in the high schools.

The conversion from the system that was in place to the new system was very complex and difficult. It went more smoothly in some places than in others, but it took years everywhere. Along the way, what had been regular schools operated by districts survived these changes in some places, either because they did a first-rate job or because qualified operators of contract schools could not be found. In most others, the system eventually converted entirely to contract schools. But that was not true everywhere. Some states, while faithful to the principles that the Commission had proposed, found ways other than systems of contract schools to get there.

The federal government learned a lot about what it needed to do to build the capacity of the states, and the states learned a lot about what they needed to do to build the capacity of the districts, the school operators, and the helping organizations. There were a few scandals when sharp operators emerged and new legislation had

to be framed to deal with them. Sometimes district officials were caught taking money from contractors to award them contracts, and district attorneys had to deal with them too. But over time, the quality of provision everywhere was raised enormously, great improvements were made in the equity of resource distribution, unexpected energy was released among the educators in the schools, and student performance improved dramatically. The innovation of autonomous schools running under performance contracts, lump-sum budgets, and a very lean local district office had gone a long way toward building nimble, high-performance organizations rather than lumbering, gargantuan ones.

Along the way, each state had found its own path to improved performance, which, while true to the principles that had guided the Commission, accomplished their aims in ways that the Commission could hardly have imagined. The laboratory of democracy proved very effective as a national learning system once again.

4. EARLY CHILDHOOD EDUCATION

Scores of studies had demonstrated the importance of the early years to children's long-term development and to their success in school and later in life. Affirmed by then emerging neuroscience research on brain development, the early years, well before formal schooling began, were regarded as both a time of unprecedented growth and a time when social inequities took root. Researchers found, for example, that even by the age of 3, children from welfare families had vocabularies that were half as large as those of their more affluent peers — a consequential difference at the onset of kindergarten with serious repercussions for the later school years.

Back then, policymakers were beginning to understand that the early years mattered, and what happened to young children during those years did as well. Moved by data indicating that learning disparities could be ameliorated, if not reversed, through the provision of high-quality early education programs, policymakers at the state and federal levels began investing in such programs. Indeed, moved by the power of preschool interventions, some policymakers even called for universal prekindergarten for all, not just at-risk, youngsters.

Although these efforts did improve the quantity of services for young children and their families, significant problems remained: first, services were not made available equitably across the states; second, services were not of sufficient quality to render the hoped-for gains; and third, there was no infrastructure to support quality. In this case, more was not necessarily merrier.

Recognizing both that high-quality early childhood education held great potential and that this potential was not being realized, the Commission turned its attention to young children as the bedrock of the new system. Taking $18 billion of the savings gained from the Commission's overall plan and adding to the existing investments in early childhood already being made, they proposed to use the funds to achieve two essential goals. The first, related to enhancing quantity, was to increase the number of services so that all 3- and 4-

year-old children whose parents wanted to enroll them in preschool (not just children from low-income families) would be able to do so; the second, related to enhancing quality, was to ensure that every program in the nation would be of high quality — quality sufficient to launch each young child off to a successful start in school.

Similar to other Commission recommendations, this one afforded states flexibility regarding implementation, with two exceptions. Each state would be obligated to use some of the new funds generated by this proposal to provide financial aid to low-income and otherwise needy families who could not afford the cost of the high-quality programs. Moreover, to ensure that programs were of high quality, a substantial amount of the total would be set aside for the creation of a statewide infrastructure that would: (1) establish and monitor standards for children's learning and for program quality; (2) provide enriched professional development and related recognition and compensation for competence; (3) establish governance systems to promote the efficient use of human and fiscal resources; (4) establish viable linkages with schools and other institutions that promote children's healthy development; and (5) provide parents and policymakers with evaluative, informative data to enable them to make effective decisions for their children and states, respectively.

Although it took years for states to put the new approach to early childhood education in place, it was worth the effort. Not only did states learn a great deal from one another and from other countries about creating high-quality and effective early childhood systems, but children, their parents, and society at large were thrilled. Children performed far better in school because programs were finally of sufficient quality to render the promised gains. Parents were more satisfied with — and committed to — their children's education because they saw education's promise firsthand. And society benefited because those long-promised cost-benefits that accrued from reduced referrals to special education, reduced grade retention, and even reduced teen pregnancy, welfare dependence, and incarceration were achieved.

5. STRONG SUPPORT FOR THE STUDENTS WHO NEED IT THE MOST

The proposals made by the Commission had a more dramatic effect on equity in American schooling. It might easily have been otherwise. Raising the standards in the way we have described could easily have made things worse for disadvantaged students, because this heavily standards-based system might have created even higher hurdles for some children than they had faced before. But the Commission had thought through what it would take to make sure that a system in which those who had the most got more and those who had the least got the most. They knew that the United States had one of the most unequal distributions of income in the industrialized world, and that was resulting in children coming to school with a whole range of very serious problems that the schools did not

have the personnel, funds, and expertise to cope with. So they proposed a number of measures intended to address the equity problem directly.

The first was the establishment of a pupil-weighted financing referred to earlier. This scheme reached right down to the school level and the student level, and was designed to provide more resources behind the students who cost more to educate and the most resources for those who cost the most to educate. It called for all state school funding to be converted to this form of funding and for all public schools to be directly funded by the state.

This single recommendation produced what was undoubtedly the most fundamental change in the fortunes of poor children since the Elementary and Secondary Education Act of 1965. The Commission debated this proposal long and hard, not because they were opposed to the principle — far from it — but because the example of California, with its devastating combination of the Serranno-Priest school finance decision, which equalized school finance in California, and the Proposition 13 limitation of the tax-raising capacity of the state, had shown what can happen when a state equalized its school finances at the same time it leveled them down. If legislation had come before the state legislatures to adopt a pupil-weighted scheme for distributing school funds without raising the total school budgets, the better-off districts would all have lost money and, knowing that, would have fought the legislation tooth and nail. But the Commission, recognizing that, proposed to take a substantial share of the money saved by restructuring the student progression through the system and add it to the pot, thus raising the total amount of money available for funding the schools in a state. In that way, it became politically possible to institute a fairly aggressive form of pupil weighting in the state formulas. The result was an enormous increase — about $18 billion nationwide — in the funds available for educating disadvantaged children.

Many schools serving large concentrations of disadvantaged children were reconfigured and resourced so they could be open from early in the morning into the evening. Qualifying students got additional schooling and tutoring, three good meals, sports and recreation, a space to do their school work, and a safe, nurturing environment. This was hardly a new idea, but the new funding pattern made it a reality in many, many schools.

Schools with large concentrations of low-income children also got, under the new finance plan, the funds needed to provide extensive services for children with physical or psychological problems that might impair learning and often go undiagnosed and unaddressed in low-income families. Many programs of this sort were set up, and, invariably, the school people involved were amazed to find out how many students who had been labeled slow learners actually had a hearing problem or poor eyesight or some motor problem that could be corrected with a simple therapy.

Another measure built into the Commission's plan was a proposed legislative requirement that school districts managed by local boards establish governmental units designed to tightly coordinate the provision of educational services with the provision of social services to low-income families. The local option for mayoral control of schools, also built into the plan, put the schools and the social service agencies under the same management and accountability systems, thus leading to much tighter coordination of these services.

Another proposal of the Commission that had a real impact on the prospects of disadvantaged children mentioned above was the idea that mayors should take the lead in bringing all the local officials together who headed the social service, foster care, juvenile justice, and health care systems, along with the schools, to create fully integrated databases that permit analysis of concentrations of community problems like high incidences of youth crime, poor health, use of hospital emergency rooms for routine health care, low education performance, and so on. The Commission, looking back at a large body of research in this arena, had learned that this kind of coordination and analysis could become the basis of very powerful plans for dealing with those problems in an integrated way, using the schools as a focal point for registering all the members of very low-income families for the services to which they were entitled. Where this was done well, it resulted in many changes in the deployment of scarce funds and the way these agencies worked, which in turn resulted in dramatic improvements in the health and education of young people in the most impoverished areas and significant decreases in juvenile crime.

It turned out that, among the things that often happened where such collaborative programs were instituted, there was an agreement to register children for school at the same time and in the same place as their parents registered for social services, so that all the relevant agencies could collaborate to assess the needs of the whole family as a unit and develop a combined, coherent plan to provide the services that the family needed to succeed.

Some of the Commission members realized that states could adopt all of these measures and there might still be big failure rates among disadvantaged children for the simple reason that if their aspirations did not substantially rise, they either would not think they needed to get to high academic standards or would not think they could, or both. Millions of students came from families, neighborhoods, and communities in which aspirations had been very low for a very long time, and it was natural for these students to adopt those aspirations. Because nothing would work unless this issue was addressed head on, the Commission, in its report, said as forcefully as it knew how that the private sector in each community needed to work as hard as it could to raise the aspirations of young people whose aspirations could be expected to be low. Some chose to do this with massive advertising campaigns, some did it in other ways; more than the Commission had thought likely worked hard to convey to young people that jobs for the low-skilled were disappearing, that hard

work in school would pay off, that students who looked and talked like them and came from the same kinds of backgrounds were succeeding in school and, as a result, in life.

None of these measures by itself proved to be a panacea, but the record of the past 15 years has shown that where local officials worked hard and together, the combination has made all the difference for a very large number of very vulnerable children who almost surely would have fallen through the cracks otherwise.

6. GETTING THE STANDARDS, CURRICULUM, AND ASSESSMENTS RIGHT

The Commission had been very much aware of the dangers inherent in proposing a system even more dependent on examinations than the one it hoped to replace, all the more so because of the nation's experience with standards and tests since the first Commission on the Skills of the American Workforce had proposed a standards-based system of education in 1990.

The first Commission had proposed a standards-driven system for the United States based on its review of the way that such systems worked in Europe, where examinations were based on very thoughtfully developed syllabi and the examinations required extensive writing and multi-step solutions in mathematics. Most of those examinations were developed by curriculum experts, not psychometricians, and so were their standards, often by the same people. The staff of the first Commission had noted that the countries with the best performance in mathematics often had mathematics standards written by one person or a very small group of people working closely together, with closely matched examinations. The result was not only unusually coherent standards and examinations, but a very coherent curricula as well.

But all too often, standards in the United States were anything but coherent, the result of a brokering process among teachers and others who had no incentive to create coherent standards. Whereas examples of excellent exam papers are often released in other countries, so that students and their teachers can get a clear view of what work looks like that meets the standards, that rarely happened in the United States. Instead, we continued to rely much too heavily on multiple-choice, machine-scored tests that produced no examples of clear thinking, good analysis, fine writing, or skillful problem solving. American test developers, in an effort to be responsive to the demand for cheap tests and to the demand for "customized" state accountability tests, created giant banks of pretested test items and asked the states to gather a group of teachers together and select items that they thought matched the state's standards. The result was a test that matched no one's idea of what a powerful, coherent curriculum ought to look like, a curriculum of the kind that drives the performance of the best-performing nations in the world.

So the Commission, in its report, had called attention to several examples of first-rate standards, syllabi, and assessments. It had called attention to the practice in some countries of letting students know that they

would be examined in some subjects orally (but not notifying them which subjects until just before the exam), and it had strongly advocated the idea of using examination boards as the linchpin of the design of its State Board Examination strategy.

An examination board is an organization that offers examinations and the syllabi on which they are based. It administers the examinations and produces score reports for everyone who needs them. And it offers training to the teachers who teach the courses that are framed by the syllabi. In countries that have examination boards, schools, usually high schools, choose the examination board they want to affiliate with, though in some countries, schools can affiliate with more than one board. Usually the ministry of education decides on the group of boards that are authorized to play this role, and no school can use public funds to offer examinations not approved by the ministry. The College Entrance Examination Board, the sponsor of the Advanced Placement tests, has many of the attributes of such a board. In most cases, though, examination boards offer what amounts to a core curriculum and electives from which a student may choose. At the time the *New* Commission issued its report, the College Board had not yet done this.

So the Commission, in its report, had suggested to the states that they follow this pattern for the State Board Examinations the Commission recommended. Each state would have its own boards and would also approve a limited number of other examinations for use as the equivalent of its own State Board Examinations. And it had also proposed that the states, as they built their own State Board Examinations, carefully study the examples of world-class standards, syllabi, and examinations provided by the Commission before they started developing these new examination systems.

In fact, the nature of that curriculum and of the standards that drive it had been a major focus of the Commission's recommendations. The research that had been done for the Commission had painted a global economy that was producing many requirements rarely, if ever, reflected in state standards or tests. Not only were math, science, and technology becoming increasingly important, but it was equally clear that many other subjects in the curriculum, from the fine arts to world history, were no less important. It was also clear, however, that the way those subjects were being taught often had very little to do with the likely requirements of employers in the future.

So the Commission saw the creation of the State Board Examinations as the occasion for a fundamental review of the goals of the state curriculum, and therefore the standards and assessments, to reflect this profound shift in the kinds of skills and knowledge that would be needed in the years ahead. Whereas earlier efforts at standard setting had relied mainly on school teachers, and, to a lesser degree, on college professors to determine what was worth teaching, this time the states cast their nets wider and relied more heavily on empirical research and rigorous analysis of data to figure out what people would have to know and be able to do to succeed in the kind

of world that was coming into view. Who would actually need what kind of math, and why? In what ways and with what skill levels would people actually have to communicate with one other? Who would have to know what about other countries and other peoples, and what would they have to know about them? What about our history and other people's history was most important to know to preserve our democracy?

These efforts to think hard and well about what was worth teaching led in some unexpected directions. It turned out that employers valued certain kinds of expertise greatly but did not expect people to be trained for particular jobs, until they got to college or graduate school, because job descriptions were changing ever more quickly. They most wanted people who had the kind of knowledge and skill that underlay many kinds of jobs, and they wanted people who were very good at learning new things quickly. This required the people setting the standards to pay much more attention to identification not only of the core knowledge required but also of the key ideas and conceptual frameworks needed to really master the new core curriculum, the frameworks that adults could hang new material on when they needed to learn it.

Educators had talked for decades about "learning to learn," but it turned out that they knew very little about how to build a curriculum that helps their students do that. They ended up turning to medical schools and other professional schools for advice on this, because medical schools had long ago given up trying to teach prospective doctors everything they would have to know and had created curricula designed to train doctors how to figure out what they needed to know and find out how to get that knowledge when they needed it.

Perhaps the biggest discovery followed from the Commission's finding that a far higher proportion of our workers, at every level, would have to be people who could think out of the box, creating new ideas for new products and services (many of them based on swiftly advancing technologies). This is a world in which there is no single right answer; there are only answers, some of which are more creative then others. No one disagreed with the proposition that being able to recall dates in history and being able to do one's times tables with automaticity was very important, but a world in which virtually all student testing was a search for single right answers chosen from a preselected list of possible answers was a world that could not possibly encourage creative work. This realization led to a profound reconsideration of the whole American approach to testing and assessment. It also led to a reconsideration of the place of the arts in the curriculum and even to the role of play.

The standard setters learned that we would need people who could manage, lead, and staff highly innovative enterprises of all sizes and network them together to bring new products and services to huge customer bases all over the world more quickly than the competition. And that led to elements in the standards related to leadership skills and the skills one needs to be an effective member of a team.

It seemed that we would need many more people who knew much more about the rest of the world, because the emerging middle class and the markets they represented were not in Europe but in Asia and South America and Eastern Europe, places few Americans knew very much about.

As we said above, it was challenge enough for the United States to meet, to say nothing of exceed, the best student performance in the world in the core subjects in the curriculum from the position the country was in 2006, when the report was issued. To do all these other things, too, not just for the elite, but for all their students, the states would have to revise their curricular aims and standards in a fundamental way.

As it turned out, the federal government played the key role in driving assessment in these new directions. The landmark No Child Left Behind legislation came up for reauthorization just as the Commission's report came out. Many people who strongly supported that legislation felt that it would be greatly strengthened if the federal government would provide less leeway for states to avoid the sanctions on low-performing schools by setting weak standards for student achievement. Many prominent voices were heard during the reauthorization hearings in favor of national standards in the core subjects in the curriculum.

In the event, the Congress, moved in part by these voices and in part by the Commission report, adopted a model very like that of several other countries. High school-leaving standards were to be set by Board Examinations approved by the states, but at key points between the beginning of school and the point marked by the Board Examinations, the federal government would

In 1998, the UK launched reforms to raise the skills and qualification levels for young adults and workers to world standards. The goals are to increase the number of employers who make training a key part of future business plans and to help workers acquire the knowledge and skills that make them employable and active in their communities and reduce potential unemployment. Among the adult basic education priorities are: (1) free basic skills courses in reading, mathematics, communication, and the English language for low-skilled adults; (2) free, face-to-face, online information, advice and referral services for adults interested in learning new skills or retraining to improve their careers, and who generally do not yet have a first full national vocational qualification (NVQ) at a Level 2 (the gateway to advanced technical education or training programs); and (3) free employability skills training through NVQ Level 2, designed for employers to address their workforce's skills needs, and intended for mostly small- and medium-size enterprises that currently do not work with training providers to train low-skill workers and give them paid time off for training. The UK 2006–2007 investment in adult and lifelong learning and skills development totals £8.7 billion.

★ ★ ★ ★

With the support of several foundations, state and local governments, and businesses, the Council for Adult and Experiential Learning is currently carrying out a multisector demonstration of individual learning accounts in: Chicago in the foodservice sector; northeast Indiana in the manufacturing and public sectors; and the San Francisco area in the allied health care sector. Under a model referred to as Lifelong Learning Accounts, employers match employee accounts at $500 per year, employees contribute a minimum annual amount of $120, third-party sources match the combined contributions, and employees are assisted in mapping out a learning plan with an education and career advisor.

set examinations in reading, writing, and mathematics, benchmarked to international standards. The legislation the Congress passed authorized the U.S. Department of Education to begin the process by setting standards and a national test for 4th-grade reading first.

The Congress also authorized other substantial additional expenditures for assessment development and administration in the revisions to No Child Left Behind. Among them was an offer of matching funds to every state willing to pay for the regular administration of the OECD Program for Student Assessment (PISA) tests. These tests were created to make possible a valid comparison of student performance among the OECD member countries, but, over time, the countries included in the system included most of the world's best performers, as well as a number of states in the United States. Before this was done, the only means of comparing state performance was on the widely admired National Assessment of Educational Progress (NAEP) test, but that test did not make it possible to compare state performance with the performance of other countries. The news media, it turned out, gave a lot of play to the publication of the OECD PISA reports, because many states that had thought they were doing pretty well were dismayed to see how they stacked up against other countries of roughly the same size as their state, countries that were direct economic competitors.

Perhaps most important, Congress was persuaded by the Commission's conclusions about the limitations of the tests that had been in use up to that point to authorize substantial funding for research and development that would lead to a whole new style of asssesment, and provided additional funds for the states and schools to purchase the new assessments that emerged from this research. What persuaded the Congress to do this was testimony during the reauthorization hearings to the effect that the states were spending only about $10 to $15 per test, per student on their accountability testing, whereas the countries with the best performance were routinely spending $50 or more, the International Baccalaureate was charging $54 for its examinations, and the College Board was charging $83 for its Advanced Placement tests. The difference, of course, was in what was being tested, and the Commission's conclusions about the importance of assessing students' creative and innovative capacity and their reasoning ability as well as their mastery of fact and procedure carried the day.

7. WORKFORCE SKILLS FOR WORKERS OF ALL AGES

The Commission was well aware that most of the people who would determine the outcome for America's economy over the decade or two following release of its report were already in the workforce. And it knew too that the literacy of our lower-skilled workers was well below that of their opposite numbers in other advanced industrial countries and far below what it needed to be if both they and the nation as a whole were going to be competitive in the years following the release of the report. These facts weighed heavily on the Commission, because it realized that the stiffest competition the United States faced was from countries that had managed to create a very sturdy foundation of high literacy among numbers of the workers that rivaled ours in size, workers who would work for a fraction of what our workers were charging for their services. High literacy would be the foundation for everything — for most work below the professional level, for acquiring professional skills, for learning new technical skills in a rapidly changing economy, for everything else that would matter. But adult literacy had for a long time been a very low priority in the United States. Though 31 million Americans 16 years old or older were out of school and had no high school credential, there were enough funds to meet the needs of only 3 million of them.

So the Commission's first priority was to find ways to get as many workers as possible up to the levels of high literacy embodied in the new State Board Qualifying Exams. If the standard set by these exams was to be the standard every school child was to meet, it seemed obvious that the first obligation was to make it possible for every American worker to meet that standard who wanted to.

One suggestion the Commission made was to amend the tax laws to make it possible for employers to enable their workers with little or no English to learn that language. For years, many Northern European countries had provided free training in the native language for families coming into their country to work, whether or not they were citizens. This tax proposal aimed at the same target.

But the most important proposal the Commission made on this score was that the federal government provide free services to all people who had completed the 9th grade to enable them to meet the mathematics, English, and related literacy standards embodied in the new state qualifying examinations. They observed that this would enable the states to use the funds they had been spending on the whole range of adult education services to concentrate those funds on getting those adults who lacked a 9th-grade level of education and fluency in English up to the point where they could take advantage of the new federal program. Not all adults, of course, chose to take advantage of these opportunities. In the event, about 2.5 million additional adults did so every year. But over time, this resulted in a sea change in the employability of people who had only been able to scrape by before and in the general productivity of the workforce as a whole. Over time, millions of school dropouts, recent immigrants, high school graduates with only 6th-, 7th-, or 8th-grade literacy, and others who had taken courses at community colleges — people who were trying to support families on the minimum wage, who were living with their parents because they could not afford to do otherwise, whose productivity at work was low and could not be improved because they lacked the advanced reading, writing, and math skills needed to do high-productivity work — all these people were able to earn more because they produced more, and, in the process, their prospects and the prospects of the society as a whole were profoundly altered.

But the standard embodied in the State Board Qualifying Exams was meant to be a foundation, not a roof. All the way through their careers, American workers, no matter how many degrees they had beyond the State Board Qualifying Exams, would need to be able to get more education and training to be able to adapt over and over again to changing markets, technologies, and tastes. Many of these people needed another degree to take the next step in their careers. Many others needed only a certificate program. Some needed to change careers. Others needed to brush up. And still others needed to acquire a specific set of new skills to progress on their chosen path.

Military men and women had long had access to the Montgomery GI Bill to support not only attendance at colleges and universities, but also technical and vocational schools, apprenticeship programs, and many other kinds of continuing education and training. The Commission had noted, though, that only 30 percent of those who were eligible had actually taken advantage of this opportunity and had successfully encouraged the Congress to provide a modest amount of funding to more vigorously promote the use of these funds by people leaving the military for civilian life.

A whole system had been in place for years, of course, to meet the needs of full-time civilian degree seekers. That fit the model of young people without family obligations going from high school directly to college, to advanced full-time study, and then into the job market. But the reality was changing, and that model fit fewer and fewer people. Something needed to be done for those who had to fit their studies around full-time jobs and in all those situations in which something less than a full degree was needed. This was,

in the minds of the Commissioners, essential for maintaining a workforce that was ready to take on the next big challenge, whenever and wherever it came from.

So the Commission proposed the creation of Personal Competitiveness Accounts (PCAs), a new program conceived on the scale of the GI Bill and intended to accomplish similar outcomes.

Under this program, a PCA account was established for every child at birth, and that account was credited at the baby's first breath with a $500 contribution from the federal government. Each year after that, through the age of 16, the federal government added another $100. These deposits earned 4 percent in interest every year and were worth $3,200 by the time the person had turned 16. At 16 and any time after that, the worker who owned the account could decide to make additional tax-exempt contributions to the account, deducting the amounts from his or her salary. So could the person's employers. Under the law, the federal government was obliged to match the employees' contributions if they earned less than twice the minimum wage. The Commission report also urged state governments to make their own matching contributions to the employee deposits in these accounts.

The legislation creating the PCA accounts said that the account owners could use the money in their accounts for tuition, fees, books, supplies, and materials for any career-related program at any accredited institution. But the legislation also made it clear that the Congress wanted corporate training programs, union apprenticeship programs, joint labor-management training organizations, and other nontraditional providers to be eligible providers of these services, along with community colleges, universities, and other traditional providers.

Later, when newspaper stories began to appear about some of the apparently trivial purposes to which these funds had been put, an effort was made to amend the legislation to limit its use to certificate and degree programs. Eventually the Congress, seeking to find a way to hold the providers accountable for their use of the funds from this program, amended the legislation to create a Commission charged with coming up with a way to balance the need for flexibility of program design in the face of rapidly changing economic needs with the need to make sure that the funds involved were used for the purposes that Congress had originally intended. After a great deal of discussion, the Commission came up with a system of voluntary education industry standards for course certification that everyone could live with. Portable credentials that guarantee to the employer that the prospective employee has the skills that are needed had turned out to be key to making the 21st-century labor market work smoothly. One of the many advantages of this system was that it could be used as a way to hold the provider community accountable for the use of the funds (by counting the proportion of those seeking certification who actually achieved it) while at the same time signaling to both the student and the providers what skills and knowledge industry valued.

The uptake on the new PCA program by employers was slow at first, but employers began to add it to their benefit packages because it was an attractive and inexpensive recruiting tool. It was also true that workers were slow at first to make voluntary contributions from their salaries to these accounts, but in time they began to see that the people around them who had made those deposits and were getting the right education and training were getting the jobs they wished they had gotten, that having the right set of training certificates under their belt increasingly made all the difference in getting a job when jobs were tight. And they started investing everything they thought they could afford in their own education and training accounts. Just as was the case with the GI Bill, when the economists started researching the effects of the bill after the first five-year anniversary of its passage, they were very surprised at the returns on both this investment and the investment that had been made in the members of the workforce who were taking advantage of the guarantee of free funding for the foundation literacy program. They were among the highest rates of return that they had seen on any federal program ever.

One of the most far-reaching recommendations of the Commission in the area of adult education and training had to do with its proposals for a sweeping reorganization of the workforce development system. The Commission anticipated a future driven by economic turbulence and churning labor markets, and a world in which businesses would succeed only if they had access to highly educated, highly skilled, and innovative workers at every level, and individuals would succeed only if they knew what skills were demanded by employers and had a chance to get them locally. It also understood that the regional economies were going to compete fiercely with one another all over the world, and were likely to succeed only if all the economic, political, and education and training forces within a region — both public and private — pulled together to identify their strengths and build on them in a conscious, planful way.

The Commission proposed that the federal government authorize governors and state legislators, working with local elected officials, to create Jobs, Skills, and Economic Growth Authorities within their states that would align workforce areas, economic development areas, and community college districts into regions based on labor markets. These Authorities would, they said, be responsible for developing and implementing unified, comprehensive economic development strategies for regional growth and prosperity that would include the measures for workforce development and adult and technical education that would be needed to make them successful.

And they would have teeth. In the Commission's plan, these business-led bodies would have the authority to issue tax-exempt bonds for both economic development and workforce development purposes, including adult and technical education, and to raise revenue from the private sector, including philanthropic sources.

These Authorities should, the Commission said, be appointed by the relevant political leaders and chaired by highly respected business executives, and their members should be drawn from the ranks of the leaders of all the relevant communities. They should be tasked with setting goals for economic development and employment and be held accountable for achieving them. The whole community would need to be involved in setting those goals.

The Authorities would run media campaigns to encourage employers to advance the education and training of their employees and young people and older workers to raise their aspirations and seek the further education and training they would need to reach those aspirations. They would adopt skill standards for the critical jobs and careers in their regions and work hard to make sure that high-quality education and training programs were available to young and old to reach those standards. They would look carefully at the effectiveness of the career centers in their regions that provided counseling to individuals looking for work and training and funds needed to get access to training to make sure that those centers were operating effectively. And they would accredit the organizations providing programs for adults preparing for their State Board Exams, and see that the English-language training programs for workers were doing the job they were expected to do. In these and many other ways, they would weave together the formerly disparate and fractionated services in the areas of economic development, workforce development, adult education, and job training into a much more powerful engine for both individual growth and development and regional economic development.

When the Congress considered the legislation that would be needed to implement the Commission's proposals, it

The McAllen, Texas, Economic Development Corporation (MEDC) for the past 20 years led an effort to build a vision and strategy for the region's economic growth. The strategy calls for diversifying the regional economy, creating jobs, and enhancing relationships with their Reynosa, Mexico, colleagues across the border. It became apparent to the region's leadership that technical education constituted an important part of the long-term solution. In 1993, the region's leadership collaborated to spur the creation of a new comprehensive community college, South Texas College, to meet employer needs for skilled workers. The community college's mission explicitly supports the region's economic development strategy: to serve as the cornerstone for the economic vitality of the region. The MEDC also relies on the Lower Rio Grande Valley Workforce Development Board for labor market intelligence to support aggressive business recruitment and expansion efforts. The strategy has helped attract more than 500 employers and nearly 100,000 jobs to the region, along with billions of dollars in private investment.

★ ★ ★ ★

The Wyoming Department of Employment produces an annual report on the kinds of jobs that the graduates from the state's seven community colleges get and how much money they make in order to identify some of the strengths and weaknesses of community college programs. These reports, which are based on data from unemployment insurance wage records, help the state legislature determine, for example, how much their investments in nursing programs result in net additions to the health care workforce within the state and how many nursing graduates migrate to other states.

made sure that there were provisions that would lead to these authorities being defined by the geography of real labor markets, not the geography of political boundaries, even when those labor markets crossed state lines. And it decided to include a section that provided extensive waivers from many of the provisions of existing legislation on job training, economic development, and many other related areas when the new Authorities submitted acceptable strategic plans — including nonfederal matching funds — for combining the use of federal, state, and local funding in creative and appropriate ways. This possibility, combined with the state-granted bonding authority, turned out to weigh heavily in the balance as key leaders in their communities decided whether they would invest the time and energy to make these new Authorities a success.

In some communities, the necessary leadership emerged quickly, in some cases more slowly, and in some not at all, but, on the whole, the change from what had been in place before was dramatic. Some communities decided to put a lot of their chips on industries at the cutting edge of international technology development, like biotech. One seacoast state decided to place some bets on creating a competitive edge in the composite technologies central to the next stage of boat building. A midwestern state concentrated some of its resources on developing its competitive position in biofuels, and a mountain state did the same in the oil sands industry. But almost everywhere, the regional authorities placed many bets. Many, for example, looked hard at ways to strengthen their health care

industry, some concentrating on providing more and better-trained health industry workers, some by investing in their research capacity, and others by strengthening the intermediary organizations that help to make their health care providers more up to date and efficient, and many used a combination of these strategies.

One industry that a number of authorities bet on that had not been anticipated by the Commission was the education industry itself. In a now-famous case, one Authority put together a coalition of local universities, telecommunications firms, software developers, community colleges, venture capital companies, and one Indian company with unique expertise in Web-based technical education to create a state-of-the-art capacity to make advanced Web-based learning support systems for technician-level jobs in emerging industries. This one strategic decision put that metro area in a position of world leadership in industrial training for a long time.

Almost everywhere, these new Authorities strengthened the capacity of community colleges to anticipate and respond to the changing needs of businesses in their region, and developed much better and more efficient systems to get English-language training to new immigrants. They also developed more effective campaigns to raise the aspirations of high school dropouts and adults who had given up on themselves and provide them with high-quality programs to get them the foundation skills they had long ago given up on ever getting. In many places, they were able to greatly improve the services available at the career centers that people went to when they lost their jobs, were searching for their first job, or needed the education or training that would put them in a position to get their next job. They made sure that each center had highly trained counselors who were familiar with the occupational needs of employers, the forecasts on future needs that local economists had done, the standards that candidates for jobs would have to meet, the best places to get training for any particular job or career, and all the various sources of funds that individuals in a wide variety of circumstances could call on to pay for the education and training they needed. They organized another set of services for employers that helped them organize more effective in-company training or collaborate with one another to offer training they all needed but none could develop alone.

One of the things that made this new system so much more effective than the old one was a requirement that was buried in the federal legislation establishing the authorities. It required the states to use the unemployment wage records to report on the employment and earnings of the graduates of all publicly supported community college and proprietary school programs. This arcane provision of the law resulted eventually in a great flow of information that the customers of these institutions almost automatically used to make decisions as to which institution they would attend. Publishers realized that there was money to be made by taking these data and arranging them in an appealing way. Grocery store checkout counters and news stores started to see regional magazine covers adorned with ratings based on these

data that had startlingly dramatic effects on enrollments in these institutions.

The measures recommended by the Commission relating to the education and training of adult workers changed the face of the public workforce development system. It is unlikely that they would have had quite the effect they did were it not for the fact that the Congress, at roughly the same time the Commission's recommendations were being considered, also passed a series of measures providing much more effective cushions for people put out of work by outsourcing, offshoring, and the relentless automation of jobs. The Congress recognized that it was very unfair for a few people to bear the social and human costs of the economic turbulence that was, in fact, bringing the economic benefits of growing productivity to the country as a whole.

SUMMING UP

Even after 15 years, it is easy to recall the acrimony of the debate about the ideas the Commission put forward. Though many had been convinced by the analysis that the Commission had offered of the dynamics of the changing global economy that dramatic changes needed to be made in the American education and training system, many had not been persuaded at all, and some disagreed strongly with particular recommendations. Though many Americans had a low opinion of their education system in general, they turned out to be quite comfortable with the schools in their own community. Many educators were afraid that the proposals made by the Commission would put their jobs at risk. Some were afraid that they would lose power or authority. Critics on the left said that many low-income and minority students would be unable to meet the higher standards and would therefore be victimized for life by the proposed changes. Critics on the right were upset that the proposed changes would create new accountabilities for schools that they had hoped would be relatively free of regulation. Unions were upset about giving up seniority rights, uniform salary schedules, comfortable retirements, and other hard-won benefits. Conservatives were upset that some states were recognizing the unions as the state's partner in the bargaining process, and the unions had won the right to organize the contract schools in those states, which were now all the public schools in the state.

But almost all of these groups came in time to recognize that they had more to gain than to lose from the Commission's proposals. The Left got real school finance equity, a clear role for unions, the end of the threat of vouchers in particular, and the privatization of public schools in general. But the Right got rid of the bureaucracy and, in its place, got real school autonomy, real competition in a very competitive public school marketplace, the end of seniority rights for teachers, a revamped teacher licensing system that made the alternative route to licensure the only route, and the introduction of the most rigorous standards the nation had ever seen. No one was completely happy, but everyone had gotten more than they had ever actually expected to get.

The result now, after 15 years of very hard work, is what is plausibly the best national public school system in the world. The real winners are the students who on the whole are more engaged, working harder, and getting more out of their education than ever before. The bottom tenth of our performers are now performing above the average of all students in the advanced industrial countries, and our top tenth are the equal of any top tenth in the world, a big advance from where the top tenth was 15 years ago.

No less important was the revolution that slowly occurred in the world of workforce development and job training. The sharp deficit of American workers' literacy with respect to its competition was slowly reversed. American workers everywhere started to assume that continuing, never-ending training was part of the air they would have to breathe to be successful and they had the resources they needed to pursue it. And, in the process, they developed an agility that enabled their employers — new and old — to come up with market-leading ideas again and again and get those ideas into production faster than their competitors, again and again.

The new regional authorities played an important role in this process. A vehicle for bottom-up, not top-down, planning, they stirred the bubbling cauldron of American ingenuity and innovation, bringing together the forces of supply and demand in a uniquely American way, enabling us to make effective plans without running the unacceptable risks of a planned economy.

And not a moment too soon. It is now clear that the Commission's predictions for the evolution of the global economy were right on the mark, and if anything, coming on rather more quickly than forecast.

Comments

Statement from
DAL LAWRENCE AND MORTON BAHR

We must register two concerns about the report. The design for contract schools can become an open door for profiteers. One of us is a citizen of Ohio, where charter school legislation has resulted in almost universal poor student achievement, minimal accountability, and yet considerable profits for charter operators, many with peculiar political agendas. If past experience means anything, concentrating policy at the state level will stifle, not encourage, creativity.

Statement from
JOEL I. KLEIN

I commend the Commission for the good and hard work that it has done and for a report that presents bold and promising proposals to deal with the issues that our nation and its workforce will face in the 21st century. There are many aspects of the Commission's report that we are in the process of implementing in New York City under the leadership of Mayor Michael Bloomberg. The Commission recommends pushing these reforms forward (for example, restructuring teacher compensation, expanding prekindergarten services), and that is all to the good. The Commission also makes wide-ranging recommendations about other matters, such as student funding, teacher hiring by the state, and the role of contract schools. While these are innovative ideas meriting further study and analysis, I am not now prepared to endorse them on the scale suggested by the report. Finally, I believe that any attempt to achieve effective, comprehensive school reform will require the transformation of the culture in our schools — from one that is excuse based and compliance driven and refuses to differentiate among staff on the basis of merit or organizational need, to one that recognizes the importance of strong school leadership, school-based empowerment, and meaningful accountability for student performance. These critical cultural concepts are embedded in the report, but I highlight them for emphasis.

Background Papers

Estimates of the Additional Expense and Savings Associated with the Commission's Proposed Reforms in Elementary and Secondary Education

INTRODUCTION

This background paper provides the working cost estimates associated with the elementary and secondary reform proposals put forward by the Commission. In it, we provide the following: a summary of how the costs of the proposals add up; the cost estimates for each major proposal, as well as descriptions of cost savings and available offsetting revenue currently in the system; and a summary of the assumptions that underlie each major cost estimate.

It is important that the reader understand the spirit in which this analysis was performed. We do not intend that these tables be used as templates for state budgets. Our purpose was to show that the proposals made by this Commission are, taken in the aggregate, financially feasible from the standpoint of the nation as a whole. Because there are wide variations among the states in the way their grade schools and higher education systems are governed and funded,

it is inevitable that a detailed analysis of the funds flows related to the Commission's proposals in one state will not track to another. Each state will have to digest the Commission's proposals and do its own analysis of the financial implications of the plan it chooses to implement the ideas put forward by the Commission.

The focus of this analysis is the funding of elementary and secondary education. We made no attempt to estimate the implications of our proposals for the costs of higher education. Our goal is that 95 percent of high school students be qualified to go to college, and the analysis here shows how that could be accomplished for little more than we spend now. But we also hope that most of those who are qualified actually go to college.

That will cost a great deal of money — perhaps another $30 billion to $40 billion a year. We have not attempted to estimate the actual cost, because doing so would entail addressing many issues in higher education finance that we were not prepared to tackle. But we believe that the arrival of these students at the doors of our community, technical, and four-year colleges ready for college-level work would represent an extraordinary victory for this country. The statistics cited earlier in the Commission report make it clear that this investment will lead to a very large boost in personal incomes, which will in turn lead to increases in tax revenues that will much more than pay for these increased education costs. Far more important, the returns in terms of increased productivity and growth in the gross domestic product should enable this country to survive whatever economic storms might arrive on our shores for a very long time.

The sections of this report are organized in the following manner. The Overview presents the overall financial impact of the five major education reform proposals put forward by the Commission, including the cumulative estimated cost impact of the totals for each of the reform elements. In the five sections that follow, the financial implication of each of the reform elements is taken up one by one. For each reform element, a brief context for the element is presented, a short description of the reform plan envisioned is provided, the underlying assumptions are reviewed, and the estimates are presented. In every instance, the tables presented in this report are backed by mini-simulation models. If a state were interested in attempting to implement the proposed reforms, it would be possible to play "what if" with state-specific data for each of the

major reform components to gauge the cost impact in a particular state.

THE OVERVIEW

The constellation of proposals put forward by the Commission includes the following:

- A redesigned teacher compensation and retirement system
- A strategic investment in early learning services for 3- and 4-year-olds
- A strategic investment in students who are not successful in school
- The elimination of public investment in remediation in postsecondary education
- A strategic reorganization of the delivery of education, especially at the high school level

TABLE 1 shows the overall results for the cost estimates behind each of the five major Commission proposals. Additional expenses, projected savings (or funds already in the system dedicated to the topic), and how the two add up are detailed in TABLE 1. At this time, the estimated additional costs taken against the projected savings show a net need for revenue for all the projected reforms of $7.8 billion per year.

TEACHER COMPENSATION AND RETIREMENT

Teacher Compensation

Context • In calculating the cost of a reformed teacher compensation system, the first step we took was to learn from existing state systems. In Arizona, the nominal cost to the state of the career ladder program averages $219 per student in the 28 participating districts. The program has been in place for a decade. The district minimum is $210 per student, and the maximum is $262 per student. The state funding formula allocates support on the basis of weighted students and a teacher

experience index, with $127 per weighted/indexed student. Hence, higher amounts go to students with special needs (for example, those at risk) — Patagonia averages $262 for each of its 77 students because they are low income, not because the district is small. East Valley Institute of Technology (EVIT) averages $242 for its 6,361 students because it has had the highest teacher experience

TABLE 1:
Overall Scorecard on the Fiscal Impact of Proposed Reforms, Fiscal 2002–03

	ADDED EXPENSES	SAVINGS AND/OR EXISTING FUNDS	NET
Teacher Compensation			
Career Ladder	$25,820,663,259		
Retirement		− $6,627,768,033	
Net Change			$19,192,895,226
Early Learning			
Cost of Serving 3- and 4-Year-Olds	$34,610,525,000		
10% Expansion and Quality Control	$3,461,052,500		
Existing Funds		− $18,790,223,000	
Net Change			$19,281,354,500
Hard-to-Serve Students			
Cost of Serving	$38,568,052,913		
Existing Funds		− $19,897,000,000	
Net Change			$18,671,052,913
Cost of Remediation			
Remedial classes		− $2,660,319,489	
Net Change			− $2,669,319,489
Reorganize System			
Additional High School Students	$9,913,127,463		
High School Reorganization		− $44,965,662,704	
Advanced Standing		− $11,564,071,826	
Net Change			− $46,616,607,067
GRAND TOTAL			$7,859,376,083

index (1.11). Kyrene, a district of 17,488 students, averages $214 per student because it has a small proportion of students with special needs. Apache Junction's 5,499 students average the least amount because they had the minimum Teacher Experience Index (TEI) (1.00) and a low concentration of students with special needs. In general, district size has nothing to do with the cost per student. It is generally the larger districts that have voted to participate and pay a higher local levy, but, once they are in the program, size is unrelated to cost.

The cost to the state is not necessarily the cost of the program. Actually, local levies pick up much of the cost of the program. In addition, the state has added programs (three divisions of a more generous classroom site fund, including performance pay, an optional performance initiative program, and a separate instructional improvement fund) that contribute funds for overlapping purposes and programs. The career ladder pay has been folded into current salary schedules. The new features — some part of the the career ladder programs in other states or districts — that Catalina Foothills has been considering will count as part of the career ladder but will in fact need to be paid for out of other revenue sources.

In some ways, the cost of career ladder programs is most obvious when the programs are new, as there can be a sudden jump in state funds flowing to a district. However, because the career ladder program involves career salary steps, this immediate flow of funds need not match up with the long-term costs of the program: if many teachers qualify for ladder salary increases, then the local district will have to bear the cost somehow, because the state payment is unrelated to how many teachers qualify for which amounts of salary. The state pays a fixed amount; the district covers the shortfall with a local levy, larger class size, a less-qualified staff, or whatever other means are available. Usually the district does not even know why it has a shortfall and instead blames a proximate cause such as benefit increases or No Child Left Behind.

In Minnesota, Q Comp includes a career ladder and altered salary schedule as main components of its $260 per student cost. Of the cost, about 73 percent comes from the state, and the remainder must be raised by local districts. Northfield, a district that has had to cut its budget the past two years, is not opting for the local levy to support the program. Q Comp is a new program and, as such, has both obvious short-term costs and unclear long-term costs. In Minneapolis, which already had ProPay, funded locally, and has been phasing in the Teacher Advancement Program (TAP) in eight schools, Q Comp support will not be enough to cover the costs of TAP for all schools. (This is true even though the Broad Foundation is kicking in an additional $130 per student for schools that implement TAP.)

When a state pays a constant amount per student, the consequences can differ from district to district. Small, rural districts often have fewer students per teacher and fewer professional qualifications (though more seniority) per teacher, so gain less per average teacher; however, when they do gain, the purchasing power of the dollar can be larger in rural areas ($3 buys in Big Stone County what $5 buys in Minneapolis's Hennepin County).

In New Mexico, a three-tier licensure system is being phased in with tiers "provisional," "professional," and "proficient." The new system has minimum salaries in a version of a career ladder program. There are complex and multifaceted qualifications for advancing a tier. By 2007–2008, the statewide minimum salaries will be $30,000, $40,000, and $50,000 for the three tiers, respectively. Metropolitan areas generally already exceed these minimums, but rural areas do not. In rural areas, the increased costs will stem from the increased minima for the lower two tiers. In metropolitan areas, the increased costs will stem from teachers moving into the third tier. No one has a good prediction for what either of these costs will be. The economic incentive to move to a third tier depends on the gap between current salary and the tier salary; for senior teachers in metropolitan areas, that gap will be small. Metropolitan areas may increase the amount they pay at minimum for each tier, but those decisions have not yet been made. New Mexico is just beginning the process of deciding how to adjust its state aid for district costs that follow the three-tier system. In a circular causal fashion, the higher the pay incentives per teacher, the more teachers will move up a tier, so an increase in the per-teacher cost has a multiplicative effect, leading to much higher total costs.

Teacher Compensation Reform Plan • As an alternative to the current education-and-experience-based salary schedule, the Commission has proposed a career ladder with a base salary and two

types of salary increases. The average base salary would be $45,000 in 2006 dollars. Each credentialed beginning teacher would earn this amount.

The main salary increases would be pay hikes on advancement to a new rung on the career ladder. There would be three tiers above the beginning teacher tier. A variety of criteria — including advanced preparation and classroom evaluation — could influence the advancement in rank. The first salary increase, for achieving the second tier, would be $5,000 (2003 dollars); the second increase would be $10,000; and the final salary increase received for achieving the top tier would be $15,000. Advancing through the tiers would be worth $30,000 in salary to a teacher. In addition to providing extra pay for demonstrated extra skills, the two upper tiers would have added responsibilities.

The second type of salary increase is yearly raises. The criteria for these yearly increases could vary, with many different criteria, or the criteria could simply be based on a summative judgment of adequate progress. On average, we expect these salary increases to be $500 per year in 2003 dollars ($850 per year for tier 4). For teachers in tier 1, annual salary increases would be given only up to 15 years of experience; thereafter, a teacher would have to move to tier 2 to receive an annual salary increase. For tier 2, the limit to receive an annual salary increase would be 25 years of experience. For tiers 3 and 4, the limit would be 30 years of experience.

The pay as described would apply to an estimated 95 percent of teachers on a 10-month teaching schedule. The

TABLE 2:
National Average Teacher Salaries by Years of Service and Career Ladder Tier

YEARS OF SERVICE (10-MONTH CONTRACT)	TIER 1	TIER 2	TIER 3	TIER 4
0	$ 45,000			
1	$ 45,500			
2	$ 46,000			
3	$ 46,500			
4	$ 47,000			
5	$ 47,500			
6	$ 48,000	$ 53,000		
7	$ 48,500	$ 53,500		
8	$ 49,000	$ 54,000		
9	$ 49,500	$ 54,500		
10	$ 50,000	$ 55,000		
11	$ 50,500	$ 55,500		
12	$ 51,000	$ 56,000	$ 66,000	
13	$ 51,500	$ 56,500	$ 66,500	
14	$ 52,000	$ 57,000	$ 67,000	
15	$ 52,500	$ 57,500	$ 67,500	
16	$ 52,500	$ 58,000	$ 68,000	
17	$ 52,500	$ 58,500	$ 68,500	
18	$ 52,500	$ 59,000	$ 69,000	$ 84,000
19	$ 52,500	$ 59,500	$ 69,500	$ 84,500
20	$ 52,500	$ 60,000	$ 70,000	$ 85,000
21	$ 52,500	$ 60,500	$ 70,500	$ 85,500
22	$ 52,500	$ 61,000	$ 71,000	$ 86,000
23	$ 52,500	$ 61,500	$ 71,500	$ 86,500
24	$ 52,500	$ 62,000	$ 72,000	$ 87,000
25	$ 52,500	$ 62,500	$ 72,500	$ 87,500
26	$ 52,500	$ 62,500	$ 73,000	$ 88,000
27	$ 52,500	$ 62,500	$ 73,500	$ 88,500
28	$ 52,500	$ 62,500	$ 74,000	$ 89,000
29	$ 52,500	$ 62,500	$ 74,500	$ 89,500
30	$ 52,500	$ 62,500	$ 75,000	$ 90,000
SALARY OF TEACHERS WITH A 12-MONTH CONTRACT (BELOW)				
LEAST EXPERIENCED TEACHERS WITHIN TIER	$ 53,360	$ 61,480	$ 76,560	$ 97,440
MOST EXPERIENCED TEACHERS	$ 60,900	$ 72,500	$ 87,000	$ 109,972

remaining 5 percent of teachers are expected to opt for a 12-month contract. Teachers interested in a 12-month contract could opt to go into this track at the end of their second year. Each year while on track 2, teachers would receive an annual stipend equal to 16 percent of their salary.[1]

The provisions and salaries for teachers of the different experience and tier are indicated in **TABLE 2**. A teacher in tier 4 on a 12-month contract with 30 years of experience would earn $109,972.

The cost of this system depends on how frequently a teacher passes from one tier to the next. We envision a system in which passage from one tier to the next is a notable achievement. Once they become eligible, we expect 65 percent of teachers to move from tier 1 to tier 2. We expect 40 percent of experienced teachers to move to tier 3 and 20 percent to move to tier 4 when eligible. A second factor associated with the cost of the system is the time it takes to acquire the skills and experience needed to advance to the next tier, and whether a particular teacher has the talent and dedication it takes to step up the career ladder. Effectively, these are estimates of the potential of teachers. On average, we expect the teachers who will eventually be tier 4 to move up a tier every 6 years. For teachers who will eventually reach but not exceed tier 3, movement is expected in the 8th and 16th years. For teachers who end at tier 2, advancement is expected after 10 years of experience.[2]

In addition to promotion rates, cost is affected by turnover rates. When a senior teacher is replaced by a junior one, the overall cost decreases. Ultimately, in a stable system, the gain from turnover matches the amount of salary increases, leading to a stable yearly cost. Turnover has been estimated from aggregate data on national patterns and detailed data on district systems. Because we are considering national costs, two types of turnover are ignored: turnover from school to school within a district and leaving one district for a comparable job in another district. Neither of these affects the cost of this program if it is run statewide.

Of the remaining new hires, most are not fresh out of school. Some have delayed entry into teaching while working at another job,[3] and others have left teaching temporarily (often to start a family) and are reentering. These new hires affect cost because those with delayed entry will retire earlier since they are older than other inexperienced teachers, and those reentering teaching return with almost all of their previously acquired skills and pay levels. The expected distribution of hiring types by experience is shown in **TABLE 3**. The expected distribution of total teachers is also reported, in the right-hand column of **TABLE 3**. (Note that we have made no provision for teachers stepping back down the tiers, though this would be possible.)

Though 20 percent of those hired as teachers may potentially be tier 4 material, the actual share of tier 4 teachers is much less. About 11 percent of all teachers who are hired subsequently leave as tier 4 teachers, and 14 percent leave as tier 3 teachers. The highest amounts of attrition are in the initial years, when — despite potential — there are few upper-tier teachers, so the vast majority of departures are from tier 1.

PRIOR TEACHING EXPERIENCE	RECENT GRADUATE	DELAYED STARTING TEACHER	RETURNING EXPERIENCED TEACHER	TOTAL
\multicolumn{5}{c}{**TABLE 3:** Distribution of Teachers by Years of Service and Experience Prior to Hiring (in %)}

PRIOR TEACHING EXPERIENCE	RECENT GRADUATE	DELAYED STARTING TEACHER	RETURNING EXPERIENCED TEACHER	TOTAL
0	9	8	0	4
1	7	7	0	3
2	6	6	0	3
3	5	6	0	3
4	5	5	0	3
5	4	5	0	3
6	4	5	0	2
7	4	4	0	2
8	4	4	0	2
9	3	4	0	2
10	3	4	0	2
11	3	4	0	2
12	3	4	8	5
13	3	3	8	5
14	3	3	7	5
15	3	3	7	5
16	3	3	7	5
17	3	3	7	4
18	3	3	6	4
19	2	3	6	4
20	2	2	6	4
21	2	2	6	4
22	2	2	5	3
23	2	2	5	3
24	2	2	4	3
25	2	1	4	3
26	2	1	3	2
27	1	1	3	2
28	1	1	2	2
29	1	0	2	1
30 & Up	3	1	4	3
GRAND TOTAL	100 %	100 %	100 %	100 %

The average salary for teachers with a 10-month contract is expected to be $54,798 (2003 dollars). For teachers with a 12-month contract, which does not include teachers in the lowest-earning first two years and adds an annual stipend of 16 percent of salary, the average is $64,785. The average for all teachers would be $55,208. With slightly fewer than 3 million teachers, the annual salary cost of this system would be $166 billion (2003 dollars). This would be $26 billion more than the current system, about an 18 percent increase in average salary and total salary cost for the school year.

The added cost comes primarily from the increased base salary. While we do not have completely reliable figures on average beginning salaries for recent graduates

beginning teaching, the $45,000 might be about $10,000 higher than the current average starting salary. Although the figures for the upper end of salaries are eye catching, it is the initial salaries that represent the most significant percentage increase and cost. Despite the high final salary and the cutoff for tier 1 yearly pay increases, the expected career earnings of a tier 4 teacher are expected to be only 24 percent above those of a tier 1 teacher. Even tier 4 teachers spend much of their career at lower tiers and salaries.

TABLE 4 compares the proposed salary structure to 2002–2003 salaries in 2002–2003 dollars. The average salary is about the same as the highest state (California) in 2002–2003, 21 percent higher than the national average, and about 70 percent above the lowest state

TABLE 4:
Proposed National Average Salary Structure Versus Existing Salaries, 2002–2003, and Possible Responses in High- and Low- Salary States, 2002–2003

PROGRAM	AVERAGE SALARY		INITIAL SALARY	
	AMOUNT	% 2002–2003 NATIONAL AVERAGE	AMOUNT	% 2002–2003 NATIONAL AVERAGE
Proposed National Average				
Proposed Salary Structure	$55,208	121	$42,857	137
Existing State Salaries, 2002–2003				
Highest-Salary State	$55,673	122	$37,401	119
Lowest-Salary State	$32,416	71	$23,088	74
Possible State Responses				
High-Salary State (15% Above Proposed)	$63,490		$49,285	
Low-Salary State (10% Below Proposed)	$50,190		$38,960	

(South Dakota). The initial salary would be 15 percent above the highest state (Alaska), 37 percent above the average, and 86 percent above the lowest state (Montana). There will be differences from state to state under the proposed salary structure, the relation to the average would be approximately the same, but the increases would be more than the proposed national average in the highest paid states (15 percent above is illustrated in the table) and less than the proposed national average in the lowest paid states (10 percent below is illustrated in the table).

Teacher Retirement Benefits

The estimate for the savings associated with a flat 6 percent district contribution to a teacher's retirement was necessarily an average of what occurs across the country state by state. We selected seven states from across the country in which we could determine what the employer and employee contributed to the pension plan. The average total contribution was 17.85 percent. From that total contribution, we subtracted 6 percent for the employer's share under the proposed plan and 6 percent for an average employee contribution. In the computation of estimated savings, we assumed that public education employers could realize a savings of 6 percent in retirement for each teacher. We then multiplied the average teacher salary in 2003 times 6 percent. Finally, we added 6 percent of the increased salary cost, the difference in salary between the proposed compensation system and the current average salary.

This proposal would also address the issue of unfunded state pension liabilities for school employees. While there is some dispute about the exact size of the unfunded part of state retirement systems, these concerns would be eliminated under this proposal.[4]

TABLE 5: Teacher Compensation and Retirement Cost Estimates for School Year 2002–2003 in 2003 Dollars					
	AVERAGE TEACHER SALARY OR ADJUSTMENT	COUNT OF FULL-TIME EQUIVALENT TEACHERS IN 2002–2003	ADDED EXPENSE	SAVINGS AND/ OR EXISTING FUNDS	NET
Current System	$46,600	2,999,526			
Proposed Career Ladder System	$55,208	2,999,526	$25,820,663,259		
Retirement	$2,210	2,999,526		$6,627,768,033	
GRAND TOTAL (Revenue Needed)					$6,627,768,033

Teacher Compensation and Retirement Cost Estimate

TABLE 5 presents the teacher compensation and retirement cost estimates for the Commission's proposed reforms.

EARLY LEARNING

Context

In calculating the cost of providing preschool education, the first step is defining the service to be provided. Determining what constitutes a quality preschool program and providing funding for such programs have recently become priorities for many states. This focus on preschool education grew out of the national Education Summit held in Charlottesville, Virginia, in September 1989.[5] In February 1990, six National Education Goals were announced by President Bush and adopted by the governors of the 50 states.[6] The **first goal** was "[by] the year 2000, all children in American will start school ready to learn." The third objective of this goal stated that "[a]ll children will have access to high-quality, developmentally appropriate pre-school programs that help prepare children for school." [7] In July 1990 the National Education Goals Panel was set up to monitor the progress of the nation and the states toward all of the goals.[8]

The National Education Goals Panel identified the following five dimensions of children's school readiness:

- **Physical well-being and motor development** — including health status, growth, disabilities, physical abilities— including gross and fine motor skills;

- **Social and emotional development** — including the social ability to interact with others, take turns, and cooperate, and the children's perception of themselves and their abilities to understand the feelings of other people and interpret and express their own feelings;

- **Approaches to learning** — inclination to use skills, knowledge, and capacities, enthusiasm, curiosity, persistence on tasks, temperament, and cultural patterns and values;

- **Language development** — verbal language including listening, speaking, and vocabulary and emergent language, including print awareness, assigning sounds to letter combinations, story sense (stories have a beginning, middle, and end) and writing processes;

- **Cognition and general knowledge** — knowledge about properties of particular objects and knowledge derived from looking across objects, events, or people for similarities, differences, and associations; also knowledge of social conventions such as assignment of particular letters to sounds and knowledge about shapes, spatial relations, and number concepts.[9]

These dimensions have served as an important guide as states seek to meet this goal and develop high-quality, developmentally appropriate preschool programs.

Defining Quality

One of the first steps in progressing toward the objective of high-quality, developmentally appropriate preschool for all is defining what constitutes a high-quality program. While traditionally the provision of child care has been distinct from the provision of nursery or preschool,[10] the goal of having all children ready for school has required that the child care and preschool sectors work together to define and construct programs that support "the evolution of a comprehensive and linked set of services for children, used at parental discretion, which will advance youngster's early development and school readiness."[11] The efforts to define and assess quality in preschool programs have incorporated much of the work that has been previously done in the child care field.[12]

Studies in the early childhood education field have identified three different dimensions on which quality can be assessed:

- **Structural** — group size; staffing ratios; teacher and administrator education; training and experience; and physical environment (space per child, for example);

- **Process** — developmentally appropriate activities; nature of teacher-child interactions; teacher attitudes toward students; health and safety aspects of the environment; layout and appropriateness of furnishings; equipment and curricular materials; how teachers and staff relate to parents;

- **Child outcomes** — child's social and emotional developmental competence;

self-perceived competence or self-efficacy; behavior; physical health; increased vocabulary; math skills, including number concepts, simple addition, and subtraction; telling time, counting money; print concepts, including knowledge of letters, letter-sound associations, and familiarity with words and book concepts [13]

An additional dimension, the adult work environment, is recognized by some studies. This dimension includes the teacher's and director's salary and benefits, the turnover rates among teachers, the teacher's work satisfaction and commitment, and the teacher's perception of job stress.[14]

Many states have initiated Quality Rating Systems (QRS) that establish a set of program and practitioner standards that are known to produce good child outcomes and are coupled with monitoring to measure compliance.[15] Assessments under these standards require student observation. The National Education Goals Panel developmental domains discussed above should be addressed in state Child-Based Outcome (CBO) Standards.[16] Specific areas addressed by such standards include the following: language/communication, literature, math, physical motor/health, social/emotional, science, cognition/general knowledge, art/aesthetic/creative approach, social studies, and self-help.[17] As of 2003, 19 states had officially adopted or endorsed CBO standards, eight states had standards that had not yet been officially adopted or endorsed, 12 states were in the process of developing such standards, and 11 states had no standards either in effect or in process.[18]

Examples of standards can be found in the federal Head Start Program Performance Standards, which are the mandatory regulations that grantees and delegate agencies must implement in order to operate a Head Start Program. The standards define the objectives and features of a quality Head Start Program in concrete terms; they articulate a vision of service delivery to young children and families; and they provide a regulatory structure for the monitoring and enforcement of quality standards.[19] States have also been encouraged to set quality criteria for early childhood education in exchange for federal Child Care Development Funds (CCDF).[20]

Comprehensive standards have also been developed in more recent years by the National Association for the Education of Young Children (NAEYC) and the National Institute for Early Education Research (NIEER). NAEYC's Early Childhood Program Standards set standards in 10 areas and are widely used by preschools nationwide.[21] The following areas are addressed:

- relationships
- curriculum
- teaching
- assessment of child progress
- health
- teachers
- families
- community relationships
- physical environments
- leadership and management [22]

The National Institute for Early Education Research also has 10 Pre-K Quality Standards on which it ranks states in its yearly *The State of Preschool* report. In 2002 one state, Arkansas, met all of the quality benchmarks, but 20 states met five or fewer.[23] The standards are as follow:

- comprehensive curriculum standards
- teacher holds a BA
- teacher has specialized training in Pre-K
- assistant teacher has Child Development Associate (CDA) credential or equivalent
- at least 15 hours a year of in-service training
- maximum class size of not more than 20
- staff-child ratio of 1:10 or better
- vision, hearing, health screening, and referral
- site offers at least one support service
- site provides at least one meal [24]

Another set of standards often cited are those of the Abbott Preschool Program in New Jersey. The following standards were set by the New Jersey Supreme Court:

- six-hour day
- 182 days a year program
- a certified teacher and assistant for each class
- maximum class size of 15
- adequate facilities
- provides transportation, health, and other services as needed
- provides a developmentally appropriate curriculum that meets child-care standards of quality and state content standards[25]

Child outcomes in the Abbott programs are determined using a variety of instruments including the Early Childhood Environment Rating Scale (Revised), the Supports for Early Literacy, the Preschool

Classroom Mathematics Inventory and the Peabody Picture Vocabulary Test, and Get Ready to Read.[26]

Research has shown that high-quality early childhood education programs have well-qualified staff (teachers having a bachelor's degree or an AA degree with a certification in early childhood education; assistants having an AA degree or CDA; all staff understand how children develop and learn and can identify and respond to individual children's needs), staff are well compensated (the teachers and staff are paid enough to prevent high turnover rates), have small classes (no more than 15 to 20 students), and appropriate staff-child ratios (1:10 maximum).[27] Positive outcomes for children are more closely linked to the teacher's manner of relating to a child than the curriculum.[28]

Finally, an important aspect of developing quality preschool programs is educating families about what constitutes quality care and education. Historically parents have not been "well-informed consumers and can not accurately judge child-care quality." Some studies have suggested that parents "place cost and convenience" above the training and certification of teachers and care givers and the quality of the interaction of staff members with children.[29]

Funds Currently in the System

To date, families pay a significant share of the cost of preschool.[30] Since 1965, however, with the advent of the Head Start Program, the federal government has taken an active role, and in the past decade states have become increasingly active. The funds discussed in the following sections are for school year 2002–2003 and fiscal year 2002. These figures will be used in the early learning cost estimate to gauge the funds currently available in the system to offset the cost of serving the students the Commission proposal hopes to serve at an appropriate level of quality.

Federal Sources • Federal funding for early childhood education comes from both the Department of Health and Human Services (HHS) and the Department of Education. HHS programs include the following:

- Head Start Program, which provides grants to public and private agencies for low-income preschoolers, spent $6.5 billion in fiscal year 2002.[31]

- Child Care Development Fund (CCDF), which provides funding for states for child care distributed through certificates or vouchers to parents, provided $6.7 billion in fiscal year 2002[32] (approximately 26 percent of children served were 3- and 4-year-olds).[33]

- Temporary Assistance to Needy Families (TANF) (states and local governments can choose to transfer TANF funds to CCDF grants or spend some of their federal TANF dollars directly on child care) transfers amounted to approximately $1.9 billion in fiscal year 2002.[34]

- Social Services Block Grants for child care, which amounted to $99 million in fiscal year 2002. An additional $105 million was transferred from TANF for child care.[35]

Department of Education funding for preschool-age children includes the following:

- Title I — Approximately 2 percent of the funds provided by the Department of Education under Title I go to preschool-age programs that help children in high-poverty communities enter kindergarten with the skills they need to succeed in school (approximately $200 million in 2002).

- Early Reading First, which consists of competitive grants to school districts and preschool programs for the development of model school readiness programs ($75 million in FY 2002).

- Even Start, which promotes family literacy programs for young children ($250 million in FY 2002).

- Special Education Preschool Grants and State Grants, under the Individuals with Disabilities Education Act (IDEA), which make funding available to provide special education and related services for 3- to 5-year-old children with disabilities ($500 million in FY 2002).

- Early Childhood Educator Professional Development Program, which provides competitive grants for educators in high-poverty areas to improve their knowledge and skills ($15 million in FY 2002).[36]

Other than Head Start and IDEA funding, it is difficult to determine exactly how much federal funding is used for preschool. States do not track Title I for prekindergarten, and although states can transfer TANF funds to CCDF or spend them directly on payments for preschool and use CCDF money to pay for preschool, there are no clear records that distinguish preschool spending from child care spending.[37]

State Sources • In fiscal year 2002–2003, state funding for prekindergarten initiatives totaled $2.54 billion.[38] State dollars for preschool programs come from a variety of sources, including the general fund, lottery funds, gaming revenues, tobacco settlement funds, sin taxes, and a dedicated percentage of income tax.[39] State funds are distributed to preschool programs in several different manners, including by competitive grants (16 states), noncompetitive grants (4 states), formula allocation (21 states), or tuition subsidy (1 state).[40]

Local Government Sources • Eighty percent of states also used local dollars to help pay for preschool. Local revenues come from property taxes, sales taxes, and, in one case, San Francisco, a spending earmark.[41]

Private • In addition, two-thirds of state preschool programs received in-kind contributions, including transportation services, meals, and maintenance of facilities.[42] One-third of state-financed programs included parental fees as part of the payment structure. Fees were usually on a sliding scale.[43]

The Number of Preschool Students to Be Served

The final part of the overall cost determination is the calculation of the number of students who will use the service. The target population must be identified. Is the program for all 3- and 4-year-olds, or only at-risk 3-year-olds and all 4-year-olds? If you specify all 4-year-olds, does that actually mean every 4-year-old or only those that will take advantage of service offered? Once the eligible population is identified, then dollar amounts can be estimated.

Data to project enrollment can be gathered from the U.S. Census Bureau, school district enrollment figures, and existing preschool and child-care attendance data. Even if the goal of the program is universal service, in making projections, it should not be assumed that 100 percent of eligible children will use the service. Some families will opt not to enroll their children in the preschool program, instead purchasing such services in the private market, and not all enrolled children will use all of the available services.[44]

In 2000 there were approximately 3.89 million 3-year-olds and 3.99 million 4-year-olds in the United States. The numbers are projected to vary little over the next decade.[45] Approximately 17 percent of all children under the age of 6 live in poverty.[46] In 2002 according to the *Digest of Education Statistics,* 1.7 million 3-year-olds were enrolled in preprimary programs. Of these, 39 percent were enrolled in public nursery schools, while 40 percent attended private preschools. Ten percent were enrolled in

public kindergartens while 7 percent were enrolled in private kindergartens. Forty-one percent attended full-day programs, while 32 percent attended part-day programs. For 4-year-olds, the data show 2.6 million were enrolled in preprimary programs. Of these, 45 percent were enrolled in public nursery schools and 44 percent enrolled in private nursery schools. Twenty percent were enrolled in public kindergarten and 13 percent enrolled in private kindergarten. Forty-five percent were in full-day programs and 40 percent in half-day programs.[47]

The Commission's early learning proposal is to serve every 4-year-old interested in participating in a publicly supported, high-quality early learning program. The goal is to serve virtually all 4-year-olds and all of the 3-year-old children who live in low-income households. To get an accurate number of 4-year-old students who would participate, we started with the 3.99 million 4-year-old students and backed off our estimate of the number of 4-year-olds whose families would elect not to participate. For this estimate, we used the number of students who attend private school (11 percent) for K–12 education and the number of students who are home schooled (1.5 percent). To get an accurate number of low-income 3-year-old students who would participate, we started with the 3.89 million 3-year-old students and took 17 percent of that figure to represent the number of 3-year-olds in the target group.

Early Learning Cost Estimate

After the services to be provided are specified, the quality standards set, and the number of children expected to use the service calculated, the cost of the program can be computed.[48] Costs can be divided into three areas: capital costs, infrastructure costs, and direct service costs.[49] The quality determinations regarding the levels and types of services to be provided are major factors in determining these costs:

- Capital costs include the building and grounds and maintenance of the facilities, play structures, classroom furnishings, books, other educational materials including computers, and transportation costs.

- Infrastructure costs include the costs of administering, monitoring, and

evaluating the program; providing resources and referrals for the program; providing technical assistance and support; and providing for planning and coordination of services. Initial training expenses for teachers and ongoing professional development may also be included in this component, as well as data collection and analysis, and public relations work.[50]

- Direct costs include the costs of specific programs and services that the children and their parents receive. Direct services may include preschool classes, child care, and family support services. The

TABLE 6:
Commission Early Learning Cost Estimate for 2002–2003

EARLY LEARNING SERVICE	COST PER CHILD SERVED	NUMBER OF STUDENTS SERVED	COSTS AND OFFSETTING REVENUE
4-Year-Olds Served in a School District Setting	$7,750	1,735,700	$13,451,675,000
4-Year-Olds Served in a Community Provider Setting	$9,000	1,735,700	$15,621,300,000
3-Year-Olds Served in a School District Setting	$7,750	330,700	$2,562,925,000
3-Year-Olds Served in a Community Provider Setting	$9,000	330,700	$2,976,300,000
10% Expansion and Quality Control Overhead			$3,461,220,000
Total Costs			$38,071,557,500
LESS THE FOLLOWING FEDERAL AND STATE FUNDS ALREADY IN THE SYSTEM			
State Contribution			$2,540,000,000
Federal Head Start			$6,536,570,000
Federal CCDF and TANF			$8,683,653,000
Federal Education Funding (NCLB and IDEA)			$1,030,000,000
Offsetting Revenue			$18,790,223,000
GRAND TOTAL (Revenue Needed)			$19,281,354,500

salaries and benefits of instructional staff, administrators, and other staff members will be a major component of this cost, so the decisions as to the number of students per classroom, number of staff members per classroom, level of education, and experience required for early childhood teachers, instructional aides, and administrators are all very important.[51]

The costs of needed early learning facilities, though very important, are not considered in this estimate. We considered three sources to derive the operating cost estimates for a high quality early learning program — an estimate from an Augenblick, Palaich and Associates education adequacy study in the state of Connecticut, an estimate provided by Anne Mitchell Associates, and an estimate developed by the New Jersey Department of Education. At its core, the cost estimates in these studies were based on an early childhood classroom with between 15 and 20 students, a teacher, and an aide. Each of the programs costed out that we examined were full-day programs with four hours of instructional time built into the day. Each study assumed the qualification of the teacher was defined as a bachelor's degree. The qualifications for the aide varied from study to study, ranging between an AA degree with an early childhood certificate to no special qualifications required. Each study costed out these core services and other needed wraparound services.

These estimates were adjusted to reflect the 2002–2003 school year and to reflect interstate cost of living differences and were

averaged to create an estimate of $7,750 per student cost for early learning programs offered by the public schools and a $9,000 per student cost for programs offered by other providers in the community. For the Commission estimate, we assumed that students would be equally divided between the two types of programs. Finally, it has been suggested that without a significant investment above the personnel needed to deliver these services to children, the expansion and quality control of these programs would be put in serious jeopardy. Therefore, the estimates include an additional 10 percent to address these concerns. TABLE 6 presents the early learning cost estimates for the NCEE proposal reform.

MEETING THE NEEDS OF STUDENTS AT RISK

Students-at-Risk Cost Estimate

The Commission's proposed reform plan as noted above has several critical elements, but central to its goals, and central to its funding scheme, is a set of decisions about how to serve students at risk of falling behind in the redesigned public K–12 education system. The following are critical interventions in the lives of students at risk of falling behind:

- Detailed screening assessments for all students that need them. The results of these assessments are used for academic and social interventions. These screenings would be available for any student, and for estimating purposes, it is expected that 50 percent of all students would use these services.

- A school intervention process that helps students stay on track and at grade level. This programming includes tutoring, double scheduling in targeted areas, and any of myriad other interventions designed to keep a student from falling behind and to intervene immediately. These services are targeted to the students, the needs of whom are identified in the screening process and in interim assessments administered by teachers. It is expected that approximately 35 percent of all students and 100 percent of all at-risk, special education, and English-language learners will need these services.

- Increased access to after-school, extended day programming, and mentors. These services offer a mix of academic and social interaction programming for all students. It is difficult to come up with a rationale to estimate the number of students who would participate in these programs. These programs should be offered to 80 percent of all students, and we expect that 50 percent of those students will participate.

- In many communities, collocating health and social services at or near the schools dramatically increases the chances of children being healthy and ready to learn. While many of these needed services are provided by public sources to begin with, coordination

TABLE 7:
Meeting the Needs of Students-at-Risk:
Cost Estimates for School Year 2002–2003 in 2003 Dollars

	COUNT OF STUDENTS AFFECTED	ADDED EXPENSE	SAVINGS AND/ OR EXISTING FUNDS	NET
Access to Screening Services	24,370,375	$6,067,593,750		
Remedial Support (tutoring, double-period classes, etc.)	16,989,263	$27,182,820,000		
After-School/Extended-Day Programming and Mentoring	19,416,300	$4,854,075,000		
Connections to Health, Judicial, and Social Services	48,541	$4,854,075,000		
Residential School	48,541	$4,368,668		
Existing Current Funds			$19,897,000,000	
GRAND TOTAL				$18,671,052,913

and organization are needed at the site level. These programs should be required for approximately 15 percent of students.

- For certain students, the only way out of very trying family and neighborhood circumstances is through a residential school. This option should be made available to the students who need it. We expect that to be one-tenth of 1 percent of the students in the public schools.

To create a reasonable estimate of the additional costs and potential savings such a system might generate, we had to make several assumptions about the per student cost of the above services. The per student costs are as follows:

- $50 per student for diagnostic screening services. It is assumed that schools can purchase the tests and tools needed to gauge regular academic progress.
- $1,975 (or 24 percent of the 2002–2003 national average) set aside per student for remedial academic intervention.
- $170 per student set aside for extended day programming and mentoring.
- $300 per student is allocated for the coordination of health and social service programming.
- $10,000 per student set aside for residential schools.

The data used in the model are taken from the National Center for Education Statistics Common Core of Data on the American Public Schools for 2002–2003. Existing revenue estimates are derived from federal and state sources for compensatory education (100 percent) and special education (40 percent) of 2002–2003 revenue. **TABLE 7** shows the cost estimate for the redesigned education delivery system for meeting the needs of at-risk students.

COST OF REMEDIATION

Postsecondary Remediation Cost Estimate

We looked to existing research to estimate the cost of remediation in postsecondary education. This was done in two parts. First, it was necessary to find out how much was being spent nationwide on remediation. Second, we needed to know how many students were taking remedial classes. By knowing these two pieces of information, we would be able to estimate a per-pupil cost figure.

A 1998 study conducted by David W. Breneman and William N. Haarlow, "Remediation in Higher Education: Its Extent and Cost," [52] provided an estimate of what percentage of the higher education budget is devoted to remediation. They estimated this figure to be roughly 1 percent of total expenditures, or about $1 billion out of the $115 billion budget for that year. Earlier estimates had the cost of remediation in the range of $911 million to $1.05 billion using data from Texas and Maryland and applying the results from those two states to the nation. Breneman and Haarlow expanded their study to include data from all 50 states to alleviate the concerns about the limited data sources in the original studies. Another study by the Alliance for Excellent Education suggested $1.4 billion was needed to fund remediation at community colleges alone.[53]

What Breneman and Haarlow were careful to point out was that this estimate does not take into consideration (1) private colleges, (2) lost earnings for students if they had not enrolled and "diminished labor productivity," and (3) "costs to society as a whole through failure to fully develop the nation's human capital." Similar comments were also made in other studies, suggesting that such estimates were conservative and did not include all costs of remediation. In any case, higher education institutions will always spend something on remediation for new immigrants and other adults who might wish to enter the higher education system and have not had the opportunity to go through the system proposed by the Commission.

With this estimate in mind, we gathered additional data from the National Center for Education Statistics (NCES). Looking at 2003–2004 IPEDS data, we found current higher education expenditures for all institutions, including community colleges, to be $267 billion. We used the estimate of 1 percent of that budget to be allotted to remediation for about $2.7 billion.

NCES also provided data on the proportion of students enrolled in remedial classes. The data showed that 35.9 percent of all freshmen and sophomores had taken at least one remedial class and in what subject areas they took remedial classes in (English, math, reading, writing, and study skills). We then applied the 35.9 percent to 2003–2004 enrollment figures to estimate the total number of students who have taken at least one remedial class. For 2003–2004 that number is about 6.5 million students.

Dividing the total remediation expenditures by the total number of students taking classes, we estimated that it costs on average $412 a student to provide remedial

	COST PER STUDENT FOR REMEDIAL CLASSES	COUNT OF FULL-TIME EQUIVALENT STUDENTS IN REMEDIAL CLASSES	ADDED EXPENSE	SAVINGS AND/ OR EXISTING FUNDS	NET
Additional Costs			$ 0		
Cost of Eliminating Remedial Classes	$ 412	$ 6,478,931		$ 2,669,319,489	
GRAND TOTAL (Revenue Needed)					$ 2,669,319,489

TABLE 8:
Postsecondary Education Remediation Cost Estimates for School Year 2002–2003 in 2003 dollars

classes. **TABLE 8** shows the cost estimate for postsecondary education remediation.

Redesigned Education Delivery System

Redesigned Education Delivery Reform Plan • The Commission's proposed reform plan, as noted above, has several critical elements, but central to its goals, and central to its funding scheme, is a set of decisions about how to redesign the public K–12 education pipeline. The following are critical aspects to the reform plan:

- Rigorous gateway tests that allow students to move into upper secondary or postsecondary experiences upon successfully passing the tests.

- A governance system that allows the easy movement of students from secondary to upper secondary or to postsecondary and technical training, in a way that ensures quality and respects student interests.

- Increased efficiency of the education system in terms of the number of students who are prepared to pass the gateway exams because the early learning experiences make all students ready to learn, teaching is more targeted and effective, and students have a more direct path to the advanced training in which they are interested.

- This dramatically reduces the dropout rate and the frequency at which students are asked to repeat a grade.

- Such a system will dramatically increase the number of 13- to 18-year-old former secondary students who will participate

in postsecondary institutions (community and technical colleges across the country). This participation in postsecondary education might tax the physical capacity of the receiving institutions, but students who take advantage of these opportunities will bring with them the same tuition and subsidies (federal, state, and local) that they would have two or three years later.

To create a reasonable estimate of the additional costs and potential savings such a system might generate, we had to make several assumptions. Critical among them were the following:

- That the dropout rate would be lowered for students in high school to 1 percent per year. This would increase the cost because more students would need to be served until they passed the gateway test.

- Though it would be possible to imagine at least a few 8th graders passing the gateway exam, the modeling presented here used the following very conservative estimates for those passing this gateway exam: 0 percent of 8th graders, 3 percent of 9th graders, 65 percent of 10th graders, and 90 percent of 11th graders.

- For those students who pass the gateway exam, there are essentially two choices: continuation in an upper secondary academic program or participation in a community college or technical program. The former continues the secondary costs associated with high school. The latter moves the student into the

			TABLE 9: Redesigned Education System Cost Estimates for School Year 2002–2003 in 2003 dollars		
	COUNT OF STUDENTS AFFECTED	ADDED EXPENSE	SAVINGS AND/ OR EXISTING FUNDS	NET
Additional Costs for High School Students Retained in School	1,200,282	$9,913,127,463		
Savings Associated with High School Students Moving to Postsecondary Education System	3,517,104		$19,134,631,869	
Savings Associated with Reduction in Grade Repeaters	1,927,340		$15,917,903,373	
Savings Associated with Postsecondary Education Advanced Standing Earned	971,288		$11,564,071,826	
GRAND TOTAL (Revenue Saved)				$46,616,607,067

postsecondary education system and reduces the need for support in the K–12 system. The modeling presented here used the following estimates for those passing this gateway exam: 50 percent of 8th graders passing the test will move to the upper secondary program and 50 percent will move into the postsecondary system in the 9th grade; 40 percent of 9th graders passing the test will move to the upper secondary program, and 60 percent will move into the postsecondary system in the 10th grade; 25 percent of 10th graders passing the test will move to the upper secondary program, and 75 percent will move into the postsecondary system in the 11th grade; and 15 percent of

11th graders passing the test will move to the upper secondary program, and 85 percent will move into the postsecondary system in the 12th grade.

- Finally, moving through the upper secondary academic program will save the individual student and the postsecondary institutions resources because the student earns advanced standing in the postsecondary institutions while in the upper secondary program.

The data used in the model are taken from the National Center for Education Statistics Common Core of Data on the American Public Schools for 2002–2003. **TABLE 9** shows the cost estimate for the redesigned education delivery system.

ENDNOTES

1   The percentages of 95 percent on a 10-month contract and 5 percent on a 12-month contract were used to calculate our teacher salary cost estimate. Over time, we would expect more teachers to opt for the 12-month contract. The additional cost for these teachers could be offset in these estimates because they would be available to work in the summers with special needs students and adult workers who need training.

2   In our model, however, entry to a tier is not tied to a specific number of years of experience.

3   Credit for that previous work experience must be determined when the person is hired.

4   Some unfunded liability figures for state systems are provided in Brainard, K. *Public Fund Survey Summary of Findings for FY 2004*. National Association of State Retirement Administrators, Sept. 2005, Appendix B. http://www.publicfundsurvey.org/publicfundsurvey/pdfs/Summary 20of%20Findings%20FY04.pdf.

5   National Education Goals Panel (NEGP), http://govinfo.library.unt.edu/negp/page1–7.htm.

6   NEGP, http://govinfo.library.unt.edu/negp/page1–7.htm. These goals were later expanded to eight by Congressional action. http://govinfo.library.unt.edu/negp/page1–5.htm.

7   National Education Goals Panel. *Getting a Good Start in School*. Washington, D.C.: National Education Goals Panel, 1997. http://govinfo.library.unt.edu/negp/page3–3.htm. Child Trends. *School Readiness: Helping Communities Get Children Ready for School and Schools Ready for Children*. Washington, D.C.: Child Trends, 2001.

8   NEGP, http://govinfo.library.unt.edu/negp/page1–7.htm.

9   http://www.ed.gov/pubs/AchGoal1/goal1.html; Kagan, S. L., Moore, E., and Bradekamp, S. *Reconsidering Children's Early Development and Learning: Toward Common Views and Vocabulary*. Washington, D.C.: National Education Goals Panel, Goal 1 Technical Planning Group, 1995; Child Trends, *School Readiness*; and Kagan, S. L., and Rigby, E. "Children Ready for School." New York: National Center for Children and Families, Teachers College, Columbia University, 2002, 10.

10   Kagan and Rigby. "Children Ready for School," 14.

11   Kagan and Rigby. "Children Ready for School," 15.

12   Kagan and Rigby. "Children Ready for School," 18.

13   Barnett, W. S., Lamy, C., and Jung, K. *The Effects of State Prekindergarten Programs on Young Children's School Readiness in Five States*. New Brunswick, N.J.: National Institute for Early Education Research, Rutgers University, Dec. 2005; Currie, J. *Early Childhood Intervention Programs: What Do We Know?* Los Angeles: UCLA and NBER, Apr. 2000; Golin, S. C., and Mitchell, A. *The Price of School Readiness: A Tool for Estimating the Cost of Universal Preschool in the States*. Washington, D.C.: Institute for Women's Policy Institute, 2004, 10; Helburn, S. W., and Howes, C. "Child Care Cost and Quality." *The Future of Children*, 1996, 6(2), 64–65.

14 Helburn and Howes. "Child Care Cost and Quality," 64–65.

15 Stoney, L., Mitchell, A., and Warner, M. E. "Smarter Reform: Moving Beyond Single-Program Solutions to an Early Care and Education System." *Community Development: Journal of the Community Development Society,* 2006, *37*(2), 105.

16 Scott-Little, C., Kagan, S. L., and Frelow, V. S. *Standards for Preschool Children's Learning and Development: Who Has Standards, How Were They Developed, and How Are They Used?* Greensboro: SERVE: Improving Learning through Research & Development, School of Education, University of North Carolina, 2003, 25.

17 Scott-Little, Kagan, and Frelow. *Standards for Preschool Children's Learning and Development,* 27.

18 Scott-Little, Kagan, and Frelow. *Standards for Preschool Children's Learning and Development,* 17. National Child Care Information Center, a service of the Child Care Bureau of the federal government, sets forth the Framework for Quality in Early Learning Guidelines that includes the following advice: Early learning guidelines should be based on research, should be focused on outcomes (what children need to know and do), be comprehensive but not overwhelming and balanced among all domains of development, and be aligned with state standards (http://www.nccic.org/pubs/goodstart/framework-quality.pdf). Standards should cover the breadth of areas of child development and also go deeply into each area. In-depth areas of assessment have been identified in the following areas: physical and motor, social and emotional, approaches toward learning, language and communication, and cognition and general knowledge. Scott-Little, C., Kagan, S. L., and Frelow, V. S. *Inside the Content: The Breadth and Depth of Early Learning Standards: Executive Summary.* Greensboro: SERVE: Improving Learning through Research & Development, School of Education, University of North Carolina, Mar. 2005, 3.

19 Head Start Performance Standards and Other Regulations are at http://www.acf.hhs.gov/programs/hsb/performance/index.htm.

20 "Good Start, Grow Smart: The Bush Administration's Early Childhood Initiative, Partnering with States to Improve Early Learning." http://www.whitehouse.gov/infocus/earlychildhood/sect6.htm.

21 Gilliam, W. S., and Zigler, E. F. "A Critical Meta-Analysis of All Evaluations of State-Funded Preschool from 1977 to 1998: Implications for Policy, Service Delivery and Program Evaluation." *Early Childhood Research Quarterly,* 2000, *15,* 441–473.

22 National Education of Young Children, NAEYC Early Childhood Program Standards, http://www.naeyc.org/accreditation/standards.

23 Barnett, W. S., Hustedt, J. T., Robin, K. B., and Schulman, K. L. *The State of Preschool: 2004 State Preschool Yearbook.* New Brunswick, N.J.: National Institute for Early Education Research Source, Rutgers University, 2004, 44.

24 Barnett, Hustedt, Robin, and Schulman. *The State of Preschool: 2004 State Preschool Yearbook,* 44.

25 Lamy, C. E., and others. "Inch by Inch, Row by Row, Gonna Make This Garden Grow: Classroom Quality and Language Skills in the Abbott Preschool Program: Year One Report, 2002–2003."

New Brunswick, N.J.: National Institute for Early Education Research, Mar. 2004; Abbott Indicators Project. *The Abbott Preschool Program: Fifth Year Report on Enrollment and Budget.* Newark, N.J.: Newark Education Law Center, Oct. 2003, iv; Starting at 3, Abbott Preschool Program, http://www.nj.gov/njded/ece/abbott/inch.pdf#search=%22Inch%20by%20inch%20Abbo tt%20preschool%20Year%20one%20report%22.

26   The Early Childhood Environment Rating Scale-Revised (ECERS-R) is used to rate programs in seven subscale areas: space and furnishings, personal care routines, language and reasoning, activities, interactions, program structure, and parents and staff. The Supports for Early Literacy Assessment (SELA) has the following six subscales to assess literacy: literate environment, language development, knowledge of print/book concepts, phonological awareness, letters and words, and parent involvement. The Preschool Classroom Mathematics Inventory (PCMI) has materials and numeracy and other mathematical concepts subscales. Measures of language assessment include the Peabody Picture Vocabulary Test (PPVT/TVIP) and Get Ready to Read (GRTR), which assesses 20 items, including book knowledge, print knowledge, letter knowledge, letter-sound correspondence, emergent writing, linguistic awareness-initial phonemes, linguistic awareness-rhyming, and linguistic awareness-compound words. Lamy and others. "Inch by Inch, Row by Row," 30–31.

27   Denton, D. *Improving Children's Readiness for School: Preschool Programs Make a Difference, But Quality Counts!* Atlanta: Southern Regional Education Board, 2002, 21; Brandon, R., and others. "Orchestrating Access to Affordable, High-Quality Early Care and Education for All Young Children Policy Brief." Seattle: Human Services Policy Center, 2004, 1; Gilliam, W. S., and Zigler, E. F. *State Efforts to Evaluate the Effects of Prekindergarten: 1977 to 2003.* New Haven, Conn.: Yale University Child Study Center, Apr. 2004, 9; Gilliam and Zigler. "A Critical Meta-Analysis of All Impact Evaluations of State-Funded Preschool from 1977 to 1998"; Golin and Mitchell. *The Price of School Readiness,* 13.

28   Currie. *Early Childhood Intervention Programs.*

29   Helburn, and Howes. "Child Care Cost and Quality," 69–70.

30   Stoney, Mitchell, and Warner. "Smarter Reform," 110.

31   In 2000, Head Start served approximately 11 percent of all 3- and 4-year-olds. Barnett, Hustedt, Robin, and Schulman. *The State of Preschool: 2004 State Preschool Yearbook,* 15. In 2002, total Head Start enrollment was 912,345. Fifty-two percent, or 474,420 of these, were 4-year-olds. Thirty-six percent, or 328,444, were 3-year-olds. This comprised 49,800 classrooms in 18,865 centers. Head Start Program Fact Sheet, http://www.acf.hhs.gov/programs/hsb/research/2003/htm. In addition to the $5,886,706,000 in federal funds allocated to the states, 176 states provided $177,572,211 to fund 28,173 additional slots for 3- and 4-year-olds. Barnett, Hustedt, Robin, and Schulman, *The State of Preschool,* 216. Head Start serves about 43 percent of the eligible children. Gilliam and Zigler, "A Critical Meta-Analysis of All Impact Evaluations of State-Funded Preschool from 1977 to 1998," 3.

32   Child Care Bureau Statistics: CCDF 2002, http://www.acf.hhs.gov/programs/ccb/research/ 02acf696/02acf696_2004.pdf.

33 Child Care Bureau Statistics: CCDF 2002, http://www.acf.hhs.gov/programs/ccb/research/
02acf800/list.htm. Child Care Development Funds are federal funds available to assist low-income
families to access quality child care. Federal funds are passed to the states through mandatory,
matching, and discretionary programs. State child care programs serve most families through
vouchers that allow parents to choose from a variety of providers. In 2002, CCDF served 1,743,100
children, helping to pay for care in the child's home, a family home, a group home, or a child
care center. http://www.acf.hhs.gov/programs/ccb/research/02acf800/table1.htm. Of these,
approximately 13 percent were 3-year-olds and 13 percent were 4-year-olds. http://www.acf.hhs.gov/
programs/ccb/research/02acf800/table9.htm. In 2002, the total federal share for care provided was
$6,690,043,335, and states provided an additional $2,215,062,928. Child Care Bureau Statistics:
CCDF 2002, http://www.acf.hhs.gov/programs/ccb/research/02acf696/02acf696_2004.pdf. The 26
percent share spent on care for 3- and 4-year-olds is approximately $23,153,276.

34 The federal data show that states spent $59,863,538 of their state-provided funds in matching
grants on Pre-K. Child Care Bureau Statistics: CCDF 2002, http://www.acf.hhs.gov/programs/ccb/
research/02acf696/02acf696_2004.pdf.

35 Child care for 2.8 million children in 44 states was funded in whole or part by the SSBG during
2002. http://www.acf.gov/programs/ocs/ssbg_focus_2002/focus_child_day_care.html.

36 "Good Start, Grow Smart: The Bush Administration's Early Childhood Initiative."
http://www.whitehouse.gov/infocus/earlychildhood/sect3.html.

37 Barnett, Hustedt, Robin, and Schulman. *The State of Preschool,* 23.

38 Barnett, Hustedt, Robin, and Schulman. *The State of Preschool,* 6.

39 Stone, D. *Funding the Future: States' Approaches to Pre-K Finance.* Washington, D.C.: Pre-K Now,
2006, 12.

40 Education Commission of the States, Pre-Kindergarten database, State-Funded Pre-Kindergarten
Programs Distribution of Funds, http://www.ecs.org/dbsearches/Search_Info/EarlyLearningReports.
asp?tbl=table4. The National Institute for Early Education Research annually gathers and publishes
statistics on state-funded preschools in *The State of Preschool Yearbook.* It defined a state preschool
program as one funded, controlled, and directed by the state that serves children of prekindergarten
age, focuses on early childhood education, and offers group learning experiences to children at least
two days a week. While a preschool program may be coordinated with a child care subsidy program,
it is not a child care program. It includes state supplements to fund Head Start programs. Barnett,
Hustedt, Robin, and Schulman. *The State of Preschool,* 23. The total state spending by states on
preschool reported in the yearbook includes all funds from state sources as well as TANF funds.
The reports do not include dollars from federal sources, including Child Care Development Funds,
IDEA funds, or local funding including school district funds or parent fees. Barnett, Hustedt,
Robin, and Schulman. *The State of Preschool,* 46. In 2002–2003, there were approximately 738,000
children attending state-funded preschool programs, or approximately 10 percent of all 3- and 4-year-
olds. Barnett, Hustedt, Robin, and Schulman. *The State of Preschool,* 4. Publicly funded preschools
have grown at a faster rate than private programs. In 1990, private programs served 64 percent of
the children attending preschool. By 1995, the private sector accounted for 52 percent of children

attending preschool. Barnett, Hustedt, Robin, and Schulman. *The State of Preschool,* 15. Overall in 2002–2003, 16.1 percent of all 4-year-olds and 2.5 percent of all 3-year-olds were enrolled in state-funded prekindergarten programs. Barnett, Hustedt, Robin, and Schulman. *The State of Preschool,* 37. When the percentage enrolled is expanded to include those enrolled in state prekindergarten programs, Head Start, and IDEA Preschool Grants Programs, the numbers are 34 percent of all 4-year-olds and 13.8 percent of all 3-year-olds. Barnett, Hustedt, Robin, and Schulman. *The State of Preschool,* 37.

41 Mitchell, A. "Preschool: Finance Facts and Trends." Presentation at Prekindergarten Leadership Institute: Building Bright Futures, Denver, Colo., June 4–6, 2006.

42 Barnett, Hustedt, Robin, and Schulman. *The State of Preschool,* 47.

43 Barnett, Hustedt, Robin, and Schulman. *The State of Preschool,* 47; 71 percent of state-funded preschool children were served in public schools, 18 percent in private child care centers, 7 percent in Head Start programs, less than 1 percent in faith-based programs, less than 1 percent in family child care, and 3 percent in other settings. Barnett, Hustedt, Robin, and Schulman. *The State of Preschool,* 34.

44 Mitchell, A., and Stoney, L. *Estimating the Cost of the Early Childhood System Services and Infrastructures: Tools, Approaches and Political Considerations.* Washington, D.C.: Smart Start National Technical Assistance Center, Mar. 2006.

45 U.S. Census Bureau, Table Sex by Single Years of Age 2000, http://www.census.gov/census2000/states/us.html. NIER Fact Sheet: PreK Cost, http://www.pewtrusts.com/ideas/ideas_item.cfm?content_item_id=2971&content_type_id=4&issue_name=Pre%2Dk%20education&issue=26&page=4&name=Facts%20and%20Stats.

46 NIERR Fact Sheet, PreK Cost, http://www.pewtrusts.com/ideas/ideas_item.cfm?content_item_id=2971&content_type_id=4&issue_name=Pre%2Dk%20education&issue=26&page=4&name=Facts%20and%20Stats; National Center for Children in Poverty. *Low Income Children in the United States.* New York: Columbia University, Mailman School of Public Health, May 2004.

47 Enrollment of 3-, 4-, and 5-year-old children in pre-primary programs, Digest of Education Statistics Tables and Figures 2005, http://nces.ed.gov/programs/digest/d05/tables/dt05_040.asp. In 2001 there were approximately 8.551 million 3-, 4-, and 5-year-olds in the United States: 3.795 million were 3-year-olds and 3.861 million were 4-year-olds. For 3-year-olds, 23 percent were in relative care, 14 percent were in nonrelative care, 42 percent in center-based programs, and 33 percent in the care of their parents. For 4-year-olds, 22 percent were in relative care, 13 percent in nonrelative care, 65 percent in center-based programs, and 20 percent in the care of their parents. Center-based care included day care centers, nursery schools, prekindergartens, preschools, and Head Start programs. Child care arrangements of preschool children, http://nces.ed.gov/programs/digest/d05/tables/dt05_042.asp.

48 Mitchell and Stoney. *Estimating the Cost of the Early Childhood System Services and Infrastructures.*

49 Stebbins, H., and Langford, B. H. *A Guide to Calculating the Cost of Quality Early Care and Education.* Washington, D.C.: Finance Project, May 2006, 8.

50 Mitchell and Stoney. *Estimating the Cost of the Early Childhood System Services and Infrastructures.*

51 Brandon and others. *Orchestrating Access to Affordable, High-Quality Early Care and Education for All Young Children Policy Brief.* As noted above, higher teacher salaries are linked to higher teacher qualifications, greater teacher retention, and ultimately higher quality. Staff wages are the second greatest predictor, after class size, of the quality of a program. Golin and Mitchell. *The Price of School Readiness,* 10. Thus, staff salaries will be a major factor in determining the cost of a program. In 2003 the average public preschool teacher earned $22,190, and the average public kindergarten teacher earned $42,380. Education Commission of the States, Pre-Kindergarten Quick Facts, http://www.ecs.org/html/IssueSection.asp?issueid=184&s=Quick+Facts. In 2002, 13 state-funded programs required that all preschool teachers be paid on the public school district scale. One-third of programs applied the public school scale only to public school employees, not to Head Start programs and private programs. Barnett, Hustedt, Robin, and Schulman. *The State of Preschool,* 48. Another important factor is whether the program is a half-day or full-day program. Full-day programs cost twice as much as half-day programs. Denton. *Improving Children's Readiness for School,* 18.

52 Breneman, D. W., and Haarlow, W. N. "Remediation in Higher Education: Its Extent and Cost." Presented at Remediation in Higher Education: A Symposium, 1998.

53 Alliance for Excellent Education, "Paying Double: Inadequate High Schools and Community College Remediation." Issue Brief, Aug. 2006.

Teachers and Teaching Policy

The outlook on teachers in this report begins with the observation that during much of the 20th century, when most of the members of the workforce needed only relatively low literacy to do the work they were expected to do, the advanced industrial countries could safely recruit their school teachers from the lower ranks of high school graduates going on to college. But now that more and more work is knowledge work, and low-cost countries can supply very large numbers of relatively well-educated workers to global employers, most high school graduates in the United States will have to be much better educated than before to justify their wages relative to those of the increasingly well-educated workers in countries with lower wage structures. Inevitably, this will mean that the schools will have to recruit and retain teachers from the upper ranks of high school graduates going on to college.

Singapore tops the list of all the nations in the international Trends in International Mathematics and Science Study (TIMSS) assessment of student achievement in mathematics and science. It cannot be an accident that it is the policy of the government of Singapore to recruit its teachers from the top third of the ranks of high school graduates

going on to college. We believe that the United States can do no less.

It is not simply a matter of wishing to match the best efforts of the leader. The Commission concluded that the future belongs to those nations whose workforces are comfortable with ideas, who really understand mathematical tools and reasoning, who are on familiar terms with the sciences and technology, who can apply what they know to a wide range of real-world problems and are creative as they do so, who can write well in many different genres and read deeply in a variety of fields, and much more. We have yet to meet anyone who believes that our children will learn to do these things from people who do not themselves have the knowledge and skills needed to do them.

Unfortunately, these are the very skills that the best employers in the world are looking for. Those employers are willing to pay well for those skills and to offer very attractive working conditions to the people they attract to the jobs they offer. The country needs about 15 percent of the workforce to serve as teachers. That being so, we cannot count, if we ever could, on the dedication of people who regard teaching as a calling and are indifferent to the more worldly incentives that attract people to other careers. We have no choice but to compete with good employers to get the teachers we need, and we will have to do so on their terms.

For a long time, teaching in the United States has stood between profession and blue-collar occupation. We like to think of teaching as a profession. Professions, however, are usually defined not by the job one holds but the training one has had. Professions are typically regulated by the members of the profession themselves. Most professionals are typically organized into professional partnerships, in which they are both employer and employee. In most professions, what one is paid is a function of one's ability to establish a track record of superior accomplishment. In most professions, the professional puts in as many hours as it takes to get the job done, regardless of what the employment agreement says. And, in most professions, the professional is expected to invest his or her own funds continuously, throughout his or her career, in continuing education and training, because the price of not doing so is the loss of clients or employers, and therefore the loss of income, because the market expects the professional to be at the cutting edge of the field, without question, all the time.

Few, if any, of these things are true of school teachers. It is also true that, on the whole, teachers have traded high cash compensation relative to other professions for job security, which comes in several forms, among them uniform salary schedules based primarily on seniority and very generous health and retirement benefits. This insulates the teacher from the judgments of principals as to their quality of their performance on the job, and makes longevity and pay a function of time in the seat rather than job performance. This is in addition to the inherent security built into the occupation as a result of the fact that the demand for teachers does not decrease in a recession. It is, in fact, among the most recession-proof of occupations.

And it is particularly attractive to people, mostly women, who want to be at home when their children come home from school. Because for many decades during the 20th century, husbands were expected to take paid jobs outside the home and wives were expected to stay at home to raise the children, the wages of the teachers were viewed as supplementary income. Giving competitive wages to teachers was viewed as taking money from the men, who were the true wage earners, and therefore it was considered wrong. In this way, it became socially acceptable to pay teachers, overwhelmingly women, a wage that was systematically less than what men typically earned in jobs typically employing men.

But teachers vote, and, more important, they are available to work for candidates for political office. Their organizations are usually the single biggest block of organized voters in state elections. As time went on, the people who represented teachers to both candidates for state office and incumbents learned that the public resisted increases in taxes for increased teachers' pay, but they could not see what legislators provided by way of increased health and retirement benefits, because much of this was paid for with unfunded future liabilities. Paying off those obligations to the teachers when they retired would become someone else's problem.

Still, when tough times came, localities would often have a hard time paying their teachers' salaries, much less giving them a raise. So they would, instead of doing so, cut back the amount of time teachers were expected to be available for professional development and training and give them stronger seniority rights, greater voice in who got which jobs, or in other ways further limit the right of the principal and the central office to make management and instructional decisions affecting student performance and limit the incentive or the obligation of the teacher to put in the time and effort required for student success. This is not to say, however, that progressive school districts have not attempted to design and implement new teacher compensation systems.

Because, during much of the 20th century, teachers' jobs were particularly attractive to women who wanted to be at home when their children came home from school, and minorities more generally (because college-educated women and minorities had few other opportunities), and first- and second-generation immigrants who were often the first person in their family to have gone to college, the society got better school teachers than it deserved. But on the whole, policy was geared to recruiting the bottom of the ability distribution of those high school graduates who chose to go to college.

So, the question for society now is: What do we have to do to recruit from the top third of the distribution of high school graduates going to college? What do we have to do to make teacher education an opportunity

and a challenge that our best and brightest want to take advantage of rather than a landscape littered with course work with little intellectual content and less utility in the classroom? How do we create schools in which the teachers' lounge is a place in which ideas have currency and teachers exchange ideas about how to improve their practice? How do we rearrange the incentives operating on teachers so they attract the risk takers rather than the security seekers? What sort of incentives are needed to get people who will put in whatever time is needed to do the job? How can we create a system that will reward people who want to be judged and compensated on their contribution to student achievement? How do we continue to make teaching attractive to women who want to be home when their children come home from school while at the same time making teaching no less attractive to others who could, and will otherwise, be engineers, filmmakers, clothing designers, college professors, attorneys, research scientists, or airline pilots?

As we consider how we might answer these questions, we need to consider who the young people are whom we are trying to attract to teaching and what kinds of things are most important to them as they make their career choices. One clue comes from Fred Ackerman, the head of the Victoria Principals' Association in Australia, who tells us that highly qualified young people today are less interested in a fair day's pay for a fair day's work than they are in an outstanding day's pay for an outstanding performance during that day. And they are much less interested in a career than they are in doing something next that is interesting and personally rewarding.

This is exactly what Peter Drucker, writing almost 40 years ago, predicted. Drucker was describing the coming transition from blue-collar work to knowledge work as the core of American business. Knowledge workers, he said, would be personal entrepreneurs, not company men. They would demand compensation based on the quality of their contribution, not how long they had been on the job. They would be driven by the need to be and do their very best, and would want to be recognized for their contributions. They would stay as long as they could work in that sort of environment and move on when the next big challenge came.

Those are the very people we need to have teaching in our schools. But will they come? Sure. We know they will come, because of the experience of Teach for America, which shows that a surprisingly large percentage of our very best college students are willing to teach in some of our most challenging schools. But they leave after a short time, for all the reasons we have already described. We know they can be recruited. What will it take to keep them in large enough numbers and for long enough to make a real difference?

The Commission began answering these questions by looking hard at the structure of teachers' compensation. For all the reasons just enumerated, teacher compensation is heavily backloaded, that is, it is light on cash compensation and heavy on benefits, particularly health and pension benefits that come after the incumbent retires. The effect of this compensation structure is to make it very attractive for teachers with years of service to stay longer and very unattractive for young people with good options to choose teaching.

Retirement is not the top consideration for most of those young people in their 20s. They want to know whether they will have the cash they will need to get married, buy a home, support their children, and so on. The Commission saw no reason to offer health and retirement benefits that exceed those typically offered by good firms in the private sector. By simply reducing these benefits to levels consistent with those offered by good firms in the private sector, the Commission's recommendations could save $6.6 billion nationally, which could be used to increase the cash compensation of teachers substantially and, in the process, make teaching more attractive to the very young people it was interested in.

Specifically, the Commission proposed converting teachers' pension plans from the typical defined benefit plan to either a defined contribution plan or a cash balance plan. The obvious choice for a defined contribution plan is TIAA-CREF, which was established many years ago precisely for the purpose of providing portable pension benefits to the nation's college teachers. Its record is widely admired, and it is large enough to take on the nation's school teachers without being overwhelmed. The great advantage of TIAA-CREF is that it can be set up so that the contributions vest quickly, and the vested contributions are fully portable to any other institution offering TIAA-CREF. If most of the nation's schools used this system, then the nation's school teachers could go to almost any school or college or university in the United States and remain in the TIAA-CREF system. One effect of this change would be to put pressure on many jurisdictions to raise teachers' salaries in order to keep them, because those teachers would no longer be in the position of losing all their retirement benefits if they went to some other state or school district.

Alternatively, the Commission said, states might institute cash-balance pension plans. Under these plans, the periodic contribution is fixed by contract, and so is a stipulated interest rate on the balance in the account. Thus, in a sense, both the contribution and benefit are fixed in these plans. Both the defined contribution and the cash-balance plans can be used to accomplish the end that the Commission had in mind.

Under the Commission's plan, the state, which would become the employer of the teachers, would require new hires to accept the new benefits plan, but would offer a choice to incumbent teachers at the time the policy was changed as to whether they wanted to stay with the old plan or join the new one.

Though $6.6 billion is a lot of money, it is small in relation to total teachers' compensation and therefore unlikely to make a big difference by itself in the incentives that young people face. But when it is added to the amount that is saved by restructuring the way students progress through the system, close to $19 billion becomes available for the purpose of raising teachers' cash compensation across the United States. This would represent a raise of approximately 20 percent across the board for teachers if evenly distributed across the current teaching workforce, a substantial increase.

This increase in teachers' cash compensation needs to be viewed against the background of the Commission's recommendation to make the state, not the district, the employer of the teachers in that state. Over the years, personnel compensation

— mainly teacher compensation — has accounted for about 85 percent of the total costs of public education, so one can see that this would be a fundamental change in the way we manage our system. This would obviously lead to statewide teachers' pay schedules. The per-state supplement from the $19 billion dividend would permit the states to pay more than they could otherwise pay to their teachers. The principal beneficiaries would be the cities and towns that had been least able to pay their teachers well before. The effects of having the state move to uniform salary schedules for all teachers in the state would combine with the dividend from restructuring student progression through the system to raise teachers' salaries in the poorer cities and towns and keep them from falling in the wealthier cities and towns. Or, in the language of the day, we could raise quality through the whole system while at the same time greatly increasing the equity with which we used teachers, our most vital resource.

The next question is how the state would choose to structure the salary schedule. For the purposes of conducting its analysis, the Commission reviewed the features of Denver Public Schools' ProComp and its pilot program begun in 1999. The ProComp agreement in 2004 was ratified by a vote of the union members, and funding was authorized by the voters in 2005. The main components of ProComp are:

1. The plan eliminates scheduled increase based solely on years of service.

2. The district pays annual salary increases for demonstrated student growth on standardized tests and on teacher-designated measures.

3. Teachers receive salary increases for the demonstrated acquisition of additional knowledge and skills related to the requirements for student growth and their instructional disciplines, including national certification for teaching and specialist skills.

4. Every three years, teachers receive salary increases following evaluations of their teaching as successful.

5. The district offers incentives for teachers of demonstrated accomplishment who choose to work in schools with the greatest academic need. Similar bonuses are offered to teachers and specialists who fill positions where there are shortages of qualified applicants and to teachers in schools judged distinguished based on academic gains.

6. The net result is that teachers who meet and exceed rigorous expectations have no fixed limits on their annual and career earnings. ProComp will raise teachers' salaries as well as provide greater differentials between those who achieve excellence and those who do not.

The reason that the Commission based its financial model in part on the Denver plan was that such a plan had actually been negotiated with a teachers' union and a big city school sitting across from one another at the bargaining table. It shows that such a plan is both technically and politically feasible and that the entire nation could afford the cost of such a plan, if one accepts the premises on which the larger features of the Commission's plan are built. That does not mean, however, that the Commission necessarily recommends

the Denver plan. There are many other ways to skin that cat, and many of them may be preferable to the solution that was agreed on in Denver.

The career ladder plan included in the Commission calculations assumed a level of base pay and three steps on the ladder above the base. In any case, the salaries just used to illustrate the way the new plan would work make it plain that under the new plan, the typical teacher working a regular school year would start at around $45,000 per year and, if that teacher made the top of the career ladder, she or he would make $95,000 per year. The whole schedule would produce lower salaries in the poorer states and more in the richer ones. At $45,000 per year, the new schedule would set the starting salaries about where average teachers' salaries now are, which would represent a transformation in teachers' pay and enormous advantage in teacher recruitment.

This assumes, however, that the teacher's job involved work on a schedule that might be a little longer than the current school year, to include more professional development and training. But this is a schedule that was invented to accommodate parents who wanted to be home when their school-age children came home from school. The Commission did not want to restrict itself to that pool of potential teachers and so, in its financial analysis, assumed that some part of the teaching force would consist of people who would want to maximize their earning power by working the same number of hours per year that the typical professionals in other fields work. When the model was run for these teachers, using the same assumptions as for all the other teachers but adding in more hours to account for the difference between the regular teachers' hours and these teachers' hours, the model showed that the typical teacher working the longer school year would earn $109,000 at the top of the scale. Thus, with the rewards for new teachers, for teachers working conventional schedules, and for teachers willing to work a longer school year, the new system would be much more attractive than the current compensation system and competitive with almost all of the professions with which teaching would compete.

In this new compensation system, not only would there be enough money to be much more competitive overall, but there would be plenty of opportunity to structure the system so that more could be paid to people willing to work in specialties in short supply, from teachers of students whose parents speak little English to teachers of mathematics and physics and teachers of the severely disabled. There would also be room to pay a premium to teachers who would not otherwise be willing to work in remote areas or in inner cities and other locations serving very high concentrations of children with multiple problems who require extra attention and skill. And it would be possible to relate teachers' compensation to the performance of their students.

All of this would happen in a very different work environment from the one that now prevails. Teachers would be employed not by school districts, but by a wide variety of organizations that contracted with school districts to run schools. Some of these organizations would be created by groups of experienced teachers who had a clear image of the kind of school they wanted to

teach in and the sort of people they wanted as colleagues. They might be organized as professional partnerships. Others might be organized by universities, nonprofits, public or private corporations, or many other kinds of existing organizations, some of which might be motivated by the opportunity to create schools embracing a particular philosophy, others by the opportunity to put their research to work, others by the chance to try out a new form of curriculum or school organization, or a new way to involve parents, or a way to get employers to support schools.

In this system, those teachers who had an entrepreneurial bent would have a chance to build schools and whole systems of schools around their ideas, and the market would determine whether they succeeded or failed. Teachers who had been longing for a chance to work with trusted colleagues to build the school of their dreams would have a chance to do so. Schools of education would be able to build demonstration schools that reflected the best research available.

Unlike many charter schools today, all of these schools would be regular public schools and subject to the same rules as any other public school with respect to curriculum, testing, accountability, and the requirements related to the qualifications of teachers. But the organizations that operated the schools themselves would decide what the staffing patterns would look like and how the money available to the school would be spent. And they would decide, within the limits set by the state, what the curriculum would be, what teaching methods would be used, what materials would be used, how technology would fit in, how to involve parents, how the school would be organized and managed, and so on. Thus, the scope for teachers' professional judgment and growth would be far larger than is typically the case now, especially in those schools owned and run by teachers.

But no school organization would be certified by the state to run schools in that state unless that organization was affiliated with a network or was itself a network that could show that it had the necessary capacity to provide high-quality continuing teacher training, access to current research, management support, and other services that teachers require to be at the top of their game. Thus teachers in this new system would be guaranteed the kind of professional support that many teachers now lack.

Under the Commission's plan, the state would have the primary responsibility for recruiting, training, licensing, and employing teachers. This authority would be vested in a Teacher Development Agency (TDA). The TDA would be a state agency affiliated with the state education agency. It would be empowered to do public opinion polling to find out what potential candidates think about teaching as a career and what it would take to get them interested in teaching, run sophisticated recruiting campaigns, and train teachers and license them for service in the schools. And it would be empowered to aggressively recruit teachers using all the techniques now used by the best companies. The TDA would look for candidates for teacher training not just from those coming out of strong undergraduate arts and sciences programs but also from the military, from civilian careers, and from the ranks of former teachers who had gone on

to other things and would consider coming back to teaching in the light of the changes in compensation and working conditions proposed by the Commission. This includes young people who might have participated in the Teach for America program and gone on to some other career but would be willing to come back to teaching and get the additional training they would have to get to pass the new and very demanding licensure examinations.

The TDAs in many states would make special efforts to source academically able young people of color with whom many of the students streaming into the school could identify, working in some cases closely with high schools in heavily minority areas to get high-school-age students to try out teaching as a career and providing them information, assistantship and intern opportunities, and the like to encourage them at every step to consider teaching as a career.

Teachers who were added to the rolls by the TDA would not actually have a job until they were hired by one of the contract schools in the state, and that employer would have the power to let a teacher go once hired. The schools would have to pay that teacher according to the state schedule. They could supplement a teacher's salary, but not pay below the schedule.

The TDA would not actually train any teachers. But it would make sure that the teachers the state engaged were trained to a high standard by defining the criteria for that training and incorporating those criteria in performance contracts that it would make with teacher training organizations. The state would also develop systems for assessing beginning teachers against its criteria. Those performance criteria would be based on visits to the candidate's classroom or videos of that teacher's performance as well as carefully constructed assessments conducted in an assessment center (perhaps along the lines of the assessments developed for beginning teachers in Connecticut in the early 1990s).

Only candidates who go through a rigorous professional training program could pass the kinds of assessments the Commission has in mind. Candidates would be expected not only to be deeply knowledgeable about the subjects they were planning to teach, but they would also be expected to know a lot about how young children and adolescents learn, how to assess students' strengths and weaknesses against the standards, how to probe a student's understanding of the subject to identify misunderstandings of the material and to correct them, how to present the material in a compelling way, how to motivate students to study hard, how to help students grasp the underlying concepts in a field and apply them to novel situations, how to help students think for themselves while mastering the basics, and how to connect with students who, for whatever reason, are not responding to their teaching.

Schools of education would be eligible to bid on these performance contracts, but so would partnerships formed by teachers, school districts, and other organizations. Those teacher preparation organizations that succeeded in preparing teachers who scored well on the state teacher assessments and that met other criteria adopted by the TDA would get more slots from the TDA, and those that did less well would get fewer slots. Among the

criteria put forward by the TDA would be the success rate of the provider with respect to the preparation of teachers who looked and talked like the students they were going to teach, as well as their success rate at producing teachers prepared to teach in shortage specialties in that state.

In this plan, prospective employers of teachers could put forward candidates for licensure who had not gone through the state teacher education system just described, but those candidates would have to pass the same examinations and meet all the other standards that the regular candidates for licensure would have to meet.

Overall, the proposals of the Commission are designed to not merely change but actually transform the compensation and working conditions of teachers in ways that will enable the nation to recruit its teaching force mainly from the top third of high school graduates going to college and create an environment for those teachers much more congenial to young people who are more interested in excelling in their work than in the security that the job affords, who will be confident that those who excel will be recognized and rewarded for their efforts, and who will have much greater scope for creating the kinds of schools that they would like to teach in, with colleagues of their choice, people who will challenge them to do their best and contribute to the intellectual vitality of the work. Every feature of the Commission's design has been bent to these purposes, reflecting the Commission's conviction that no single factor is more important in determining the quality of our children's education than the quality of their teachers.

Early Childhood Education

One of the strongest and most consistent set of findings from American education researchers has to do with the positive effects of high-quality early childhood education. Despite those findings, however, the United States has long been far behind many nations around the world — even some developing countries — that provide universal, high-quality early childhood education. Instead, there is a patchwork quilt of providers and services, differing widely from state to state, all of which, when added together, provides mostly low-quality services to only a small fraction of the children who need them.

The proposals made by the Commission would change this landscape dramatically. The Commission, in calculating the way the additional funds made available for early childhood education might be used, assumed that all the money now going into early childhood education would continue to do so, and the new money proposed by the Commission — more than $19 billion — would go in on top of those funds.

Proceeding on that assumption, it calculated that the additional funds would make it possible to provide four hours of high-quality organized instruction to all the low-income 3-year-olds who want and need it and another four hours per day of high-quality early childhood education to every 4-year-old not currently in private preschool, regardless of family income. The basis of these calculations can be found in the background paper on the financing of the Commission's recommendations.

The Commission intends that these programs be staffed by highly competent teachers, who would be compensated accordingly, and it expects that the institutions that provide the early childhood education would be licensed by the state for quality and safety.

In the United States, policy with respect to early childhood education has tended to focus only on the provision of programs. The result is that very little attention has been given to the other components of effective early childhood education systems. Indeed, we can hardly be said to have an early childhood education system in the sense in which we have school systems, or health systems, or foster care systems. And, without an effective, well-organized, and well-managed system in place, we will never have consistently high-quality early childhood education for our children.

Eight Components of a System for Early Care and Education

1. QUALITY PROGRAMS

- Support and foster the effective use of materials, curriculum, and pedagogy, including multi-age and flexible grouping of children, effective staff deployment, attentiveness to cultural and linguistic variation, and appropriate balance between academic and play activities.
- Foster concerted attention to children's physical and mental health by providing appropriate screenings, immunizations, and services.
- Provide incentives to encourage early care and education services to participate in accreditation and in other quality-enhancement efforts.
- Foster ongoing relationships with schools, resource and referral agencies, and other community services.
- Support family child care and family child care networks.

2. RESULTS-DRIVEN SYSTEM

- Define appropriate results across all domains of development, with appropriate benchmarks. Include parents and professionals in defining such results.
- Establish data-collection mechanisms that consider the ages and abilities of young children.
- Establish appropriate safeguards so that data collected will not be used to label, track, or stigmatize young children.

3. PUBLIC ENGAGEMENT

- Support parents as consumers, ensuring that parents have options in early care.
- Provide incentives for U.S. businesses to be family-friendly in their policies and practices and provide community support for early care and education.
- Increase community awareness of early care and education.

4. INDIVIDUAL CREDENTIALING

- Credential all who work with young children. Licensing of facilities should be separate from the credentialing of individuals.
- Create the credentialing system and compensate teachers accordingly.
- Create credentials for administrators, directors, master teachers, and leaders.

5. PROFESSIONAL DEVELOPMENT

- Ensure that all certification and teacher preparation programs are up-to-date and focused on developmentally appropriate outcomes.
- Ensure that the professional development content and incentives for administrators, directors, and master teachers are appropriate for their diverse roles and responsibilities.
- Foster the development of leadership in all sectors of the early care and education system.

6. PROGRAM LICENSING

- Eliminate exemptions. Ensure that all programs serving young children are subject to state regulations.
- Streamline, coordinate, and adequately fund facility licensing.
- Create or support the development of national licensing standards that states can use as guidelines.

7. FUNDING AND FINANCING

- Identify the costs of a quality system. Include the cost of funding the infrastructure and the full cost of care.
- Ensure that staff compensation in early care and education is commensurate with that of public schools, given equal education and experience of staff.
- Identify both short- and long-term revenue sources.
- Develop a long-term financing plan. Create a time line for its implementation.

8. ACCOUNTABILITY

- Establish state governance mechanisms. Create boards, cabinets, or other structures that take responsibility for oversight of early care and education through planning, assessment, distribution of resources, and agenda setting.
- Create local mechanisms to coordinate the delivery of service, ensure the effective use of funds and provisions for the infrastructure, and coordinate these efforts.

Adapted from Not by Chance: Creating an Early Care and Education System for America's Children. © 1977 Sharon L. Kagan. *Used with permission of the author.*

The material in the box on the previous page describes the components of an effective system for early childhood education.

The first item on the list in the box addresses characteristics of the programs to be delivered. All the other items on the list constitute the infrastructure that needs to be built around the programs to make sure that they are of uniformly high quality throughout the state. They range from properly conceived and implemented accountability systems to sound systems of accreditation and data gathering and monitoring. The problem with American early childhood education, as we said above, is as much the lack of robust infrastructure as it is the lack of quality programs, In fact, these are but two faces of the same problem.

When the Commission calculated the cost of quality early childhood programs, it added 10 percent to the costs of the entire delivery system to account for the cost of building an effective, high-quality infrastructure to complete the early childhood system. This fraction was applied not just to the new money we would put into early childhood education, but to the money that is now being spent as well.

So we would strongly urge the states to examine these infrastructure requirements closely and take the steps needed to make sure that a robust infrastructure is in place to ensure high-quality early education for all the children.

THE ADULT WORKFORCE

The U.S. labor force, totaling 165 million people in the year 2021, will not include any child born in 2006 or later. It will, however, include nearly 100 million people who *today* are already out of school and at work. About two-thirds of these workers are likely to be part of the active workforce at least through the next decade. While K–12 school reforms begun now would clearly benefit the children and grandchildren of the current workforce, they would not directly affect the skills, compensation, and productivity of this essential core of workers.

SKILLS OF THE ACTIVE WORKFORCE

According to a just-released OECD survey, the United States has the highest dropout rate of any nation studied. Over 30 percent of entering high school students do not graduate with their class in four years. Thirty-one million Americans age 16 and older — 20 percent of adults age 25 and over — are out of school and do not have any type of high school credential. While a majority of dropouts eventually earn a high school credential, it is typically a GED. And one-third of foreign-born adults, and

44 percent of Hispanic adults, do not have any high school credential.

In 2001, over one-third of applicants for jobs with larger American employers are reported to have lacked the literacy and/or math skills necessary to perform the jobs they sought.

In fact, U.S. adults with a high school diploma but no college ranked dead last among their peers from 19 developed countries in terms of their literacy proficiency. According to the National Adult Literacy Survey and the International Adult Literacy Survey, more than two in five U.S. adults had only basic or below-basic prose literacy skills in the 1990s; nearly three in five demonstrated only basic or below-basic quantitative skills. These are not high standards; basic proficiency is the skill required to perform simple and everyday literacy activities. The average composite literacy level of native-born adults in the United States ranked 10th among 17 developed countries, while the literacy of foreign-born adults in the United States ranked 16th internationally — a mediocre performance in comparison to 19 other developed nations, in the eyes of the report's authors.

A decade later, the prose literacy of U.S. adults remains unchanged. Quantitative skills have increased modestly. However, the average literacy skills of Hispanic adults, the largest and fastest-growing minority segment of our workforce, declined dramatically. Today three of four Hispanic adults demonstrate only basic or below-basic prose literacy skills; four in five have comparably low quantitative skills.

Current U.S. investments in the basic education of adults are sorely inadequate. Investing in adult education and literacy is not considered a priority linked to the economy. The federal government invests just over $500 million in adult basic education. States are required to provide at least a 25 percent match in dollars or in-kind resources. This total investment provides services to fewer than 3 million adults each year.

ENABLING EVERY MEMBER OF THE ADULT WORKFORCE TO GET THE NEW LITERACY SKILLS

The Commission report argues that American workers will in the future require a workforce almost all of whose members have at least two years of college — not a series of remedial courses, but real college-level work. That is a level far higher than the levels of literacy by which we have up to now measured adult literacy. If we are to take that goal seriously and respond to the point that, for a long time to come, the workers we will have are the ones already in the workforce, then it follows that one of our first priorities must be a massive

effort, far beyond what is now being made, to provide a foundation level of literacy for the workforce now in place. That is the rationale for the Commission's first recommendation in this arena — for the federal government to guarantee to every adult member of the workforce the right to a free education to the standard set by the first state qualifying examination.

Two other measures that could do much to improve the literacy of our workforce should be considered. The first has to do with the language skills and productivity of immigrant workers.

If current trends continue, the educational attainment of the workforce is likely to increase only about 3 percent over the next 15 years, even though college-going rates are at their highest levels. This is in part because the prime-age, native-born workforce in the U.S. will not grow through 2020.

Growth in the U.S. labor force over the next 20 years will be fueled solely by the entry of immigrants to our shores and into our workplaces. As was the case for the Northeast states during the 1990s, immigration will be the only source for our nation's growth between 2000 and 2020 — an increase that the Census Bureau projects of about 6 million persons aged 25 and over. While many new immigrants will be well educated, many will not, and most will need to acquire English proficiency to be most productive in our workplaces. In order to get the most that these workers have to offer the economy, we need to promote English-language skills in the workplace. One incentive device currently in place to help meet this need is Section 127 of the Internal Revenue Code.

Section 127 makes employer-provided educational benefits tax exempt to the employee. This provision stipulates that up to $5,250 of assistance from the employer for undergraduate and graduate courses is considered tax-exempt income for the individual.

Section 127 should be amended to allow employers to use tuition benefit programs to pay for literacy and English as a Second Language (ESL) or other pre-undergraduate education. This would help new immigrants and low-skilled workers to develop the basic education and language skills required for more advanced work and learning opportunities.

CREATING PERSONAL COMPETITIVENESS ACCOUNTS—THE GI BILL FOR OUR TIMES

A U.S. Bureau of Labor Statistics study found that workers typically hold about 10 jobs during the first 20 years of their working lives. Technology and other structural changes are accelerating turnover, and therefore the pace at which workers' skills lose value or become obsolete. In such a dynamic labor market, enabling workers to better manage their own careers by upgrading their skills at a time and place of their choosing becomes critical.

But most workers are not in a position to take advantage of it, because most of the available financial aid is intended for full-time students studying for regular degrees. These workers, many of them married with children and some financially responsible for their parents, simply cannot go to school full time, and many, in any case, do not need a degree, but rather a certificate program or the equivalent, in order to acquire some focused skill or knowledge that is just what he or she needs to take the next step in a career or to gain a competitive edge in a swiftly moving field.

For all these reasons, the Commission proposes that the federal government establish for each newborn child a Personal Competitiveness Account (PCA). The U.S. government would make contributions on their behalf through age 16 to "prime the learning pump," and authorize all workers to make voluntary contributions to their own portable, tax-advantaged accounts thereafter. Employers could choose to match individual employee contributions, and these payments would qualify for a tax benefit under an amended Section 127 of the Internal Revenue Code. The federal government would match individual contributions for low-income workers, say, those earning less than twice the federal minimum wage. The PCA accounts would function as follows:

- In the year of birth for each U.S. child, an account would be created and credited with $500 in federal contributions. Each year thereafter, through age 16, the federal government would credit an individual's account balance with another $100. By age 16, an individual's account would contain $2,100 plus accrued interest — at 4 percent compounded annually, the account balance would total $3,200.

- At age 16 and thereafter, any worker could elect to make tax-exempt contributions to the account up to some annual limit. Employers could choose to match individual employee contributions; these payments would qualify for a tax benefit under the amended Section 127 of the Internal Revenue Code. The federal government would be required to match individual contributions for low-income workers, say, those earning less than twice the federal minimum wage. State governments also would be encouraged to match individual contributions of low-income workers.

- PCA account resources could be used only for tuition and fees, books, supplies, and materials for any career-related education and training with certified public or private training providers. PCA account balances would not affect eligibility for any other federal or state training assistance program such as Pell grants. Career counseling would be available through career centers, and an annual performance report would be required of each certified training provider and widely published.

To illustrate the concept, if a worker earning twice the minimum wage or about $400 per week were to put just $5 a week into a PCA account and the employer and federal government matched the contributions, the individual would accrue an additional $4,000 after five full years of employment, assuming a 4 percent interest rate. When added to the individual's account balance at age 16, this would yield a total of over $7,000 available for further education and training.

CREATING REGIONAL COMPETITIVENESS AUTHORITIES THAT BLEND REGIONAL ECONOMIC DEVELOPMENT WITH REGIONAL WORKFORCE DEVELOPMENT TO MAKE AMERICA COMPETITIVE

A future marked by economic turbulence and churning labor markets, driven by a knowledge-based, technology-driven global economy means U.S. businesses will need more flexible, skilled, and innovative workers. The United States needs human resource policies, systems, and strategies that are driven by regional growth and business requirements and encourage more and better use of educated and skilled labor. Our nationwide federal, state, and local workforce development systems need to be refashioned, equipping them with new powers and tools so they can more consistently meet these difficult challenges and support regional growth.

While global competition is seen as a national challenge, it is at the regional level where most experts agree that U.S. competitiveness will be determined. It is there that supply chains, complementary industries, investors, university-based and other research efforts, and skilled people can join forces to achieve the critical mass necessary to stimulate economic activity and innovation. It is vital that the U.S. foster strategic, regional partnerships to identify the strengths, challenges, resources, and needs of communities, to support regional, knowledge-based innovation economies.

The federal government has recognized the power of regional growth strategies in the U.S. Department of Labor's WIRED (Workforce Investments for Regional Economic Development) initiative, focusing on building strong regional economies. WIRED brings together key players, including research universities, venture capital, economic and workforce development, and education, optimizing their regions' ability to innovate.

The Workforce Investment Act of 1998 (WIA), the nation's primary public workforce development system through which other services and programs may be accessed, was written to encourage collaboration among workforce and economic development efforts in states and regions. The WIA provisions that govern the establishment of local workforce investment areas, however, may unintentionally hinder regional development, with boundaries and jurisdictional authority for workforce efforts organized around political jurisdictions rather than true labor market regions. This has led to over 600 WIAs operating across the country today.

In the economic development arena, 323 Economic Development Districts (EDDs) are established across the United States for receipt of federal Economic Development Administration funds. EDDs are intended to provide a mechanism for coordinating the efforts of individuals, organizations, local governments, and private industry around economic development. EDDs are required to develop and maintain comprehensive economic development strategies for their regions; assess local and regional strengths, weaknesses, and development needs; implement strategies to attract economic development funds; develop specific projects; and provide technical assistance to local entities.

In the postsecondary education arena, while there are many postsecondary education institutions in the United States, community colleges are the primary providers of postsecondary education and training in most states and local areas. With over 1,200 community colleges nationwide, each with its own identified service area, they currently educate and train about 11.6 million students representing 46 percent of all U.S. undergraduates, and vary in sophistication about how they assess and meet local labor market needs.

To promote the alignment of economic development, adult education, and workforce development activities around regional economic strategies, the Commission proposes that the federal government authorize governors and state legislatures, together with local elected officials, to align workforce areas, economic development areas, and community college districts into common regions based on labor markets, economic activity, and other objective criteria. States would establish new jobs, skills, and growth authorities at the state and regional levels. The regional authorities would be chaired by business, with members appointed by local elected officials from business, labor, economic development, and education leaders.

Regional authorities would develop and oversee implementation of the region's unified comprehensive economic development, workforce development, and adult and technical education strategy for regional growth and prosperity. The authorities would provide strategic leadership for and ensure coordination with community colleges on regional workforce education and economic development efforts. They would oversee an adult learning system for young adults without diplomas, immigrants, and other low-literate adults.

The authorities would be granted power to issue tax-exempt bonds for both economic and workforce development (including adult and technical education) and to raise revenue from the private sector, including philanthropic sources. State and regional authorities with federally approved plans that match federal funds with nonfederal resources would be granted broad waivers and flexibility in their use of federal monies to accomplish strategic goals.

The authorities would establish and publicize, through public hearings and media, comprehensive strategic goals (for example, job growth, business success, education and skills levels, employment, earnings, and prosperity) for the region and be held accountable by local elected officials for achieving them. An authority's comprehensive plan would govern the specific strategies, tactics, service mix, and providers necessary to achieve the stated goals. Business services, for example, could be provided through the coordinated efforts of a wide range of organizations such as small business corporations, rural

development councils, manufacturing extension centers, U.S. export assistance centers, and others to promote innovation, business expansion, entrepreneurship, and job growth.

Employers in the region would be challenged through media and outreach campaigns to advance the further education and training of their frontline workers. Technical assistance to small and mid-sized enterprises to become high-performance workplaces that value higher education, skills, and creativity in their frontline employees would be brokered through appropriate intermediaries. Credential-based skills development for employers, workers, and job seekers would be available throughout the region, emphasizing innovative strategies to meet the needs of employers, incumbent workers, and job seekers, such as targeting multiple employers in a specific industry, using career ladder approaches for training, and offering workplace literacy programs and upgrade training for incumbent workers.

Each region would operate a network of career centers, offering universal access to career information and labor market intelligence, job listings and placement assistance, training vouchers to eligible individuals, and referrals. Unemployed and dislocated workers could access information about and benefits from unemployment insurance and a new wage insurance scheme.

Regional authorities would be responsible for a reformed adult education delivery system, ensuring the establishment of standards for program providers and instructors, a process for identifying and accrediting providers who meet the standards, and for monitoring quality. To connect adult and career-related learning and to encourage continued learning, community colleges (where they exist) would be designated as the primary adult education provider, assisted by other providers in the region. The authority would design and organize a coherent and comprehensive referral and support system, incorporating career centers, libraries, and other entities for adults participating in literacy, ESL, and basic education.

The entire system just described, like the elementary and secondary education system, should be designed as a performance-based system. This requires accepted measures of performance and a data management system that will make sure the measures are made and information gained from them is made available to all who need it.

For that reason, we believe that the Higher Education Act should be amended to support state demonstration projects that use unemployment insurance wage records to measure the employment and earnings of graduates from two-year public institutions, to measure institutional performance accountability. Alternatively, the law that authorizes the National Center for Education Statistics (NCES) could be amended when renewed to support these accountability demonstrations. States should enact legislation to institute higher education accountability measures of employment outcomes for community colleges and proprietary institutions.

The goal of such legislation would be to improve programs of study and develop a clearer understanding of their impact on labor market outcomes for each institution by providing accurate data to the institutions, potential students, and the state. Targeted data should include student characteristics (for example, demographics, work, and education history), employer characteristics (for example, industry code, firm size), and possibly employer survey information (for example, occupation, suitability of worker skills).

The systems for producing these data should have consistency and comparability across locations and time while allowing for adaptation to the variety of institutional and economic environments. These data should be prepared by established state statistical agencies that have access to the universe of confidential employer and worker information and meet standards of privacy, analytic rigor, and community credibility. This state-based collection of student records with Unemployment Insurance and other administrative records also should be coordinated on an interstate basis by state employees.

All information should be produced in a manner that protects the confidentiality of each student and employer and should be covered by strict statutorily defined confidentiality requirements, including those of the Family Educational Rights and Privacy Act (FERPA). Educational institutions should also establish and document explicit and standardized statements of consent relating to the use of student information.

COST ESTIMATES

New Literacy for Adults

This guarantee would provide all individuals who have completed at least the 9th grade the opportunity to access the secondary education necessary for passing the new state qualifying examination, enabling them to continue their postsecondary education and acquire further credentials that will increase their productivity and prosperity. An NCES survey estimates that 58 percent of individuals age 16 and over who are without a diploma or GED and currently not attending high school have completed the 9th through 12th grades. This is a target population of approximately 18 million individuals. The current uptake rate of people without a high school diploma who prepare for and take the examination for a GED is about 7 percent. We propose to triple the take-up rate, adding another 14 percent, or 2.5 million people. Assuming a $1,000 cost per student, we estimate that helping these adults pass a state qualifying examination would cost about $2.5 billion annually.

Personal Competitiveness Accounts

In the year 2021, the annual federal contributions to the accounts for youth would be:

$500 x 4.7 million live births	=	$ 2.350 billion
$100 x 18.3 million 1–4-year-olds	=	$ 1.830 billion
$100 x 22.7 million 5–9-year-olds	=	$ 2.270 billion
$100 x 22.1 million 10–14-year-olds	=	$ 2.210 billion
$100 x 8.6 million 15–16-year-olds	=	$ 0.860 billion
Subtotal		$ 9.520 billion

In examining individual learning accounts for workers, the Swedish government estimated that 10 percent of its workforce would start a learning account in the first year of such a program and over the first 10 years, about 30 percent would have active learning accounts. Applied to the United States, this implies about 15 million accounts in the first year and an average of roughly 30 million accounts annually over 10 years. If a third of such workers earn less than twice the minimum wage, and save 1.25 percent annually ($5 per week at minimum wage), the federal match to their personal accounts would equal nearly $2 billion annually — more than twice the current federal expenditure on job training for disadvantaged adults under the WIA.

Current Coverdell and 529 Savings Plans encourage families to save for future college costs. For tax purposes, they are treated as Roth-like IRAs and create a tax expenditure to the federal government of about $600 million per year.

In sum, the PLC accounts are estimated to cost the federal government about $13 billion annually: $9.5 billion per year in contributions for each youngster, $2 billion annually in matching contributions to the accounts of low-wage workers, and less than $1 billion in the tax-favored treatment of the accounts.

Regional Development Program

We estimate no net increase in costs for this change in policies.

ESL Proposals

Under current law, exclusion of employer-provided education assistance benefits is estimated to cost the federal treasury about $900 million per year. The ESL proposals should not increase these costs by more than 50 percent or about $450 million.

New Data System for Accountability

Federal support for the expansion of demonstration projects that integrate state unemployment insurance wage records with educational administrative data would cost about $50 million. This would enhance state data systems in the 12 states now known to track graduates of two-year public institutions and expand pilot efforts to 10 additional states. Additional interstate coordination of records by the Bureau of Labor Statistics and the contracting of

state employees by BLS would cost about $10 million. Added costs for the proposed measures are moderate because of the reliance on existing data and on state and federal agencies that currently administer those systems.

Totals

New Literacy for Adults	$ 2.500 billion
Personal Competitiveness Accounts	$13.000 billion
Regional Development Program	$ 0
ESL Proposals	$ .450 billion
New Data System	$ .060 billion
Total	$ 16.010 billion

Commentary on the Report

Commentary

'Tough Choices': Change the System, or Suffer the Consequences

Education Week
Vol. 26, no. 26, pp. 32–33, 44
January 17, 2007

Marc S. Tucker

Imagine that a really good, high-paying job opens up, one demanding quite high skills. It comes down to two candidates. One candidate, Amit, has higher skills than the other, Bob, and is willing to work for half the salary Bob demands. So Bob doesn't get the job. He goes from employer to employer, only to find that they are all aware there are growing numbers of very highly skilled people like Amit willing to work for lower wages than our high-flying job seeker. What do you suppose happens? Well, in time, of course, Bob and all the other people in his situation face reality and lower their salary demands until they come into line with the market. There go the nice houses, fancy vacations, and private schools for the kids. Quite a comedown.

That, in a nutshell, is what the *New* Commission on the Skills of the American Workforce predicts for the standard of living of the American people if we do not get our act together quickly.

Sixteen years ago, in 1990, the first Commission on the Skills of the American Workforce said that the jobs of Americans with low skills were threatened by low-skill people in poor countries who were willing to work for much less. That turned out to be true. But now, with the economic ascendancy of China, India, and other countries, large numbers of highly educated people are joining the global workforce willing to work for half or less of what Americans have been getting. And they are available to employers worldwide at the click of a mouse, without moving an inch.

It also is true that the cost of automating jobs is declining rapidly, and, as these costs go down and labor costs go up, it becomes possible—and, in fact, necessary—for employers everywhere to automate more and more jobs.

The people whose jobs are in the most immediate danger are those who do routine work. If it is routine, it can be reduced to an algorithm, and if it can be reduced to an algorithm, it can be automated. That is true of many high-skill, high-pay jobs, as well as for low-skill, low-pay jobs.

The commission points out that there is a way to avoid a decline in our standard of living. Companies will be able—and happy—to pay outsize salaries to American workers if those workers are able to produce, year in and year out, new products and services that are in high demand and for which they are the only supplier. But it is not just the blowout new products and services that will produce these high-margin products and services; it is also the endless stream of more modest innovations and improvements that turn very good products and services into great ones.

Thus the only way to keep our heads above water will be to have countless firms and industries blazing new trails that lead to an endless supply of new and exciting products and services, many of them powered by state-of-the-art technological advances.

These factors combine to create a specification for the kinds of workers we will need at almost all levels of the economy if we are to avoid a steady decline in our standard of living. We will have to match the best national education achievement in all the core subjects in the curriculum, produce the most creative and innovative graduates available anywhere, and have a nation of workers who are the fastest learners on the face of the globe. Learning quickly, by the way, is much easier for people who have a good command of the core ideas and concepts in the disciplines they have studied, because these ideas and concepts provide the framework on which new knowledge can be hung.

The commission compared this specification to what we have now. The United States, for decade after decade the world's leader in educational attainment (the proportion of our workforce with the equivalent of the high school diploma), is being overtaken by nation after nation, some of them developing countries. In the report of the *New* Commission on the Skills of the American Workforce, we focused on the three most respected comparative measures of educational achievement—the Trends in International Science and Mathematics Study, the Program in International Student Assessment of the OECD, and the Adult Literacy Survey (also from the OECD)—and found that the United States places anywhere from the middle to the bottom of the rankings on all of them. The United States leads the developed world in the proportion of students who drop out of school. On measures of both quality and quantity, our performance is mediocre.

And it gets worse. Over the past 30 years, the scores of our children on the 4th-grade National Assessment of Educational

Progress literacy assessment have been virtually flat (although our performance on mathematics is better). Yet the cost per pupil over the same period has risen by 240 percent, after correcting for inflation. We appear to be getting less for our education dollars than any other nation for which we have data. To put it another way: we have tried over the past 30 years almost every intervention that anyone could think of, and they have all failed. The only thing that has greatly increased is the amount of money we are spending.

But there is one thing that we have not tried, and that is to change our system of education, a system that has remained remarkably stable since the early part of the 20th century, a system that was designed for an entirely different era.

And a new system design is exactly what the commission is proposing. Here are the highlights.

We begin with a thought experiment. Suppose, the commission said, that the states create syllabus-based board examinations set to the standard required for entrance into their community and technical colleges without remediation. Suppose that students could take these tests anytime they wished, but that the majority passed by the age of 16, and 95 percent passed by age 18. Assume further that those who passed were automatically admitted to the community or technical college of their choice as soon as they passed the exam. And further suppose that those who hit a higher score could stay in high school to take an International Baccalaureate program, a program made up of Advanced

Placement courses, or the equivalent, put together by the ACT admissions-testing service or others. Those who were not able to pass on the first try would be able to try again, as often as they wished, and their high schools would be obligated to help them do that.

The gross savings from such a scheme would be about $60 billion, coming from the reduced time in high school for those now completing 12 years of schooling and from the elimination of remediation in college. Add back $10 billion in costs to account for the students who would stay in high school under this scheme who now drop out. Then throw in another $8 billion, and you have an investment fund of about $58 billion to use to make sure that this thought experiment becomes reality.

In the report, we invested a little over $19 billion in high-quality early-childhood education, enough to meet the needs of all 4-year-olds and all low-income 3-year-olds. We invested another $19 billion or so in teachers' salaries, enough to raise starting pay to the current median, about $45,000 per year, and top salaries to $95,000 for teachers working a regular school year and $110,000 for teachers working a full year. Our polling research tells us that this is enough to attract teachers from the top third of the students entering college.

The commission proposes to move the governance, organization, and finance of our system into the 21st century in several ways. First, we would have school boards, instead of running schools, contract with third parties (we hope many will be groups of teachers, organized as partnerships) to run schools. They would do this with performance contracts, so the ability of the organizations running schools to keep their contracts would depend on the performance of the students.

Schools would no longer be financed by their local communities but, instead, directly by the state. The United States, almost alone among advanced industrial countries in relying for school funding on the wealth of local communities, would join the ranks of nations in which school funding does not depend on local wealth. Schools statewide would be funded on a formula, with each student worth a certain base amount, with increments on top of that for students from low-income families, students from families in which English is not spoken at home, students with mild disabilities, students with severe disabilities, and so on. After equalizing in this way, we would add our last $19 billion to the pot to top up school budgets nationwide, so that we would not have to rob the wealthier schools to pay for the poorer schools, thus making equalization politically possible.

Teachers, in our plan, would be hired by the state, on the sort of salary schedule described above, but they would not have jobs until they were engaged by a school. This plan would put teachers in the top ranks of our professionals and empower them in ways they have only dreamed about until now. It would give students and parents real choices among excellent schools. It would give poor and minority students a real shot at a first-rate education everywhere. It would build lean, performance-oriented management systems at every level. And it would give the United States the best purchase on a bright future it could possibly have.

Some who have seen the report wonder whether those who have benefited from the system the way it is now organized will allow these kinds of changes to take place. The commission, composed of people no one would characterize as revolutionaries, believes that the enormous pent-up frustration with the system as it is currently organized will carry the day.

Bad systems are now defeating good educators everywhere. We have no choice but to create a state-of-the-art system in which good educators can do extraordinary work every day.

Marc S. Tucker is president of the National Center on Education and the Economy.

Commentary

'TOUGH CHOICES': RADICAL IDEAS, MISGUIDED ASSUMPTIONS

EDUCATION WEEK
VOL. 26, NO. 24, P. 38
JANUARY 17, 2007

DIANE RAVITCH

There is a line between visionary thinking and pie-in-the-sky theorizing. The recent report of the New Commission on the Skills of the American Workforce, *Tough Choices or Tough Times,* is most assuredly on the wrong side of that line. Not only is this widely publicized and much-praised report an exercise in pie-in-the-sky theorizing, it would—if enacted—dismantle American public education. The report itself says as much. It says that the present system of education is no good, and we must start over.

Like many previous reports, this one lays out a string of criticisms of our education system, most of which are unassailable, and then proceeds to propose a variety of changes. In this case, however, most of the report's prescriptions are not only radical but dubious. Some of them are risky gambles with one of our most vital social institutions.

Frankly, it is difficult to understand how a commission composed of so many distinguished men and women produced such an ill-conceived document. One imagines the horse-trading that enabled each commissioner to get his or her favorite proposal added to the mix. That is the way such committee structures usually work. Yet the commission has the nerve to insist that no one should cherry-pick "only those ideas that cost the least and offend the fewest." No, they demand a wholesale adoption of their recommendations.

Let us briefly review the most important of them.

First, the report proposes that all students at the end of 10th grade take a board examination (created by states, the national government, or international organizations) in core subjects. Those who score "well enough" will have the right to go to a community college for a two-year technical degree or a program leading to a four-year state college. Those who score even better can stay in high school longer to prepare for a second set of exams; if they do well on those exams, then they can go to a selective college.

What's wrong with this? Lots of things. The first set of exams will supposedly be set at the same level as those of "the countries that do the best job educating their students," but the commission asserts that 95 percent of all students will meet this standard. Indeed, they also say that "no one would fail," because students can take the exams again and again. So this exam is actually a very low bar that will be used to divide students into two groups: those bound for two-year colleges and those bound for four-year colleges. (No further mention is made of the 5 percent who can't pass this low hurdle.) One may safely predict that the two-year group will be composed mainly of students who are African American, Hispanic, recent immigrants, and poor. It is not clear how this proposal will improve academic performance or why the nation needs to construct this elaborate examination system to sort young people into careers.

Second, the report calls for "a major overhaul of the American testing industry" to ensure the development of tests that measure such things as creativity and innovation, teamwork, abstract thinking, and self-discipline. The report says portentously,

"If that is not done, then nothing else will matter."

What's wrong with this? If the proposed examination system, indeed the entire report, hinges on the creation of tests that measure creativity, innovation, self-discipline, and so forth, then the whole enterprise is a house of cards. The report fails to identify a single test, not in this country or anywhere else, that successfully measures these qualities.

A third recommendation is universal preschool education, not exactly a radical or original idea. It is one that nearly everyone applauds.

What's wrong with this? Nothing. It requires only a political willingness to pay the cost of a high-quality educational program, not just day care.

A fourth recommendation is that teachers should be recruited from the top third of high school graduates going on to college. The report says that the way to do this is to pay teachers more (a starting salary of about $45,000 per year and a top salary of about $110,000 a year) while cutting their pensions and health benefits. The cost of higher salaries would be funded by cuts in benefits.

What's wrong with this? The relatively meager increases in compensation proposed by the commission are nowhere near enough to induce teachers to give up their retirement benefits. Nor are the proposed salaries large enough to recruit "the best and the brightest" to enter teaching as a career instead of law, medicine, or investment banking. If the commission really wants to achieve the goal of getting the best-educated graduates to become teachers, then it should propose a starting salary of, say, $70,000 and a top salary of, let's say, $300,000, so that teaching could truly compete with the jobs that are currently attracting the top students. Better yet, to avoid invoking an arbitrary number, why not take the median income of the members of the commission and use that as a target for compensation of the top-performing teachers?

A fifth recommendation is to change radically the governance structure of public education. Every school would be "operated by independent contractors" instead of the local school board; the new role of the local board would be to write performance contracts, monitor the work of the contractors, and collect data.

What's wrong with this? To date, there is no evidence to demonstrate that independent contractors are better able to operate schools than local school districts. No high-performing nation has assigned control of its public schools to independent contractors. The contractors that are ready to run public schools are few in number. Some, like Edison Schools Inc. and the Knowledge Is Power Program (KIPP), have good records; others have failed or gone bankrupt. It is inconceivable that the nation is ready to turn over tens of thousands of schools to contractors that have thus far managed only a few dozen schools or never run more than one school, or that do not now even exist. This is the riskiest and most incomprehensible gamble of all.

A sixth recommendation is to abandon local funding of education in favor of state funding, with dollars matched to the needs of individual students. Thus, schools with large numbers of disadvantaged students would have more funding than schools that serve a more advantaged population.

What's wrong with this? Not much, other than the resistance of local communities that don't want to relinquish control of their budgets. Since the trend of state court decisions is pushing school finance toward a state-funded system, this recommendation is one of the few that stand a chance of influencing public policy.

A seventh recommendation is to create "Personal Competitiveness Accounts," that is, savings accounts for individuals that can be used only for work-related training. The government would establish such an account for every new baby with an initial deposit of $500. The initial cost of this program, which the commission calls a "new GI Bill," would be $31 billion per year. Employers and states could eventually add to the accounts.

What's wrong with this? It is not clear why employers and states would have an incentive to pay the billions necessary to enlarge these accounts. Nor is it clear that the establishment of such accounts would be more cost-effective than making high-quality job training available at low cost when needed, either by employers or community colleges.

An eighth recommendation is to "create regional competitiveness authorities to make America competitive." The report says that Congress should encourage states to establish "regional economic-development authorities involving the key leaders from many sectors in those regions in the development of economic-development strategies that make sense to them." These authorities would coordinate the work of the region's education and training institutions "to make sure that each region's workers develop the skills and knowledge needed to be successful in that labor market."

What's wrong with this? In a report that supposedly focuses on nimble, high-performance management, this is a bizarre proposal. It sounds a bit like a Soviet five-year plan. Why does Congress need to "encourage" states to establish regional authorities? Do regions really need such authorities to coordinate education and training institutions? Why would these authorities be the best guide to the skills and knowledge that workers need? This proposal promises nothing but a layer of bureaucratic management to try to steer the economy, a strategy that has never worked in the past and is not likely to work in the future.

Taken together, the report's fervent advocacy of structural change stands in sharp contrast to its indifference to curriculum and instruction. Structural changes, the commission argues, will save American education. They will bring about higher academic performance, a better-educated workforce, and a high-wage economy. Unfortunately, the commission's report contains not a shred of evidence that its prescriptions will work. And common sense suggests that at least some of these prescriptions might harm the patient. One wishes that the commission members had begun their deliberations with a simple caveat: Do no harm.

Diane Ravitch is a historian of education, a research professor at New York University, and a senior fellow at the Hoover Institution and the Brookings Institution. Her books include Left Back: A Century of Battles over School Reform, The Language Police, *and, most recently,* The English Reader, *which she edited with her son, Michael Ravitch.*

Commentary

Education's 'Grand Departure'

Defending the Skills Commission's Vision for the Future

Education Week
Vol. 26, no. 24, p. 38
February 21, 2007

Thomas W. Payzant, Charles B. Reed

We respectfully disagree with Diane Ravitch's characterization [in the previous commentary] of the *Tough Choices or Tough Times* report of the *New* Commission on the Skills of the American Workforce as "pie-in-the-sky theorizing" and its recommendations as "risky gambles with one of our most vital social institutions" ("'Tough Choices': Radical Ideas, Misguided Assumptions," *Commentary,* Jan. 17, 2007).

As members of the bipartisan commission, we can assure the reader that, contrary to Ms. Ravitch's assertions, there was no "horse-trading" involved in its creation. We proposed a total redesign of the system because we knew from past experience with piecemeal reforms that, however worthy, they have little hope of producing the improvements needed now.

Interestingly, Ms. Ravitch says the criticisms we made of the American education system are "unassailable." Most prominent among those criticisms is that while we have the second-most-expensive system in the developed world, our results are mediocre. There is a strong likelihood that we will suffer a steep long-term decline in our standard of living if we do not make major changes. In these circumstances, the biggest gamble we can take with our system is not to change it.

Because we propose getting 95 percent of high school students to a new bar, Ms. Ravitch concludes that it must be set very low. Not so. We recommend the bar be benchmarked to our best competitors' and set at what it would take to get into state community and technical colleges without remediation. We propose to move the bar to a 12th-grade level, from the current 8th-grade level.

Ms. Ravitch dismisses our call to provide high-quality early-childhood education to young children with the observation that no one has yet demonstrated the political will to pay for it. She ignores a distinguishing feature of our report: we actually show where the money will come from. Our plan is based on a major reallocation of resources.

One of the commissioners, John Engler, was a three-term governor of Michigan. Early in his governorship, he concluded that the welfare system was broken. When he told his staff what he intended to do about it, they told him he would never get elected dogcatcher if he went ahead with welfare reform. Well, the rest, as they say, is history. Why should grand departures like this occur in welfare but not in education?

As a historian, Ms. Ravitch knows America is one long history of social revolutions, each one a case of overturning long-established institutions and ways of doing business. This only happens, however, when the people have reached the limits of their frustration with the status quo. Continuing to do something because it is the way it has always been done, and because there will be those who vehemently object, is, in fact, not the American way.

Some wag has observed that if Rip van Winkle were to wake up today after a century asleep, the only social institution he would find essentially unchanged is the public school. A little less than 100 years ago, disgusted with the way the politics of the ward heelers had corrupted the management of our schools, we introduced professional district management, nonpartisan school boards, and civil service appointments to teaching positions. The reformers succeeded because enough people were fed up with the system as it was to fundamentally change it. The response our report has already produced suggests we may have reached the same point again, with the same readiness for fundamental change. It has happened before. There is no reason to believe that it cannot happen again.

Contrary to Ms. Ravitch's assertions, there is plenty of evidence from the experience of other nations that these ideas can work. Unfortunately, it is also true that there is plenty of evidence that the status quo does not work. It is time to draw the obvious conclusion.

Thomas W. Payzant is a senior lecturer at Harvard University's graduate school of education and a former superintendent of schools for Boston. Charles B. Reed is the chancellor of the California State University system.

MAKING TOUGH CHOICES

Phi Delta Kappan
VOL. 88, NO. 10, PP. 728–732
JUNE 2007

In December 2006, the New Commission on the Skills of the American Workforce, of which Mr. Tucker is co-chair, released its report *Tough Choices or Tough Times*. The report sets forth detailed recommendations for retooling the U.S. education system in light of the changes being brought about by the global economy. In this *Kappan* special section, Mr. Tucker summarizes the commission's proposals, four commentators respond to those proposals, and Mr. Tucker answers their critiques.

MARC S. TUCKER

Nations have many important goals in mind when they design their education systems, among them instilling in young people both a desire for democracy and the knowledge needed to perpetuate it and enabling them to understand and appreciate the highest achievements of humanity, to reason for themselves in a world of difficult choices, and to understand and empathize with others in a world full of conflict. But a nation that ignores the need to also educate its voting people to earn a living does so at its—and their—peril.

That is more true now than ever before. Research conducted by the *New Commission on the Skills of the American Workforce* shows that the middle class is shredding. It is not true that all of its members are getting poorer. It is much more

accurate to say that there is a clear divide between those who have some college and those who do not. The former are becoming ever better off. The latter are sinking fast. The fact is that education holds the key to personal and national economic well-being, more now than at any other time in our history.

But it may well be that even those Americans who are very well educated will find their incomes falling, simply because companies all over the world are getting access to very large numbers of people who are as well educated as our best-educated students and are willing to work for much less.

These people are in India and China and a rising number of other poor countries that have a long history of educating their elites very well. It used to be that large fractions of these elites sent their children to the West for their graduate education and that they stayed here, because the opportunities in their home countries were very limited. But now, many are staying in their home country to begin with or come here for their graduate work and return shortly thereafter, because enormous opportunities are opening up back home.

The Internet now makes it possible for companies to employ these people wherever they are, without moving anywhere. And that is what puts our well-educated people in direct competition with millions of people in these less-developed countries who are just as well educated and willing to work for much less.

Fifteen years ago, we realized that poorly educated people in this country were for the first time in direct competition with minimally skilled people in poor countries, who were willing to work for much less. Today we are finding that highly skilled people in this country are in direct competition with highly skilled people in other countries, who are willing to work for much less. Raising achievement standards for our students who are the least well educated is still absolutely necessary—and is proving very difficult—but it is no longer enough to prevent a long, slow slide in our standard of living.

The commission concluded that in the future, the only employers that will be willing and able to pay consistently high wages will be those that produce highly desirable products and services that can be obtained only from them and for which, therefore,

they can charge the kinds of high prices that will enable them to pay high wages. American movies are one example.

The Apple iPod is another. And it demonstrates an important point. Like our movies, it rests on a foundation of state-of-the-art technology: But also like our movies, it represents enormous amounts of creativity and innovation, not just in the technology itself, but in every other aspect of its creation and distribution, from marketing strategy to industrial design. There are many other such examples.

The commission's analysis of the global economy is long and much more nuanced than I can be here (go to www.skillscommission.org for more information). But the bottom line is that most people in the United States will see their incomes falling in the years ahead unless we can match the best-performing countries in the academic achievement of our students, produce the most creative and innovative high school graduates in the world, and figure out how to educate our children so as to enable them to learn new things very quickly and well.

This is a very tall order. And the United States is not very well positioned to fill it. We have the highest school dropout rate in the industrialized world. We have the second most expensive primary and secondary education system in the world. And the results it is producing are mediocre at best, as measured by all of the most widely accepted international comparative measures of achievement. To add insult to injury, after accounting for inflation, the cost of our system has risen by 240 percent over the past 30 years, while the scores on the 4th-grade reading test of the National Assessment of Educational Progress have barely moved at all (though we have done better on mathematics).

We have tried money. And it has not worked. We have tried every kind of program initiative, and none of them have produced the kind of improvement we need at scale. The only thing we have not tried is changing the basic system we have for elementary and secondary education, which has been largely unchanged in a century.

So the commission proposed to do exactly that. In the space that remains, I will summarize the design the commission put forward. First, we proposed basic changes in the way our students progress through the system. Schools in the best-performing countries typically send their students on to what we call college when they are 16 years old, not 18 years old. If we are designing a world-class system, we thought, we should do the same. It is also true that in most of the best-performing countries, students do not go on to college unless they can show that they can do college-level work. Virtually all labor economists these days say that in the future, Americans will have to have at least two years of college to earn a decent living, so we set as a goal having 60 percent of our students ready for college by the age of 16 and 95 percent ready for college by the age of 18.

To implement these goals, we envisioned a new state examination to be offered to our high school students at age 16. This would be a syllabus-based examination covering all the core subjects in the curriculum, from math and science to history and the arts. It would be set to the standard required for college-level work in our community and technical colleges. Students who met the standard would be able to go immediately to the community and technical colleges in their state without any further admissions test and would not be required to take any remedial courses (because they would not need them).

These curriculum-based examinations would be modeled on the International Baccalaureate (IB) exams and the Advanced Placement tests as to form, though the standard would be lower. Thus these would be much higher-quality (and more expensive) tests than the states are now using for their accountability systems. As a general matter, the commission is strongly in favor of having many fewer mandated tests but vastly improving the quality of those that remain.

Students who were able to pass this new examination at a higher level could stay in high school to take a program of studies leading to an IB diploma, a program of studies made up of Advanced Placement courses, or a similar program put together by individual states or perhaps by the American College Testing organization. These students would be preparing to seek admissions to selective colleges, some of which would grant college credit for these courses, while others, as today, would not.

Some have suggested that this sounds like a take on the European tracking system, assigning our children to life destinies at age 16. It is not. Our aim here is exactly the opposite: to get almost all students to college and ready to actually succeed in college. Even the choice as to whether to go to community college or to stay in high school to tackle the IB exams or their equivalent is not an irrevocable assignment to two different stations in life, since it is quite possible for our students to go to a community college and then transfer to our most prestigious state universities.

By insisting that our students be ready for college before they are admitted to college, we will give them an incentive to take tough courses and work hard in high school. The majority of our upper-division high school students today have no such incentive. Thus they come to see high school more as a place to hang out with their friends than as a place to get on with their lives by working hard on academics.

Sending our high school students to college early and eliminating remedial education in our colleges will save $60 billion a year. Add back $10 billion to account for the students who now drop out but in our plan would stay in school, and we have saved a net $50 billion. The commission threw in $8 billion (a tiny fraction of the total $500 billion we spend each year on elementary and secondary education), and we have an imaginary investment fund of $58 billion. We took that imaginary money and thought about how it might be invested so as to enable 60 percent of our children to be ready for college by the age of 16 and 95 percent by the age of 18.

As long as our low-income students entering kindergarten continue to have vocabularies half as large as those of the other kin-

dergartners, we will never make it, because those students will never be able to catch up to their peers. So we invested the first third of our new fund in early childhood education. That is enough to pay for high-quality early childhood education for all 4-year-olds and all low-income 3-year-olds.

We invested the next third of our fund in teachers' compensation. Our aim here is to put the country in a position to recruit a large share of our teachers from the top third of the young people entering our colleges. The policies we have long had in place should have given us the lowest third of the distribution. But because we have long had access to women and minorities whose choice of professional careers was often limited to teaching, we got much better teachers than we deserved. That is no longer the case, and we are about to get the very teachers we have long deserved, just when we need far better.

Our economic analysis suggests that our students need to have much higher levels of academic accomplishment, need to have a much firmer grasp of the conceptual foundations of the subjects they study, and need to be more creative, more innovative, and better able to learn new material quickly. It is hard to see how our teachers will produce students with these characteristics unless the teachers themselves have them. These are just the characteristics that our best firms look for in the people they hire. So we will need to have policies, especially compensation policies, designed to attract such people.

The commission proposed many more changes in our system for recruiting, training, and compensating teachers than there is room to describe here. Suffice it to say that our proposals would result in setting average starting pay for teachers at the current median pay for teachers. Teachers at the top of a four-step career ladder would make about $95,000 a year, and those at the top of the ladder who are willing to work a full year would make about $110,000 a year on average. Those who work in high-cost states could make substantially more.

Some accounts of our report have suggested that we would take teachers' pensions away and would pay for their raises by doing so. That is not the case. We would convert teachers' pension plans to defined contribution plans or cash balance plans, providing benefits comparable to those offered by the better private employers or by our colleges to their faculties. Newly recruited teachers would have to accept the new compensation system, with its greatly increased cash compensation and somewhat reduced retirement benefits. But teachers already serving would be offered a choice between staying with their current plans or joining the new one. Thus no teachers would lose anything they did not choose to give up. Some of the gain in teachers' pay in our plan is paid for by the change in retirement plans, but by far the largest share is new money.

And now we get to the changes we proposed in the governance, management, and financing of the system. School boards would no longer operate schools. Instead, they would be responsible for contracting with third parties that would run the

schools under performance contracts. The commission hopes that most of the organizations running schools would be partnerships formed by classroom teachers, who would reach out to other classroom teachers whose work they admire and whose values they share to design and operate the school of their dreams.

We would also end local financing of public education. Instead, the schools would be directly funded by the state, on the basis of the composition of their student bodies. Each student would be funded at the same base rate, but there would be additional increments for students who come from low-income families and for students who come from families in which English is not spoken at home. Mildly disabled students would get another increment in funding, and severely disabled students would get still another.

This idea for funding our schools has been around for decades, but it has never been implemented, because if there is no more money statewide for the schools, the increase in funding for the poorer schools must come from the wealthier ones, which is politically a nonstarter. So the commission took the last third of our imaginary fund and used it to top up financing for the schools statewide. That would make it possible to pay Paul without robbing Peter. Thus it should be possible for the states to finally create truly equitable school finance systems, without which we do not have a prayer of getting all students to internationally benchmarked standards.

Teachers, in the commission design, would be recruited and employed by the state, according to the salary schedule briefly described above. But they would not have a job unless they were engaged by a contract school. If they were let go by a school, they would have to find another school willing to hire them.

This design would transform the opportunities facing our disadvantaged students. No longer would they arrive at kindergarten with half the vocabulary of their peers. No longer would they get the teachers that wealthier districts did not want. Schools serving a high proportion of disadvantaged students would have the resources they need to open early in the morning and stay open until late at night. They would be able to diagnose students with vision problems and get them glasses and students with hearing problems and get them hearing aids. They would be able to get the mentors and hire the tutors these students need to succeed. They would be able to afford the extended-day and extended-year programs that these students need to catch up.

This is a plan for a school system that is highly performance oriented and entrepreneurial in spirit, and it would finally make it possible for our teachers to enter the ranks of the true professions in the United States. It would support competition and choice among schools, but it would not privatize them. It would make incomparable improvements in the prospects of our disadvantaged students, but it would also greatly improve the performance of our most advantaged students.

The commission's new design will cause considerable pain to some, not least because we are proposing a major reallocation of resources. However, the commission would not insist on any of its specific proposals. Instead, we challenge those who disagree with our proposals to put forward better ideas for reaching the same goals. The penalty for failing to do so will be dire.

Marc S. Tucker *is president of the National Center on Education and the Economy.*

Commentary

THE *NEW* COMMISSION ON THE SKILLS
OF THE AMERICAN WORKFORCE

OLD NEWS OR NEW NEWS?

PHI DELTA KAPPAN
VOL. 88, NO. 10, PP. 733–734
JUNE 2007

Mr. Doyle focuses his response to Mr. Tucker on three of the commission's recommendations. He fully supports the notion of increasing student effort but has doubts about performance contracting and serious doubts about the commission's approach to funding its recommended reforms.

DENIS P. DOYLE

The recent report of the *New* Commission on the Skills of the American Workforce is a startling document, both for its findings and for its recommendations. It finds, for example, that the American middle class is "shredding. It is not true that all of its members are getting poorer. It is much more accurate to say that there is a clear divide between those who have some college and those who do not. The former are becoming ever better off. The latter are sinking fast." Human capital or the lack thereof is the subtext of the whole report.

Now this is hardly news. To my knowledge, for example, Cornell University professor John Bishop and his colleagues, among others, have been writing about the divide between the education haves and have-nots for at least two decades, possibly more. Strictly speaking, of course, human capital includes more than formal education; it includes health, talent, ability, acquired knowledge and skills, and such dispositions as creativity, energy, imagination, work ethic, and so on. In the *New* Commission's case, educational attainment is used as a proxy for human capital, as it is by many analysts.

But the notion that education (developed human capital) is the source of most wealth is by now old news. (Nobel laureate Gary Becker's book, *Human Capital,* was published in 1964, after all.) What is new news is that the phenomenon is now global and includes the developing world, not just the member nations of the OECD (Organisation for Economic Co-operation and Development). And, thanks to high technology, human capital is ever more fungible.

Not so long ago, human capital was similar to physical capital in one important respect: proximity was paramount. Bench scientists and engineers (human capital personified) worked side by side. No longer. At least, they no longer need to be physically close: virtual proximity will do.

That is why Pune, India, has become an English-language call center for American businesses that still provide customers with access to a human being on the other end of the line. It is finally the case that a telephone is a telephone is a telephone. (About one thing you may be sure: as voice recognition software and artificial intelligence become more sophisticated, human beings at the other end of the line will become as scarce as hens' teeth.)

Speaking of human contact, think of what is by now an old standby, the ATM. Who could do without automated tellers now? 'Twas not always so. When they were introduced, they caught on very slowly. The typical bank customer wanted —indeed, expected—to see and talk to a human teller. Today, the ubiquity, simplicity, convenience, and speed of the ATM have overcome the initial reluctance of customers to engage with a machine. The future has arrived already.

But Marc Tucker and the *New* Commission are right in their assertions about globalization, even though it is no longer

a novelty. A genuine revolution is taking place, with a global workforce of 3 billion (as contrasted with a domestic workforce of slightly more than 150 million). And Americans need to be educated better than ever before to compete, both at home and abroad.

What is new, of course, is scale and timing. Xerox scientists and engineers are no longer confined to PARC (Palo Alto Research Center); today, they can work together across the globe in real time, only a phone, fax, e-mail, or WebEx away from colleagues in Tokyo, Amsterdam, or Stamford. And what American business can do, so can Indian and Chinese business.

The policy key is education.

Indeed, it is no surprise that more than two decades ago management guru Peter Drucker foresaw this general phenomenon. He sagely observed then that every nation would become absorbed with education because it is the source of wealth in the postindustrial era. And so it has come to pass, with India and China, no less than the United States, consumed with educational improvement.

That the *New* Commission would zero in on these issues is, then, not startling. What is startling are the nature, extent, and sweep of the panel's recommendations.

The full range of the recommendations and how they came to be made are beyond the scope of this article. Permit me to explore just two of the more controversial ones, about which I have mixed feelings, and to offer one bit of commentary.

The first is accelerated graduation: expecting American students to complete a demanding course of study by age 16 (as is the case in Europe and Asia). The second is the recommendation that school boards abandon their prerogative to oversee the schools in their bailiwick, and instead contract with education providers to offer education. The bit of commentary has to do with the *New* Commission's "imaginary fund."

These three items boggle the mind, but for very different reasons. For example, the accelerated graduation recommendation is no more than a thinly disguised scheme to reintroduce the concept of student effort into the education reform debate. As such, it is a welcome and long-overdue development. But, unhappily, it has little chance of enactment. To put teeth into it would require us to do what the rest of the world does: institutionalize serious incentives and rewards. In the case of secondary school students around the world, the pot of gold at the end of the rainbow takes the form of the opportunity to attend a selective post-secondary institution. It is the passport to lifetime success.

But American education policy has moved resolutely in the opposite direction for the past 50 years. Access and equity have been the rallying cries of the higher education community. God forbid they be accused of elitism. With 3,500 institutions of higher education, merit scholarships (or grants) are the furthest thing from the minds of most people involved in higher education policy (nomenclature that, given the context, leads one to ask, Higher than what?).

The opportunity to use higher education as the gatekeeper of quality was forfeited long ago. Imagine what the effect of a technically simple but politically explosive reform initiative would be: award guaranteed student loans and Pell Grants on the basis of academic merit alone. No more, no less. Or how about using a mixed, sliding scale, made up of income along one axis and academic accomplishment along the other? Do what the competition does. Enough said.

To me, at least, the *New* Commission's most truly startling recommendation is to strip school boards of their authority to "operate" schools: "instead, they would . . . contract . . . with third parties . . . that would run the schools under performance contracts." Am I the only one who remembers the U.S. Office of Economic Opportunity's performance-contracting fiasco more than a third of a century ago? Apparently, because the *New* Commission offers this not as a trial, or demonstration, or experimental solution, but as the final word on school management and organization.

Finally, the *New* Commission (apparently as both a literary device and a thought experiment) costs out its reform suggestions by creating an "imaginary fund" from which to finance its reform recommendations. For example, the "savings" realized by early graduation would be available to early childhood education; the savings realized by ending remediation in college would be available for . . . follow the bouncing ball.

What is missing from this picture? A sense of the harsh reality of public finance. As everyone who follows the field knows, every year since the founding of the Republic, public expenditure for education has increased. It has never decreased; there have never been savings; there has never been an education dividend occasioned by program improvement or budget slimming. Indeed, the *New* Commission's name for the fund is more apt than the members may have intended: "imaginary fund" indeed.

Denis P. Doyle *is cofounder and chief academic officer of SchoolNet, New York, New York. He is also the author of* The Doyle Report, *a weekly e-newsletter that covers the intersection of school improvement and technology.*

Commentary

BIG CHALLENGES, BOLD IDEAS

Phi Delta Kappan
Vol. 88, no. 10, pp. 735–736, 740
June 2007

Mr. Petrilli admires the job that Mr. Tucker and the *New* Commission on the Skills of the American Workforce have done in responding to the challenges of globalization. At the same time, he has suggestions for taking their recommendations even further.

MICHAEL J. PETRILLI

Just a few years ago, when Thomas Friedman published *The World Is Flat,* I rushed to give it a read. And like hundreds of thousands of other people around the planet, I found it riveting. His description of a world transformed by the Internet, globalization, and new ways of doing business seemed like a revelation.

Yet, as I wrote in a review of the book for *Education Next,* I became crestfallen when I reached his conclusions about the nation's schools. Surely, I thought, Friedman would argue that competition would have the same positive, transformative effects on our education system as the liberalization of India's economy has had on its development. Without a doubt, I thought, he would compare our schools' stultifying unions to those of Europe, whose labor

markets he derides as "inflexible, rigidly regulated . . . full of government restrictions on hiring and firing." Absolutely, I was convinced, he would look at this new flat world, where Americans must compete with people not from their own community or state but from all over the planet, and declare our patchwork education system—with its 50 sets of academic standards and tests—no longer up to the challenges at hand. The time has come, he would say, for rigorous national standards and tests, political obstacles be damned.

Alas, Friedman merely offered a handful of underwhelming suggestions regarding math and science teaching and making college more affordable. What a letdown!

Thankfully, Marc Tucker and the *New* Commission on the Skills of the American Workforce picked up where Friedman and *The World Is Flat* left off. For all of its imperfections (and there are several, as I describe below), its recommendations are as bold as the challenge is big. The *New* Commission is willing to upset the applecart, challenge long-standing assumptions, and think way outside the box.

Not everyone is impressed. Jay Mathews, the *Washington Post*'s estimable education writer, has criticized the group's report because it "ignore[s] reality." Historian and critic Diane Ravitch (who serves as a trustee of the Thomas B. Fordham Foundation) calls it "pie-in-the-sky theorizing." [See Ravitch's article in this book: 'Tough Choices': Radical Ideas, Misguided Assumptions.] I don't agree. The reality is that the world is changing in leaps and bounds; tweaking our education system incrementally is not enough if we want to keep up. And who is in a better position to communicate a compelling (if politically difficult) vision than a blue-ribbon panel?

The *New* Commission's smartest ideas revolve around recruiting and retaining talented young teachers. Its report states a simple truth that today's education system would rather ignore: "More and more, the brightest and most able college graduates [are] not interested in committing themselves to lifetime careers." In an economy that is constantly churning, young employees expect challenge and opportunity, not stability and predictability. Our task in education, then, is not to replace the baby boomers with another generation of teachers who will spend 30 underpaid years in a bureaucratic system before retiring with

full benefits. Few young teachers will sign up for that deal. No, our challenge is to recruit talented people into teaching; get them up to speed quickly through rigorous preparation, on-the-job training, and meaningful support; and try to hold onto them for 10 years instead of 5, or 15 years instead of 10—all the while maximizing their effectiveness in the classroom.

So how do we do that? Tucker suggests by making starting salaries more competitive; by offering bonuses for high performance, specialized skills, or the willingness to take on tough assignments; by making our schools less hierarchical and bureaucratic; and by funding retirement accounts that are portable and flexible. In other words, by treating young teachers as we treat other young professionals in the information economy.

Another solid idea of the *New* Commission is to encourage a sizable proportion of teenagers to exit the K–12 system early. This notion springs from the insight that high school can no longer be the terminus of anyone's education; to have a shot at succeeding in the 21st-century economy, individuals need at least some college-level skills. That reality changes the equation for high school reform. Rather than ask how schools can keep students from dropping out and give them all the knowledge and skills they need to survive in the economy (a task not nearly accomplished even when the economy was less competitive), we ought to ask how high schools can prepare students for the next phase in their education and speed them on their way.

Under the *New* Commission's plan, most students would pass a test at age 16 and head off to a community or technical college. Those who demonstrated high potential would participate in rigorous high school programs like the International Baccalaureate (IB), then apply to selective four-year colleges and universities. Those who failed the test at 16 would get extra help until they passed it and would then move ahead to further education.

The benefits of this approach are myriad. For the majority of adolescents, it would equate to a "get out of jail free" card, liberating them from the boredom, irrelevance, and claustrophobic structure of the American high school. Community colleges—most of which possess an entrepreneurial gene unknown to the K–12 system—would have lots of incentives to meet the needs of these young learners and engage their minds. Those students who did well in the community colleges would continue on to a four-year college. Their peers who stayed behind and participated in IB programs and the like in their junior and senior years of high school would be immersed in achievement-oriented cultures, free of classmates who would rather not be there. And struggling students who needed remedial help would get it.

It's a compelling vision. Still, it's easy to understand why the proposals of the *New* Commission have been misinterpreted as creating a massive tracking system. By celebrating the examination systems found in other advanced nations (where, according to the report, most students have risen "to meet the expectations set by the ex-aminations, because they understood that that was the only way they could achieve their aims"), the recommendations bring to mind the kind of high-stakes, life-defining test that most Americans find abhorrent. After all, America is the land of second and third and fourth chances; we want strict assurances that our kid isn't going to be confined to sweeping streets because he flubbed a single test.

To its credit, the *New* Commission tries to provide those assurances. It insists, "Not passing [the examination] does not consign a student to a life of struggle. In fact, the idea [is] to organize the system with the aim of sending every student to college and, at the same time, making sure that every student [has] the skills to succeed in college once there."

But the *New* Commission hurts its case by not paying enough attention to the fundamental changes that will need to take place from kindergarten onward if most students are to be ready for a community college by the end of 10th grade. Sure, providing high-quality preschool to everybody (especially low-income children) would go a long way. And yes, recruiting better teachers could dramatically improve the quality of instruction in the nation's schools. But left out of the equation, except in passing, is the most basic of basics: the curriculum. If 16-year-olds are to possess a broad liberal arts education covering "all the core subjects in the curriculum," then grades K–8 are going to need to be completely rethought too.

The reason is that, by all accounts, the curriculum in many elementary and middle schools is being stripped of most content. Squeezed by No Child Left Behind's demands to raise reading and math scores and shunned by constructivists who refuse to deem any particular knowledge more valuable than any other, a broad common curriculum rich with literature and science and history and the arts is eroding. This trend is especially pronounced in schools with a concentrated population of minority students, where reading and math blocks now dominate, and everything else is deemed expendable. The *New* Commission is right to want all 16-year-olds to be broadly and liberally educated, but its recommendations fall far short of providing a road map for making that happen.

In addition, for all of their ambition for redesigning our education system, Marc Tucker and the *New* Commission are strangely humble when it comes to our students' potential. Should we settle for their goal of 20 percent or so of our students staying in rigorous high school programs and going on to selective colleges—the places most likely to spark the creativity and innovation the *New* Commission says are so in demand in today's economy? Why not aim to double or triple that number,

both by raising standards in the elementary and secondary system and by creating additional capacity in selective institutions at the tertiary level? Such an objective would be more than inspirational; it would be a good-faith indication that the *New* Commission's recommendations aren't an excuse to keep sorting students (and citizens) into winners and losers.

No, this *New* Commission hasn't figured out the magic solution for fixing our ailing schools. (Of course, there is no magic solution.) But its ideas—especially those affecting teacher compensation and high school reform—are at least worth taking seriously, trying out in a few places, learning from, and improving on. That's not the all-or-nothing approach the members of the *New* Commission might prefer, but it would take us closer to a day when, for all Americans, the "flatness" of the world won't inspire fear, but rather hope and opportunity.

Michael J. Petrilli *is a vice president of the Thomas B. Fordham Foundation, Washington, D.C.; a research fellow at Stanford University's Hoover Institution; and an executive editor of* Education Next.

Commentary

FALSE ALARM

Phi Delta Kappan
Vol. 88, no. 10. pp. 737–740
June 2007

Mr. Mishel and Mr. Rothstein challenge the economic analysis on which many
of the recommendations in *Tough Choices or Tough Times* are based.

LAWRENCE MISHEL, RICHARD ROTHSTEIN

Marc Tucker and the *New* Commission
on the Skills of the American Workforce
believe that revolutionary improvements
in education and skills are the antidote to
globalization and a corresponding deterio-
ration in U.S. living standards. As we demonstrate below, this claim is untrue.

Nonetheless, the *New* Commission's
approach to improving education gets some
things right: address income inequality and
the housing, health, and other constraints
that disadvantaged students face; boost
teacher compensation to upgrade recruitment and retention; provide prekindergarten for all 3- and 4-year-olds; and augment
school time with after-school and summer
programs. These admirable proposals need
not be justified by false notions of impend-
ing economic calamity.

This new report is a sequel to one
that the first commission issued in 1990.[1]
Then, as now, it made some reasonable
recommendations about educational improvement, but its economic analysis was
spectacularly wrong, as events have proved.
Like the new one, the earlier report saw
skill development as virtually the only policy lever for shaping the economy. The earlier report charged that inadequate skills,
which resulted from flawed schools, had
caused industrial productivity to "slow to
a crawl" and would, without radical school
reform, lead to a condition of permanently
low wages for the bottom 70 percent of all
Americans.

Yet within a few years of the 1990
report's publication, Americans' ability to
master technological change generated an

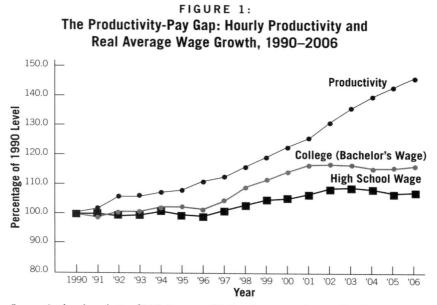

FIGURE 1:
The Productivity-Pay Gap: Hourly Productivity and Real Average Wage Growth, 1990–2006

Source: Authors' analysis of U.S. Bureau of Labor Statistics, *Current Population Survey, Outgoing Rotation Group Files and Productivity Cost Series* (www.bls.gov). Further detail on this analysis can be found in L. Mishel, J. Bernstein, and S. Allegretto, *The State of Working America 2006/2007* (Ithaca, N.Y.: Cornell University Press, 2007), appendix B.

extraordinary leap in productivity. This acceleration, exceeding that of other advanced countries, was accomplished by the very same workforce that the first commission said imperiled our future. And it created new wealth that could have supported a steady increase in Americans' standard of living.

Indeed, for a brief period, it did so. As Figure 1 shows, the late 1990s saw broad-based wage growth, increasing the living standards of all families, including both those headed by high school graduates and those headed by college graduates. Even the wages of high school dropouts climbed. But then, after 2000, wage growth stopped, and living standards fell. Yet the skills of the

workforce continue to boost productivity. In the last four years, wages of both high school- *and* college-educated workers have been stagnant, while productivity grew by an extraordinary 11.5 percent.

Workforce skills can spur productivity growth, which in turn increases national wealth, but skills cannot determine how that wealth is distributed. This is a function of policies over which schools have no influence: tax, regulatory, trade, monetary, technology, antidiscrimination, and labor market policies organize the demand *for* skilled workers and help determine how much they are paid. Continued upgrading of skills is essential for continued growth and especially for closing historic racial and ethnic income gaps but is no guarantee of economic success without policies to ensure that productivity gains are passed on to employees.

A commissioned paper, on which the *New* Commission relied, acknowledges that young college graduates "have not escaped labor market problems in recent years. Fewer young college graduates have been able to obtain college labor market jobs, and their real wages and annual earnings have declined accordingly due to rising malemployment. These young college graduates also take jobs that displace their peers with lower levels of schooling."[2]

In plain language, some college graduates are forced to take jobs requiring only a high school education. Yet Mr. Tucker, and the *New* Commission report, ignores this evidence and insists that skill shortages require us to send all (or nearly all) students to college. Mr. Tucker asserts in his article: "There is a clear divide between those who have some college and those who do not. The former are becoming ever better off. The latter are sinking fast. The fact is that education holds the key to personal and national economic well-being, more now than at any time in our history."

Not only are college graduates not becoming "ever better off." The assertion regarding those who have "some college" (not only four-year degrees) is even more inaccurate. The average real (inflation-adjusted) hourly wage for men with "some college" was no higher in 2005 than in 1973. Women's wages in this group rose only 20 percent, despite a 75 percent growth in national productivity. Wages for men and

women with "some college" have been stagnant since 2000. What economic theory did the *New* Commission employ to conclude that when wages of the most-skilled workers are stagnant or falling (and the wage gap between high school- and college-educated workers is flat), American employers must be suffering from a shortage of workforce skills? Economic data clearly indicate that we now generate sufficient skills to support healthy productivity growth and national economic competitiveness.

These workforce skills are not being rewarded, partly because the fruits of productivity growth have been redistributed from wages to profits. As for wages themselves, some college graduates—managers, executives, white-collar sales workers—have commandeered disproportionate shares of the gains, with little left over for scientists, engineers, teachers, and others with high levels of skill. No amount of school reform can undo regulatory and labor market policies that redirect wealth generated by skilled workers to profits and executive bonuses.

Mr. Tucker properly notes that those without some college are "sinking fast." But it is naive to conclude that this reflects a pure market response to relative demand for skills. An important reason that wages of workers with only a high school education have been falling faster than those of the college educated is a reformulation of labor market institutions to the disadvantage of the less educated: specifically, the real value of the minimum wage has plummeted, and as legal protections for unions have withered, so have wages in industries where unions were once powerful. Congress recently adopted an increase in the minimum wage. As a result, "returns to education" will decline as wages of less-educated workers rise. It would be foolish to conclude from this that college degrees are no longer valuable, just as it was foolish to conclude from rising returns to education—because of a falling minimum wage—that college degrees were in critically short supply.

Certainly, globalization is placing extraordinary stress on American living standards. But as Alan Blinder notes in a recent article in *Foreign Affairs,* the distinction between jobs under pressure from international competition and those that are more secure is not one of skills or education: "It is unlikely that the services of either taxi drivers or airline pilots will ever be delivered electronically over long distances. . . . Janitors and crane operators are probably immune to foreign competition; accountants and computer programmers are not."[3]

With respect to highly skilled jobs that are threatened, no school improvement can be sufficient to solve the problem on its own. The *New* Commission's report asserts that "Indian engineers make $7,500 a year against $45,000 for an American engineer with the same qualifications" and concludes that employers will continue to hire Americans only if we are better than, not only as good as, the Indians. Should American schools really be expected to graduate engineers who are five times, or even twice, as productive as those living elsewhere? School reform cannot be the

primary answer to such problems. We distract ourselves from grappling with serious economic challenges by a myopic focus on school improvement alone.

It should not be necessary to invent simplistic economic nightmares to support school improvement, and we agree with some of the *New* Commission's recommendations. But flawed economic analysis leads the panel to go beyond reasonable recommendations to several that are reckless. Space permits us to address only one: slashing contributions to teacher retirement and ending defined-benefit plans, as part of a scheme to raise teacher salaries.

The *New* Commission properly observes that if we want to recruit and retain better teachers, we must pay them more. But in an attempt to accomplish this without fully paying the price, the *New* Commission creates a myth that teacher benefits are so generous that we can reduce them and use the savings to boost salaries.

Believing this, the *New* Commission proposes to end teachers' defined-benefit pension plans (funded in advance to pay retirees a guaranteed annuity) and substitute defined-contribution or cash-balance plans (in which employers make contributions to teachers' individual retirement accounts, but in which the size of each teacher's pension depends on how savvy an investor he or she becomes). This is supposed to cut schools' contributions in half, from 12 to 6 percent of salaries, thus matching the plans of "better private employers."

We have scoured the *New* Commission's report and find no evidence to support its claim that better private employers have a lower benefit load than school systems. We don't doubt that the commission could identify some school districts with very generous benefits and some private employers with miserly packages. But the commission is using this comparison to fund a national restructuring of teacher compensation. For this purpose, only national average comparisons matter. Our own investigation suggests that the *New* Commission greatly exaggerates the relative superiority of teacher benefits and thus of the resources available to increase wages by reducing those benefits.

Pension contributions of many school districts do exceed those of many private employers, but all private employers also pay social security taxes on salaries paid to professional workers, who receive a defined-benefit social security retirement annuity to supplement their 401k's. Many teachers, however, are still not covered by social security, a fact that reduces the national average cost of teacher benefits.

The appropriate comparison would be between teacher and private sector total retirement costs, including payroll taxes (primarily social security). As Table 1 shows, K–12 teachers and all other professionals (most of whom are in the private sector) now have the same share of compensation—11.5 percent—in overall retirement and payroll tax costs. If teachers must give up defined-benefit plans, those without social security will be alone among professionals in lacking any defined-benefit safety net. There is simply no painless, cost-free way to boost salaries by raiding the benefits piggy bank.

TABLE 1: Share of Total Compensation, June 2006

	K–12 TEACHERS	ALL OTHER PROFESSIONALS
Direct wages	73.2	71.6
Paid leave	5.1	7.5
Supplemental pay	0.2	1.8
Total W-2 wages	**78.5**	**80.9**
Insurance	9.8	7.6
Pension	6.1	4.8
Payroll taxes: legally required	5.4	6.7
Other	0.2	0.0
Nonwage benefits	**21.5**	**19.1**
Total compensation	**100.0**	**100.0**
Pension and payroll taxes combined	11.5	11.5

Source: Bureau of Labor Statistics (www.bls.gov/news.release/archives/ecec_09222006.pdf, Table 2). The "paid leave" and "supplemental pay" categories are called "benefits" by BLS, but we include them here as wages because they are paid monetary compensation and included as wages in W-2s.

The *New* Commission's recommendation shifts the risk of retirement insecurity from school systems onto teachers. That this has happened more generally in the American workforce does not excuse adding teachers to this race to the bottom. The nation had a serious debate about this two years ago, when President Bush proposed a partial privatization of social security. The plan was rejected, largely from a recognition that the retirement security of all workers (or all teachers) cannot rely on their success in playing the stock market. There are always some market losers and, at times, a great many.

A great accomplishment of the past 50 years has been the provision of security to senior citizens by giving them a decent defined benefit. The nation now runs a huge risk as the private sector has, in recent decades, eroded this security by destroying private defined-benefit plans. School systems should resist this socially destructive trend, not exacerbate it. Reducing retirement security for teachers, as the *New* Commission proposes, will not help attract and retain high-quality teachers.

Note that as shown in Table 1, teacher health insurance costs exceed those of all other professionals. The *New* Commission does not propose to slash those benefits, probably because it understands that with teacher salaries lower than those of many other professionals, the same health benefits can be a larger percentage of wages for teachers than for others. As teacher wages rise, this source of phantom savings will also dry up. In any event, cutting teacher health benefits would also be socially irresponsible and will make it harder to attract and retain high-quality teachers.

We have posted our analyses of other *New* Commission recommendations on our Web site (www.epi.org/ResponseToTucker),

as well as more detailed data and illustrations regarding our discussion here of trends in productivity, wages, and benefits.

NOTES

1. *America's Choice: High Skills or Low Wages!* (Washington, D.C.: National Center on Education and the Economy, June 1990).
2. Andrew Sum and others, "Educational and Labor Market Outcomes for the Nation's Teens and Young Adults Since the Publication of *America's Choice*: A Critical Assessment," paper commissioned by the National Center on Education and the Economy, 2006, available at http://skillscommission.org/pdf/commissioned_papers/Education%20and%20Labor%20Market%20Outcomes.pdf.
3. Alan S. Blinder, "Offshoring: The Next Industrial Revolution," *Foreign Affairs,* March–April 2006, www.foreignaffairs.org/20060301faessay85209)/alan-s-blinder/offshoring-the-next-industrial-revolution.html.

Lawrence Mishel is president of the Economic Policy Institute, Washington, D.C., where Richard Rothstein is a research associate.

The Economic Case for Education Reform

Phi Delta Kappan
Vol. 88, no. 10, pp. 741–743
June 2007

To conclude this special section devoted to the report *Tough Choices or Tough Times,* Mr. Tucker reviews the points on which he and his respondents agree and defends the ones on which they disagree.

Marc S. Tucker

The most striking aspect of these three critiques [by Denis Doyle, Michael Petrilli, and Lawrence Mishel and Richard Rothstein] is the position each takes with respect to the economic analysis contained in the first half of *Tough Choices or Tough Times,* the report of the *New* Commission on the Skills of the American Workforce. Michael Petrilli and Denis Doyle characterize the economic analysis as obviously accurate and old news. Lawrence Mishel and Richard Rothstein spend most of their space assailing the same economic analysis as obviously flawed.

The economic analysis in the report is a red flag to Mishel and Rothstein for different reasons. Mishel is affiliated with a group of economists who are committed to the view that government has an obligation to create policies to ameliorate the effects of capitalism on the poor. This group views arguments of the kind made in the commission's report as weapons that their political opponents can use to prove that education alone will get people out of poverty and that the nation therefore need not invest in everything from food stamps to social security to tax credits for the working poor. Rothstein represents the views of educators who deeply resent being blamed for the failings of American business when the economy is doing poorly and never being thanked when the economy is doing well.

I am actually quite sympathetic to both sentiments, but they have little bearing on the commission's report.

Mishel and Rothstein attempt to discredit the report by demolishing statements that the report never actually makes. They set up their argument by saying that the commission sees "skill development as virtually the *only* policy lever for shaping the economy" (emphasis in original). Actually that is not true. On page 22 of *Tough Choices or Tough Times,* we say, "Successfully running a national economy based on technological growth depends on assured strength in many areas," and we go on to provide a long paragraph filled with examples that have nothing to do with elementary and secondary education, including strong research universities, sustained national investment in basic research, good protections for intellectual property, and the availability of venture capital. The fact is that we never said that skill development is virtually the only policy lever for shaping the economy.

And no serious economic analyst would say that it was. But why was it so important for Mishel and Rothstein to attribute that view to the commission? Because, short of that extreme position, one can maintain only that skill development is an important tool for shaping the economy. That is in fact our position. But Mishel and Rothstein know that it is very hard for them to attack that position, much as they might wish to do so. Three distinguished economists—Theodore Schultz, Robert Solow, and Gary Becker—won the Nobel Prize in economics for their contributions to the conclusion that education is a major contributor to economic growth, which is the very position that the commission's report takes. That is why Denis Doyle said that "the notion

that education . . . is the source of most wealth is by now old news."

But what about the other complaint: that the report's premises are obviously wrong, given that the United States experienced extraordinary economic success in the 1990s, immediately following the release of the first commission's report in 1990, in which we said that our country's economy was in jeopardy because of our poor educational performance? Surely, they say, such economic success following such dire predictions shows how unfounded those predictions were!

No, actually, it doesn't. Though economists believe that investments in people's knowledge and skills are among the most important investments we can make in economic growth, they also point out that these investments have among the longest lead times of any public investments we can make. Consider the current report. Judging by past events, it could easily take 20 years or more for the ideas in this report to be implemented at scale. From that point forward, it could take close to 20 additional years before most of the 3-year-olds affected by those policies operating at scale have entered the workforce. And it would be years beyond that before the people who had been educated under the new system constituted a majority of the workforce.

That amounts to a 50-year lead time between the point at which the recommendations are made and the time that the full effects of those recommendations are felt in the workforce. The economic boom of the 1990s was largely the result of the enormous productivity improvements that we achieved as a result of the flight of highly talented refugees from Hitler during World War II; the magnet we subsequently became for talent from China, India, and other Asian countries; the enormous investments we made during World War II and in the postwar years in basic and applied research; the wisdom of the investments made through the GI Bill; the great expansion in secondary and higher education during the 1950s and 1960s; and so on. All of these investments, combined with the unique advantages the United States enjoyed in terms of availability of venture capital, protections of intellectual property rights, and our high tolerance for business failure and support for those willing to take risk, made the 1990s possible. Far from disproving the connection between investment in people's skills and economic outcomes, the 1990s actually prove the point.

Because of the long lead times involved in this sort of investment, it is particularly important to ask how the student body is likely to change over the period in question. We point out in the commission's new report that the current heavy flow of immigrants from countries with poor education systems means that we will have to greatly improve the performance of our education system just to maintain current levels of student achievement, a point that Mishel and Rothstein ignore.

Mishel and Rothstein sarcastically ask what economic theory suggests that employers are short of skilled workers when wages for people with some college are flat. Actually, what the data show is that the

returns to education are greater now than they have ever been before, meaning that the correlation is tighter between what you know and what you earn than ever before, and the difference in earnings between those who have more education and those who have less is growing steadily greater. We point out in the report that the middle class is getting smaller, but not because all of its members are getting poorer. Those with less education are getting poorer, and those with more are getting richer. This is exactly what the theory of supply and demand would predict. The price of highly educated labor is going up because the demand for it is going up faster than the supply. The price of low-skill labor is going down because the supply is ever larger and the demand is steadily decreasing.

Interestingly, Mishel and Rothstein never mention the section of the report that chronicles the steadily rising costs of our elementary and secondary education system, over time and in relation to the systems of other countries; the failure to substantially improve student achievement despite that rise in costs; and the steady increase in the number of other countries that outperform the United States in measured student achievement and attainment. Can they seriously believe that these statistics do not threaten the ability of the United States to maintain or improve the standard of living for the American people? Their comments appear to suggest that the only important issue is how our wealth is shared among us. That is an important issue, though not one that this commission was established to investigate. But surely, it matters just as much how much wealth there is to divide and what it will take for individuals to succeed in the intense competition that lies ahead. That is the issue we addressed.

I turn now to the critiques of the report's recommendations. Doyle's primary quarrel with the recommendations is not that they would not be effective ways to improve the system, but rather that the powers that be will not allow them to see the light of day. Only events will prove him right or wrong, but I have another, less pessimistic, view.

Doyle notes that the accelerated graduation recommendation is no more than many other countries have been doing for years, but says it has no chance of enactment here. Why? Because we are so committed to access and equity in higher education. We have had a chance to talk with a number of state P–16 councils, representatives of national higher education associations, state higher education boards, and state legislators since the report was released. They know that the current system is not working, that the majority of high school students never get to higher education, and that a majority of those who do, drop out because they cannot do the work. They know that is neither access nor equity. When we point out that our plan would prepare a much, much larger proportion of high school students for college and make sure that they are ready to do college-level work when they arrive, we get very positive responses. Based on what I have seen so far, I think there are much stronger grounds for optimism than Doyle allows.

Referring to the commission's recommendation concerning contract schools, Doyle asks whether he alone remembers the performance-contracting "fiasco" run by the Office of Economic Opportunity. But he does not say whether he regards that fiasco as a failure of design, implementation, politics, timing, or something else altogether. It is clear that some charter schools are brilliant successes and others abject failures and that some of the difference is attributable to the degree to which they are held strictly accountable for the performance of the students in their care. A large part of our economy runs quite successfully under the concept that an organization will be paid to deliver services under a contract that stipulates the standards of performance that must be met in order to retain that contract. It is hard on the face of it see why this concept should not be applied to those who would educate our children.

Finally, Doyle challenges the commission's proposal for reallocation of funds within the system, again, not on the grounds that the ideas are misguided, but on the grounds that the system will not permit the proposed savings to be realized. That may or may not be true, but if it is true, our country's prospects for significantly improving our education system are very poor. Based on the response that our report has gotten among elected officials since it was released, I am actually quite confident that we are going to be able to find a few states lucky enough to have political leaders willing to take on these issues and succeed. And all we need are a few states. That is how real reform always starts.

Petrilli finds a lot to like in the report but wonders whether we go far enough. He points out that if we are to make the kinds of changes the commission wants in the secondary school curriculum, then the elementary school curriculum will have to be rethought, too. Amen, I say.

And he asks whether we were sufficiently ambitious in projecting the proportion of students who could benefit from a demanding curriculum like the International Baccalaureate program or a program made up of AP courses. It is true that our estimate of that proportion, though larger than the present number, was still modest relative to the whole cohort of students. We aimed to be realistic, but we would applaud any state that chooses to set its sights higher.

Which brings me back to Mishel and Rothstein. They actually begin their assault with praise for the commission's attention to income inequality, the special challenges faced by disadvantaged students, improved teacher compensation, preschool for all, and augmented school time when necessary. The only recommendation they chose to take issue with was the one having to do with teacher compensation. They do not object to our recommendations for greatly adding to teachers' cash compensation. But they do object to changing teachers' retirement benefits from the current defined-benefit plans to defined-contribution or cash-balance plans, as the commission recommends. Their claim that teachers' benefits are not out of line with those of most other Americans is based on a complex analysis. Our analysis, which comes up with a very different conclusion, is equally complex, so we have put it up on our Web site (www.skillscommission.org) for all who wish to peruse it.

But Mishel and Rothstein do not argue with our assertion that what we propose is nothing more than providing for school teachers the same retirement systems and benefits that college teachers now have. It is hard to see why teacher unions, many of whose members are college teachers, should object to having K–12 teachers living with the same system, about which the college teachers have never complained. But more to the point, we would have the states offer practicing teachers their choice: either join the new system or stick with the one you have. No serving teacher, under our proposals, would be forced to enter the new system. But by offering young people a whole new deal that provides much higher cash compensation, we could attract the best and brightest of our college entrants to teaching. And Mishel and Rothstein never tell us why they object to that.

Marc S. Tucker is president of the National Center on Education and the Economy.

Improper Diagnosis, Reckless Treatment

Phi Delta Kappan
Vol. 89, no. 1, pp. 31–32, 49–51
September 2007

Continuing the debate begun in the *Kappan* last June, Mr. Mishel and
Mr. Rothstein present more evidence to counter what they view as erroneous assertions
and unsound recommendations from the *Tough Choices or Tough Times* report.

Lawrence Mishel, Richard Rothstein

In the June *Kappan,* Marc Tucker summarized the *Tough Choices* report. We (and others) critiqued it, and he responded. We charged Tucker with trying to stampede policymakers into adopting reckless school reform recommendations by asserting, without evidence, that an emerging international economy made our K–12 schools obsolete and by claiming that adoption of the report's proposals could prevent middle-class living standards from falling.

International digital competition is real, but increasing the supply of college graduates will not make wages rise for a group whose earnings are already stagnant. *Tough Choices* insists that our future competitiveness requires 95 percent of all students to be college-ready at a new, higher academic standard, but it provides no jus-

tification for contradicting the Bureau of Labor Statistics (BLS) projection that fewer than one-third of future jobs will require college degrees at today's lower standard. The BLS also expects not more than another quarter or so of new jobs to require some college training.[1]

Tough Choices is the sequel to a report issued in 1990 by a predecessor group, which attributed the nation's low productivity growth in the 1970s and 1980s to inadequate American schools. But in the June *Kappan,* we showed that this analysis proved to be "spectacularly wrong." Since the mid-1990s, the productivity of American workers (educated in the 1970s and 1980s) has accelerated at historically unprecedented levels and indeed has been rising faster than in any other industrialized nation. This productivity renaissance relied on the very workforce whose skills were criticized in the earlier report. If American middle-class living standards are threatened, we argued, it cannot be because workers lack competitive skills.

Rather, the richest Americans have commandeered the fruits of this productivity growth and denied fair shares to the workers, educated in American schools, who have created increased national wealth.[2] The middle class, in short, is threatened not by lack of skills but by poor pay for skilled jobs. Social and economic policy reform, not school transformation, must be the remedy for this middle-class squeeze.

As we said in June, we are not satisfied with our schools. We are concerned about the academic, cultural, civic, and moral preparedness of today's young people; we consider it urgent to reduce gaps in outcomes that fall along lines of race, ethnicity, and income. But school inadequacies are not generating economic crisis, and so school reforms motivated by false expectations of economic collapse are bound to be misguided. In any field, proper diagnosis is a precondition for effective treatment.

In his June response, Tucker belittled our analysis, claiming that Mishel only wanted to deflect attention to economic policies advocated by his institute and that Rothstein only represented the views of educators who resented being blamed for national economic failures. We will not use our space here to respond in kind to this attack on our motives but urge him to stick to the issues in his rejoinder to this article.

Tucker also denied our charge that his report sees "skill development as virtually the only policy lever for shaping the economy." But here is how he himself summarized the report: "The fact is that education holds *the key* to personal and national economic well-being, more now than at any time in our history" (emphasis added).[3] We judge our summary of this theme to be fair.

Tucker next claimed that the past decade's productivity surge does not reflect the skills of workers graduating from contemporary American schools; rather, he attributes it to returning World War II veterans educated by the GI Bill and to education advances during the 1950s and 1960s. There is a 50-year lag, he asserted, between educational improvement and productivity growth.

While technological change certainly accumulates over many years, returning World War II veterans were in their prime working years back in the 1950s and 1960s. However good their educations, they can't have caused productivity growth from 1996 to 2006. That growth was created by workers whose skills the first commission bemoaned: those educated in the 1970s and 1980s in schools that, like today's, the commission alleged were bad enough to risk our economic future. The prime-age workforce (ages 25 to 54) in 2006 would have finished high school between 1970 and 1999. No reader of the *New* Commission's report could possibly infer that it intends to link today's inadequate schools only with economic conditions 50 years in the future. The report concerns the plight of today's middle class and attributes it to today's schools, not to those of two generations ago.

Tucker claims to follow in the footsteps of Nobel Prize winners who properly showed that education is a major contributor to economic growth. But those Nobel prizes had nothing to do with Tucker's analysis, which rues the stagnation of middle-class living standards and growing wage inequality, not lack of economic growth. Generating higher productivity will not lead to higher living standards unless we distribute the fruits of growth equitably to the workers who produced it. This has not been happening.

Tucker finds it significant that there are high "returns to education" (wages of college graduates relative to wages of those with only high school). Yes, college graduates have higher wages than others, yet the wage gap between those with college and those with only high school has been relatively flat for a number of years. Average salaries of college-educated workers have been rising rapidly for only some college graduates: sales and managerial workers, not professionals with the scientific and technical skills that Tucker claims are in short supply.

Here's one illustration. The multiple of CEO to average-worker pay jumped from 100 in 1996 to 262 in 2005.[4] Such a jump (with almost-as-dramatic increases for managers below the CEO level) pushes up the "returns to education" statistic, but it says nothing about alleged shortages of skills that schools provide to average workers. A lower minimum wage, eroded

unionism, deregulation, immigration, and imports of manufactured products all contribute to the wage gap (by lowering the wages of workers without college educations). The jobs these workers perform (increasingly in service industries) will not disappear because we improve schools. To combat these trends, we must look to the nation's economic policies.

We agree with the *New* Commission proposal to improve teacher quality by raising teacher compensation—talk of raising quality without doing so would be hollow. But the report urges that such raises be financed in part by abolishing defined-benefit pensions and substituting defined-contribution plans at half the cost.[5] This, the report asserts, will bring teacher pensions in line with those of professionals employed by the "better private employers." Raising salaries without having to pay new money is seductive, but, unfortunately, there is no teacher-benefits piggy bank. As we showed in the June issue, private employers now contribute the same share of total compensation for professionals' retirement, on average, as do states and school districts for teacher retirement. Certainly teacher pension costs are not double those of the "better firms."

Tucker stresses the defined-contribution plans of college teachers, suggesting that if teacher pensions were similar, there would be big savings to be used for teacher compensation. The BLS collects data on the share of total compensation attributable to retirement (pensions plus payroll taxes, which are mostly social security) for K–12 teachers and for all teachers (including college): 11.5 percent for K–12 teachers, but 11.7 percent for all teachers combined, meaning that retirement payments are greater, not less, for postsecondary faculty than for K–12 teachers.

We did a brief Web search and e-mail survey of colleagues who teach at colleges around the country, including public and private, elite and nonelite institutions, and confirmed that colleges make consistently higher contributions for retirement than K–12 schools do.[6] Take California, for example, the largest state. If Tucker's calculations don't work here, they are unlikely to work in most states. California K–12 teachers are covered by the kind of defined-benefit plan that he denounces. School districts contribute 8.5 percent of salary to the plan, and the state contributes another 2 percent. California has opted out of social security for teachers, so social security payroll taxes are not incurred.

At the University of California and the California State University, faculty members are covered by defined-benefit plans, contrary to Tucker's claim that college teachers don't have such unreasonably generous pensions. In the case of the University of California, contributions to the plan have been so substantial that it is now overfunded, and no contributions were added in 2007. But the university does cover faculty members under social security. California State University also provides a defined-benefit plan, plus social security. As for private institutions, the University of Southern California contributes 10 percent of faculty salaries to defined-contribution plans, plus social security, which together

account for a total employer retirement cost of about 15 percent.[7] Stanford University, Pomona College, and Occidental College do the same.

Information on many college retirement plans is publicly available on the Web. We are distressed not only that Tucker would make such flawed claims without careful research but that the distinguished group of Americans who make up the *New* Commission did not ask for better evidence before signing on to an ill-conceived proposal to wipe out the teacher retirement system nationwide.

Tucker claimed that the pension analysis was "complex" and referred *Kappan* readers to the *New* Commission's Web site for more detail. We urge readers to go there. They will see that the *New* Commission came up with its savings by saying that to be comparable to college faculty plans, states and schools would have to contribute only 6 percent of salary. But the *New* Commission's own consultant report observes that the figure should be 10 percent, not 6 percent. The estimates by the consultants excluded states in which K–12 employees are not covered by social security; they eliminated large states from their comparisons, for no reason other than that the states were large. After these (and a few other) contortions, the consultants examined retirement plans only in the unrepresentative states of Arkansas, Idaho, Indiana, Maryland, Mississippi, Utah, and West Virginia to conclude that schools nationwide could save money by converting to college faculty–type pensions. This cannot be considered research serious enough for policymakers or anyone else to follow.

There is a point of view abroad in the nation today that sees teacher self-interest and unionism as the biggest impediments to school improvement. Perhaps this is why the *New* Commission's poorly reasoned assertion that teacher pensions can be cut in half without serious consequences has been greeted without protest by editorial writers and policymakers.

We have devoted so much space to this retirement issue, a small part of the *New* Commission's report, because it reflects a pattern of unsupported claims. Here is another claim that does not hold up: the report asserts that we hire "a disproportionate share of our teachers from among the less able of the high school students who go to college" and that reforms are needed to "recruit from the top third." Admittedly, even a single low-ability teacher is "a disproportionate share," but *Tough Choices* was no more specific. In e-mail correspondence, however, *New* Commission representatives made clear to us that they intended to reference the "fact" that most teachers now come from the bottom third of the ability distribution of college students.

This claim about teacher ability is also not supported by evidence. An urban myth, it originally arose from analyses of questionnaires completed by high school students when they took the SAT. Teenagers with lower scores were more likely to say they hoped to be teachers. That's it. There was no survey to determine if these SAT test takers actually entered college, actually completed it, or actually became teachers.

Two well-known studies the *New* Commission ignored have made a mockery of the claim. One found that in 2000, 58 percent of all female teachers from the high school class of 1992 came from the top two quintiles of the ability distribution of high school graduates. Only 21 percent came from the bottom two quintiles.[8]

Another study, conducted by the Educational Testing Service in 1999, compared the verbal SAT scores of those who passed the Praxis II exam (and were thus likely actually to become teachers) to that of all college graduates. Praxis II passers in most secondary education fields (including English, social studies, math, and science) had higher ability than the average college graduate. Praxis II passers in elementary and special education had lower ability than the average college graduate but still had higher ability than the average SAT test taker.[9]

We should certainly try to recruit more teachers from the highest-ability quintiles, but we are not likely to make smart recruitment and certification changes if we understate the ability of current teachers.

The report also repeats the conventional view that one-third of all entering high school students drop out. In previous work, we have demonstrated that this finding relies on flawed uses of school administrative data and that all available longitudinal and household surveys find high school completion to be 80 percent or more.[10] The ongoing subject of scholarly examination, our conclusion remains controversial, and understandably, the report does not simply adopt our view. But it is remarkable that it does not even acknowledge the debate among professional experts regarding its dire conclusion. On our Web site (www. epi.org/ResponseToTucker), we offer new evidence regarding this attainment controversy.

Tough Choices also makes the extraordinary claim that only 18 percent of ninth-graders complete an associate or a bachelor's degree. This statistic may fit Tucker's dour preconceptions of educational performance, but it is wildly off the mark. Census data show that in 2006, 8 percent of 25- to 29-year-olds had a bachelor's degree and another 9 percent had an associate degree. Even those most skeptical of the census don't claim that the data are off by 100 percent.

The *New* Commission report, in sum, rests on a wildly exaggerated indictment of public education: that it has left Americans unprepared for economic competition, that it focuses on overly generous benefits for teachers at the expense of student achievement, that its teaching force is of the poorest quality, and that it fails to graduate large numbers of youths. If readers accept this dire picture, they are less likely to scrutinize the report's more radical recommendations with the care they deserve. And the report itself condones such carelessness by insisting that the crisis is so severe that its recommendations must be adopted in their entirety, all at once, without examining each separately on its merits.[11]

As we noted in June, some *New* Commission recommendations (such as better early childhood preparation and higher teacher compensation and quality) make sense. Others, like the abolition of the teacher retirement system to increase salaries, are reckless and based on false information. Here is another. The report proposes to abolish school districts and have all schools operated by contract between private providers and school boards. These schools would be "accountable for the results" and have "meaningful consequences for failure." The report says these are not quite charter schools, because all would hire state-certified teachers and adopt a standardized curriculum. But in essence, this is the charter school idea, made universal.

Has charter school experience in the past 15 years been so positive as to justify abolishing districts and operating every school on contract? We have elsewhere concluded that charter school achievement has not been superior to that of regular schools for similar students, presumably because, while some charter schools are excellent, others are inferior.[12] This finding is now widely accepted. The authors of the report must have thought that this evidence was irrelevant because they believe that standardized teacher certification and curriculum alone can ensure that no contract school will perform poorly.

Such confidence is misplaced, not in the least because nobody knows how to identify, before certification, superbly competent teachers, and there are no standardized curricula that command widespread support. Poor performance will still sometimes result. Charter school advocates' most conspicuous embarrassment has been their failure to deliver "meaningful consequences for failure." There is nothing in the *New* Commission's proposals that would lead to more effective accountability for its contract schools.

Chester Finn, one of the nation's most prominent advocates of charter schools, has long insisted that poor charter schools would be closed by public authorities. When the *New* Commission report was issued, Finn observed, "In the specialized universe of blue-ribbon panel reports on reforming U.S. education, this new planet gets an honors grade."[13] Recently, however, he had this to say:

"It's far harder than theorists thought to actually close a mediocre (or even bad) school. I plead guilty to having helped to propagate a naive doctrine here. Unless its students face imminent danger or someone has fled to Bermuda with the payroll, shuttering a school is a tricky business. Parents and kids usually like their school, no matter its low test scores and torpid curriculum, and don't want it closed any more than do the clients of a surplus district school. Worse, there may be no better educational option in the vicinity. (Remember why these families opted for the charter school in the first place.) Moreover, many charter boards and operators have deep community, political, and institutional ties about which one must think twice before severing. What if the school is the darling of local business leaders and philanthropists? A "ministry" of a major local church? A path down which a wary school district might be drawn into chartering? One doesn't casually close (or non-renew) such a school."[14]

In other words, the very premise on which charter schools have been supported—accountability for ends, not means—has proved a chimera. Wouldn't it be prudent to see if this aspect of chartering can be fixed before proposing to convert the entire system to this model?

Space does not permit us to examine the report's many other recommendations, some meritorious, others dubious. It is remarkable that this distinguished group of commissioners, many of whom we hold in high esteem, would adopt such radical proposals with so little oversight or demand for evidence. The *New* Commission report says more about the state of debate about education in America today than about the state of American education.

NOTES

1. Daniel E. Hecker, "Occupational Employment Projections to 2014," *Monthly Labor Review,* November 2005, pp. 70–101 (www.bls.gov/opub/mlr/2005/11/art5full. pdf). See also Lawrence Mishel, Jared Bernstein, and Sylvia Allegretto, *The State of Working America 2006/2007* (Washington, D.C.: Economic Policy Institute, 2006), Table 3.48, available at www.stateofworking america.org.

2. A figure from our June article, showing the widening gap between productivity growth and wages, is posted on our Web site at www.epi.org/ResponseToTucker.

3. Marc Tucker, "Making Tough Choices," *Phi Delta Kappan,* June 2007, p. 729.

4. Mishel, Bernstein, and Allegretto, *The State of Working America 2006/2007,* Figure 3Z.

5. The *New* Commission would do this gradually and would grandfather the pensions of current teachers.

6. Our survey results, along with further comments on Tucker's response to this article, are posted at www.epi.org/ResponseToTucker.

7. The social security employer contribution rate is 6.2 percent of salary, up to a maximum of $90,000. Because some faculty members earn more than $90,000, we estimate an average payroll tax of 5 percent.

8. Sean P. Corcoran, William N. Evans, and Robert M. Schwab, "Teacher Quality: Changing Labor Market Opportunities for Women and the Quality of Teachers, 1957–2000," *AEA Papers and Proceedings, American Economic Review*, May 2004, pp. 230–235.

9. Drew H. Gitomer, Andrew S. Latham, and Robert Ziomek, *The Academic Quality of Prospective Teachers: The Impact of Admissions and Licensure Testing* (Princeton, N.J.: Educational Testing Service, 1999), available at www.ets.org/praxis/researchrpt.html.

10. Lawrence Mishel and Joydeep Roy, *Rethinking High School Graduation Rates and Trends* (Washington, D.C.: Economic Policy Institute, 2006), available at www.epi.org/content.cfm/book_grad_rates.

11. When confronted with our evidence, several commission members have told us that they had supported the report's conclusions only as a way to stimulate discussion. The commission report, however, says: "We do not intend to encourage cherry picking only those ideas that cost the least and offend the fewest. . . . We do not propose a collection of initiatives. We propose a system that has its own integrity."

12. Martin Carnoy, Rebecca Jacobsen, Lawrence Mishel, and Richard Rothstein, *The Charter School Dust-Up: Examining the Evidence on Enrollment and Achievement* (Washington, D.C.: Economic Policy Institute, 2005), available at www.epinet.org/content.cfm/book_charter school.

13. Chester E. Finn Jr., "Short Reviews of New Reports and Books: *Tough Choices or Tough Times: Report of the* New *Commission on the Skills of the American Workforce,*" *Education Gadfly*, December 14, 2006, available at www.edexcellence.net/foundation/gadfly/issue.cfm?edition=&id=269#3160.

14. Chester E. Finn Jr., "From Checker's Desk: Two Years, Ten Lessons," *Education Gadfly*, May, 24, 2007, available at www.edexcellence.net/foundation/gadfly/issue.cfm?id=292#3415.

Lawrence Mishel *is president of the Economic Policy Institute, Washington, D.C., where* ***Richard Rothstein*** *is a research associate.*

Reckless and Wildly Exaggerated? We Don't Think So!

A Response to Mishel and Rothstein

Phi Delta Kappan
Vol. 89, no. 1, pp. 52–54
September 2007

Mr. Tucker takes issue with Mr. Mishel and Mr. Rothstein's critique [in the preceding article] of the *New* Commission on the Skills of the American Workforce report and refutes the critics' claims.

Marc S. Tucker

Here is how Lawrence Mishel and Richard Rothstein put the core of their critique: "The *New* Commission report, in sum, rests on a wildly exaggerated indictment of public education: that it has left Americans unprepared for economic competition, that it is focused on overly generous benefits for teachers at the expense of student achievement, that its teaching force is of the poorest quality, and that it fails to graduate large numbers of youths. If readers accept this dire picture, they are less likely to scrutinize the report's more radical recommendations with the care they deserve."

Let me take this indictment of the report apart, piece by piece.

- *The failure to build a first-class public education system has endangered our ability to compete.* First, we certainly did say that this country's failure to build a first-class public education system has endangered America's ability to compete. The data from the Organisation for Economic Co-operation and Development (OECD) and the Third International Mathematics and Science Study clearly show that we have one of the most expensive and least effective public education systems in the world. These critics never take issue with those findings. What they do appear to argue is that these findings don't matter.

In support of that argument, Mishel and Rothstein cite Bureau of Labor Statistics

(BLS) projections concerning the numbers of jobs that will require people with some college education and with college degrees, and they say that our report provided no justification for contradicting these predictions.

The *New* Commission on the Skills of the American Workforce did recommend greatly increasing the quality and quantity of well-educated high school graduates in the workforce, but we said nothing about how many of them should go on to college. So, whether our recommendations differ from the BLS projections is hard to say.

But the whole first part of the report is devoted to the presentation of an argument that the integration of the global labor market is creating a new economic environment in which workers in the United States are competing head on with other workers at the same skill levels around the world. Moreover, these foreign workers are willing to work for much less than American workers, and this competition will drive American wages (and the American standard of living) down. The only way to deal with this challenge, we argued, is to produce the most highly skilled, most creative, and most innovative workforce in the world. And we showed in the report, using OECD data, that the United States, instead of improving its relative standing, is falling further and further behind other nations, including some less-developed nations, in the proportion of the workforce with the equivalent of a high school diploma. The same thing is now true of the proportion of the U.S. workforce with higher education credentials.

Mishel and Rothstein never rebutted this analysis. They simply ignored our whole central economic argument.

- *A focus on overly generous benefits for teachers at the expense of student achievement.* Teacher benefits are not even mentioned in the executive summary of the commission report. This is one of many instances in which Mishel and Rothstein either critique the report they wished we had written, rather than the one we actually wrote, or pick up on a minor theme in the report on which they think we are vulnerable, apparently in the hope of destroying our credibility on the points they really care about.

When Augenblick, Palaich and Associates analyzed teacher compensation, including benefits [see their analysis in this volume], the aspects of which vary wildly among the states, the aim was to pick a set of states for the analysis that was broadly representative, including states that others would view as similar to themselves and that had data to make it possible to do valid—"apple to apple"—comparisons. That is how we got our list. That approach seemed to the commission to be careful and responsible, far more responsible than considering only the case of California in characterizing the state of teacher compensation in the United States, which is what Mishel and Rothstein appear to be suggesting.

On another important point, the trade-off we discuss is not between teachers' benefits and student achievement but between teachers' salaries and teachers' benefits. We propose substantially raising teacher salaries, funded in part by switching to a defined-contribution system more typical of college teachers. Mishel and Rothstein appear to imply that the commission's proposals would have the teachers pay for their own raises with a comparable decrease in their benefits. That is simply not true. The $6 billion that is saved by reducing teachers' benefits is only 10 percent of the roughly $60 billion that is reinvested in the commission's recommendations. If all of the savings from the new benefits program were invested in raises for teachers, that amount is still only one-third of the total increase in teachers' salaries proposed by the commission. And, I say again, in our plan, not one teacher would have his or her benefits changed from a defined-benefit to a defined-contribution plan unless that person volunteered to participate in the new plan.

- *The teaching force is of the poorest quality.* Here again, Mishel and Rothstein take issue with things we did not say. In this case, what we said was not that the teaching force is of the poorest quality but that *in the future,* this country will have a teaching force of very low quality if we do not do something now to prevent that outcome. We were careful to point out that the majority of the current members of our teaching workforce were recruited to teaching in an era in which women and minorities with college degrees had few choices of

professional careers open to them other than teaching. As a result, the United States got much better teachers than it deserved. But we also pointed out that young women and minorities with college degrees have many more attractive opportunities today and that in the future we can expect—as a result of the current policies related to teachers' compensation and working conditions—to have teachers of much lower quality than those who are in the job now. This change will come about as the teachers hired years ago are replaced by those currently being recruited.

We stand behind that assertion and will use the more rigorous of the two studies that Mishel and Rothstein cited to make our points. That study is a 2002 paper by Sean Corcoran, William Evans, and Robert Schwab, titled "Changing Labor Market Opportunities for Women and the Quality of Teachers 1957–1992," available for a fee on the National Bureau of Economic Research Web site. Here, in a nutshell, is what the authors of that paper said about their findings.

First, they pointed to prior research, which they summarize as saying that "[the test scores of] students choosing teaching as a profession during the 1970s and 80s did not compare favorably to those of their graduate student peers." They highlight Phil Schlechty and Victor Vance's 1982 study (because of its superior quality), which showed that college graduates from the class of 1972 (identified as teachers in

1979) "came disproportionately from the bottom two quintiles of the SAT score distribution." And then they cite several cross-sectional studies that found "a negative relationship between academic ability and the likelihood of entering teaching among college graduates."

Then they look at the data from the four longitudinal studies on which they focused their own analysis. After presenting the data, they conclude that "results thus far suggest that the positive relationship between academic ability and entry into teaching among female high school graduates has indeed weakened over time."

And then they focus particularly on the individuals with the highest measured ability in math and literacy. Whereas close to 20 percent of females in the top decile in 1964 chose teaching as a profession (teaching was the most frequently reported occupation among this group in 1964), "only *3.7 percent* of top decile females were teaching in 1992" (emphasis in original).

In sum, teachers have not compared favorably to the other professions with respect to mathematics and literacy ability for a long time, and in the two decades ending in 1992, the situation had gotten steadily worse, with women of the highest ability levels abandoning teaching for other careers at an astonishing rate.

The story told by this study ends in 1992, 15 years ago. It is only in recent years, well after the end of the period covered by this paper, that women have outnumbered men in law schools, business schools, and other professional schools in which their numbers were far lower during the period covered by the paper. It is reasonable to infer that the trends described by the authors of this paper can only have accelerated since 1992. This paper offers a very powerful confirmation of the commission's thesis.

- *The system fails to graduate large numbers of youths.* Mishel and Rothstein charge that we have grossly exaggerated the proportion of the student body that drops out of high school. At the same time they accuse us of greatly exaggerating this number, they acknowledge that our view is the "conventional" view! If it is the conventional view, it is, by definition, held by most of the people who have done research on it. Certainly, a very well-documented Educational Testing Service Policy Report confirms our view, along with a whole shelf of other studies, which continue to come out regularly. According to the OECD, the United States has the highest dropout rate in the developed world. It turns out that the reason Mishel and Rothstein described our analysis as controversial is simply because they are among the few who disagree with it.

IN SUM

The whole critique of the commission's analysis put forth by Mishel and Rothstein comes down to a charge that we have played fast and loose with the facts. No, we haven't. In fact, the commissioners said over and over again how impressed they

were with the range and depth of the research the staff had done over a two-year
period of intensive work.

Apart from the dispute over pensions,
Mishel and Rothstein took issue with only
one of our recommendations, the one concerning contract schools, which they characterize as charter schools in disguise. And
they present the idea of charter schools as
a failure, in the light of the low quality of
many of these schools. Few chartering authorities (for the most part, states and districts) have come to grips with the need to
shut down their charter schools if they fail
to perform. We would do exactly that. If
these contract schools are charter schools,
they are not the kind of charter schools
that the United States has had up to now,
and they will be much more effective.
What the commission did was get beyond
the arguments about vouchers and charter
schools and propose a way to get all the
advantages of competition and choice without abandoning either public schools or the
need for strict accountability for results.

Mishel and Rothstein would address
this country's social and economic problems by resurrecting the policies of the
New Deal, an era long gone, when America's economic borders were effectively
sealed, long before the Internet became the
world's communication highway. It is time
to face the facts posed by the new realities
of an era in which our workers are competing directly with workers all over the globe,
workers who are increasingly better educated, many of whom are willing to work
for much lower wages. We cannot turn
back the clock. Families in Hyderabad and
Bangalore, in Shanghai and Xian, and in
Copenhagen, Brussels, Sydney, and Perth
are absolutely convinced that education
and skills are the key to their future, and
they are determined to seize that future.
We don't have to beat them, but we do
have to join them in that conviction.

To succeed, we will have to renovate
the American education system from stem
to stern if we are to match the performance
of those countries that are doing the best
job of educating their children. Will that be
hard? Sure. Can it be done? Sure. Will we
do it? Only if we are convinced that our future and that of our children depend on it.

This is why Mishel and Rothstein's critique is so disappointing. They would have
you believe that the performance of our
education system has no bearing on our
children's economic future. Nothing could
be further from the truth. Denial is not
only dangerous. It is utterly irresponsible.

*Marc S. Tucker is president of the National
Center on Education and the Economy.*

Appendixes

THE STUDY

The Commission staff began the research on which the Commission itself relied 18 months before the first meeting of the Commission and continued the research right up to the last meeting.

Each substudy is briefly described below, and the associated papers listed. In most cases, those papers prepared by our staff and the papers commissioned from others are available on the Commission Web site.

Extensive field work was required to complete these studies. A list of the nations and organizations visited is also included below.

All but one of the background papers in the report itself were prepared by the staff. The financial analysis of the Commission's recommendations was prepared by Augenblick, Palaich and Associates (APA) of Denver, Colorado. The authors of that study were Robert Palaich, John Augenblick, John Myers, Douglas Rose, Amy Anderson, Justin Silverstein, and Amanda Brown.

ECONOMICS AND LABOR MARKET STUDY

This study focused on the flows of the international economy as they affect the prospects for economic growth in this country, with particular attention to the effects on employment and income of advancing technology and the rise of countries that can offer high skills at low wages. The study addressed seven areas, in the following sequence:

- Estimated the contributions of education and innovation (such as patents, R&D spending) to U.S. and global economic growth

- Analyzed the relationship between education and access to middle-class status since 1967 and projected to 2012

- Projected the supply and demand for education in the United States to 2012

- Analyzed the relationship between educational attainment and occupational competencies (knowledge, skills, abilities, work styles, work contexts, values, and interests) based on the U.S. Department of Labor's Occupational Information Network (O*NET) data

- Measured educational adequacy against criteria that included employability and middle-class jobs

- Estimated the vulnerability of U.S. jobs to offshoring based on the characteristics of the jobs and the skills of current job holders, as reported in O*NET

• Estimated the stock and growth of the global supply of educated workers

A report, *America in the Global Economy,* by Ray Uhalde and Jeffrey Strohl, is available on the Commission's Web site.

INDUSTRY STUDIES

We examined eight industries to understand the forces operating on these industries to produce new winners and new losers with respect to companies, countries, and workers; the prospects for growth and decline for these industries and the specific factors affecting those prospects; and the way in which the availability of workers with specific skills in this country and abroad affects investment and location decisions in these industries. On the Commission Web site, a paper by Peter Carlson and Mark Troppe synthesizing the Industry Study findings is available along with findings in each industry studied:

• Biotechnology
• Automotive
• Telecommunications
• Textiles and Apparel
• Entertainment
• Health Care
• Personal Computers
• Software

EDUCATION SYSTEMS STUDIES

We have identified nations that have consistently scored high on international comparisons of educational achievement on the dimensions that our economic studies identify as important; benchmarked education and training policies and practices in those countries that have the potential for producing substantial gains in system productivity in the United States; and reviewed and synthesized the literature on the sources of creativity and innovation in individuals and identified curricula and pedagogical techniques that have proven effective in promoting those qualities. The result of this work is the following reports and commissioned papers, many of which are available on the Commission's Web site:

STAFF PAPERS

Early Childhood Education: Lessons from the States and Abroad, Lynne Sacks and Betsy Brown Ruzzi

International Education Tests: An Overview, Betsy Brown Ruzzi

Overview of Education Ministries in Selected Countries: Roles, Responsibilities and Finances, 2005, Lynne Sacks and Betsy Brown Ruzzi

Profile of the Indian Education System, Gretchen Cheney, Betsy Brown Ruzzi, and Karthik Muralidharan

The Challenge from Asia, Marc Tucker

COMMISSIONED PAPERS

Comparative Governance, Administration and Finance for Elementary and Secondary Education in Selected Countries, Brian Caldwell and Jessica Harris, Educational Transformations Ltd.

Rethinking and Redesigning Curriculum, Instruction and Assessment: What Contemporary Research and Theory Has to Offer, James W. Pellegrino, University of Illinois at Chicago

Educational and Labor Market Outcomes for the Nation's Teens and Youth Since the Publication of America's Choice: A Critical Assessment, Andrew Sum, Tim Barnicle, Ishwar Khatiwada, and Joseph McLaughlin with Sheila Palma, Center for Labor Market Studies, Northeastern University

High Performance and Success in Education in Flemish Belgium and the Netherlands, Toon Dijkstra, European Orientation Programs, Maastricht University of Professional Education

Improving Teacher Training Provision in England: 1990–2005, Adrian Ellis, PA Consulting Group

Out-of-School Youth, Tim Barnicle

Sources of Innovation and Creativity: A Summary of the Research, Karyln Adams, University of Pennsylvania

The Delhi Public School: A Case Study in High Student Achievement, David Marsh, University of Southern California, and Judy Codding, America's Choice, Inc.

WORKFORCE DEVELOPMENT SYSTEMS STUDIES

The staff prepared case studies of the workforce economic development systems in five states:

- Florida
- North Carolina
- Oregon
- Texas
- Washington State

The staff also produced the following paper on American workforce development systems:

State and Local Workforce Systems: An Overview, 2006, Mary Clagett

The following paper was also commissioned:

New Foreign Immigrant Workers and the Labor Market in the U.S.: The Contributions of New Immigrant Workers to Labor Force and Employment Growth and Their Impact on Native Born Workers, 2000 to 2005, Andrew Sum, Center for Labor Market Studies, Northeastern University

All of these papers are available on the Commission Web site.

EXPERT INTERVIEWS AND FOCUS GROUPS

We conducted a series of interviews with leaders in education, employment, and training policy and practice in the United States and held two focus groups with international graduate students from around the world to hear from them what it takes to succeed in the global economy and what skills and knowledge they and their peers bring to the table.

EXPERT INTERVIEWS

ROGER ALTMAN
Chairman
Evercore Partners, Inc.

THOMAS BAILEY
George and Abby O'Neill Professor of
Economics and Education
Institute on Education and the Economy
Teachers College, Columbia University

LAURIE BASSI
Chief Executive Officer
Human Capital Capability

KEITH BIRD
Chancellor
Kentucky Community and Tech College System

DAVID CALLEO
Dean Acheson Professor and Director of
European Studies Program
Johns Hopkins University, School of Advanced
International Studies

PETER CAPELLI
George W. Taylor Professor of Management
and Director of the Center for Human
Resources
The Wharton School
University of Pennsylvania

ANIL GUPTA
Ralph J. Tyser Professor of Strategy
and Organization, Management and
Organization
Robert H. Smith School of Business, University
of Maryland

JERRY JAZNOWSKI
Past President
National Association of Manufacturers

PETER MORICI
Professor of International Business, Logistics,
Business and Public Policy
Robert H. Smith School of Business, University
of Maryland

KARTHIK MURALIDHARAN
Ph.D. Candidate, Harvard University
Study Director, World Bank Study on
Education in India

PAUL OSTERMAN
Nanyung Technological Institute Professor
Institute for Work and Employment Research
Sloan School of Management
Massachusetts Institute of Technologys

BOB TEMPLIN
President
Northern Virginia Community College

GRAHAM TOFT
Senior Fellow, Hudson Institute

YONG ZHAO
University Distinguished Professor
Educational Psychology and Educational
Technology
Director, Center for Teaching and Technology
Director, U.S.-China Center for Research on
Educational Excellence
College of Education, Michigan State University

Two focus groups were held with graduate
students from Johns Hopkins University,
School of Advanced International Studies.
The countries represented were:

- Australia
- Belgium
- Denmark
- Hong Kong
- India
- Japan
- Korea
- The Netherlands
- Singapore
- United Kingdom

Finally the staff visited organizations around the world (an asterisk denotes a factory tour in addition to a meeting or interview):

Australia

Sydney

- Department of Education and Training, New South Wales
- NCVER
- Cherrybrook Technology High School
- Dusseldorf Skills Foundation
- Centre for Regional Education
- Institute of Teachers
- Schools Resourcing Taskforce
- Group Training Australia

Melbourne

- The University of Melbourne, Parkville
- Australian Council for Education Research
- Department of Skills, Victoria

Belgium

- Forem Formation
- Ministry of the Flemish Community
- AVC/CSC
- VDAB
- Institute for the Promotion of Innovation by Science and Technology in Flanders
- European Commission and Union

Canada

Victoria, British Columbia

- Ministry of Education

China

Beijing

- Ministry of Education
- China Center for Economic Research
- Peking University, Guanghua Business School
- Beijing Academy of Education Sciences
- Beijing Normal University, U.S.-China Center
- Experimental School, Beijing Normal University
- Beijing 123 Middle School
- U.S. Commercial Service, U.S. Embassy
- Center for Pharmaceutical Information and Engineering Research, Peking University
- All-China Federation of Industry and Commerce
- China Textile Network Co., Ltd.
- China Textile & Apparel Education Society
- Topnew Knitting Group Co., Ltd.*
- Intel China Ltd.
- United Technologies International Operations

Shanghai

- Shanghai Municipal Education Commission

- Shanghai Jiaotong University
- Shanghai Trade Office, City of Denver
- State of Washington Trade Development, China Office
- State of Michigan China Office
- Asia Division, Vermont Chamber of Commerce
- Eaton Automotive, Engine Air Management Operations*
- Bill Wiggenhorn, founder of Motorola University and director of Global EduTech Management Group, an educational investment group building a network of new campuses and colleges as well as managing existing education institutions and delivering world-class teaching to major institutions in Southeast Asia

Shenzhen

- Orient Product Services
- Weal-Lam Parts and Tools Ltd., metal fabrication plant*
- Rice Lake Weighing Systems, Wisconsin manufacturer of industrial scales
- XtremeMac (iPod accessories emerging business)
- International Information Products (Shenzhen) Co, Ltd., a Lenovo Company, manufacturer of IBM Think Pad computers*
- FLX (HK) Ltd., manufacturer of consumer electronics for U.S. export (large manufacturer of personal karaoke machines)*

- Sound Choice, Charlotte, North Carolina, a provider of re-recorded music for karaoke
- Sure Advance PCB Ltd., manufacturer of printed circuit boards*

Dongguan

- Dongguan University of Science and Technology
- Dongguan Vocational/Technical School
- Dongguan Secondary School
- Beijing Normal Jhu Hai Campus
- SAE Magnetics (H.K.) Ltd. — HDD (subsidiary of TDK), manufacturer of magnetic recording heads, head gimbal assemblies, and head stack assemblies for computer disk drives*

Hong Kong

- Education and Manpower Bureau
- Hong Kong Examinations and Assessment Authority
- Chair of Education, University of Hong Kong
- Pui Ching Middle School
- St. Paul's Convent School
- St. Paul's Co-educational College

Czech Republic

Prague

- Education Policy Centre, Charles University
- Ministry of Education, Youth and Sport
- Institute for Social and Economical Analysis
- National Institute of Technical and Vocational Education
- CzechInvest

England

London

- Prime Minister's Delivery Unit
- Department for Education and Skills
- Qualifications and Curriculum Authority
- Office of Standards in Education, England's Education Inspectorate
- The Leitch Commission
- Learning and Skills Council
- National Employment Panel
- Sector Skills Development Agency
- BT Group
- City and Guilds
- Confederation of British Industry
- Trade Union Congress

Finland

Helsinki

- Ministry of Education
- Finnish National Board of Education
- University of Helsinki, Department of Applied Sciences of Education
- Helsinki School of Economics
- Mikkola Comprehensive School
- Sotunki General Upper Secondary School
- Confederation of Unions for Academic Professionals
- Association of Finnish Local and Regional Authorities (who run secondary, vocational, and polytechnics)
- Aike Group, Vocational and Adult Education Centers
- Tekes

Porvoo

- Edupoli Regional and Local Vocational Adult Education Centres
- Ministry of Labor
- Porvoo Employment Office
- Neste Oil

France

- Organisation for Economic Co-operation and Development (OECD)

Germany

- Institute Arbeit Und Technik

India

Delhi

- FIITJEE Limited, test prep company for IIT entry
- Oxus Research and Investments, Economics Research Firm
- Gurcharan Das, author of *India Unbound*
- NIIT Limited, supplemental private education tutoring firm
- Editor, *Business World*
- Confederation of Indian Industries
- Delhi College of Engineering
- Delhi University
- Sardar Patel Vidyalaya School
- Delhi Public School
- National Council of Educational Research and Training
- Navodaya Vidhyalaya (a typical Indian school on the outskirts of Delhi)
- Salwan Public School
- Mira Model School

Chennai/Madras

- Bala Vidya Mandir Senior Secondary School
- Indian Institute of Technology Madras
- Crescent Engineering College
- Brilliant Tutorials Ltd., supplemental private education test prep company
- AAM Matriculation Higher Secondary School
- SRF Vidyalaya School, 90 percent first-generation learners

Bangalore

- Infosys Technologies
- Wipro
- Indian Institute of Management, Bangalore
- Indian Institute of Science
- Confederation of Indian Industries Institute of Quality
- Biocon Ltd., biotech firm
- Azim Premji Foundation, Wipro-funded foundation on education and health care
- Vidyashilp Academy
- Sri Kumaran Children's Home, English nursery and primary school

Mumbai/Bombay

- *Economic Times*
- Aptech Limited, supplemental education provider working in 30 countries
- Jamnabai Narsee School
- Bajaj Lane Municipal School

Ireland

- FAS, Training and Employment Authority
- Department of Education and Science
- Irish Business and Employment Confederation
- Enterprise Ireland
- FORFAS
- Aderra
- Einet
- Irish Congress of Trade Unions
- Ireland-U.S. Chamber of Commerce
- National Qualification Authority of Ireland

Italy

Bologna

- Ministry for Education and Labor
- Fondazione Instituto per il Lavoro
- Format, Employer Association
- CISL
- L'Instituto Salesiano

Rome

- Ministry of Education, University and Research
- Montessori Foundation
- Montessori School in Rome

New Zealand

Wellington

- New Zealand Ministry of Education
- New Zealand Department of Labor
- New Zealand Qualifications Authority
- Ministry of Social Development

Biographies of
the Members of the Commission

CHARLES B. KNAPP
COMMISSION CHAIRMAN
Director of Educational Development,
CF Foundation

 Chuck B. Knapp is an economist, educator, and former university president. He currently serves as Director of Educational Development for the CF Foundation and as Chairman of the Board of the East Lake Community Foundation, the organization responsible for leading the revitalization of the East Lake community in Atlanta. Dr. Knapp was President and Professor of Economics at the University of Georgia from 1987 to 1997 and is now President Emeritus of the university. He was President of the Aspen Institute from 1997 to 1999, and from 2000 to 2004 was a partner with the executive search firm Heidrick and Struggles. Earlier in his career, Dr. Knapp served as the Executive Vice President of Tulane University and was the U.S. Deputy Assistant Secretary of Labor for Employment and Training during the Carter Administration. He was a member of the faculty at the University of Texas at Austin from 1972 to 1977. From 1996 to 1997, he was the Chair of the National Association of State Universities and Land-Grant Colleges.

MARC S. TUCKER
VICE CHAIRMAN AND STAFF DIRECTOR
President, National Center on Education
and the Economy

 Marc S. Tucker is President of the National Center on Education and the Economy, a leader in the movement for standards-based school reform in the United States. Mr. Tucker authored the 1986 Carnegie Report, *A Nation Prepared: Teachers for the 21st Century;* created the National Board for Professional Teaching Standards; created the Commission on the Skills of the American Workforce and coauthored its report, *America's Choice: high skills or low wages!;* was instrumental in creating the National Skill Standards Board and served as the chairman of its committee on standards and assessment policy; with Lauren Resnick, created the New Standards consortium; and, with Judy Codding, created America's Choice, a comprehensive school reform program. With Ray Marshall, Mr. Tucker coauthored *Thinking for a Living: Education and the Wealth of Nations,* selected by Business Week as one of the 10 best business books of 1992; with Judy Codding, coauthored *Standards for Our Schools: How to Set Them, Measure Them, and Reach Them* (1998); and with Judy Codding, coeditored *The Principal Challenge* (2002).

MORTON BAHR
President Emeritus, Communications Workers of America

Morton Bahr led the 600,000-member Communications Workers of America (CWA) for 20 years and was named President Emeritus in August 2005.

During his tenure, Mr. Bahr expanded CWA into new areas, such as health care, the public sector, and higher education. President Bill Clinton appointed Mr. Bahr to head the Commission for a Nation of Lifelong Learners, which recommended an agenda for expanded adult education and training. He served as Vice President of Union Network International, a global labor organization representing some 15 million workers in 800 unions in communications, media and entertainment, and commercial, technical, and professional fields. Prior to his election as CWA President, Mr. Bahr served for 16 years as CWA Vice President for District 1 covering New York, New Jersey, and New England.

WILLIAM E. BROCK
Former Secretary, U.S. Department of Labor

Former Senator and Ambassador, William E. Brock served in the U.S. House of Representatives, the U.S. Senate, and the President's Cabinet as U.S. Trade Representative and subsequently as U.S. Secretary of Labor. During his more than 30 years in public service, Senator Brock spearheaded numerous national reform efforts on education, including Workforce 2000, the Commission on the Skills of the American Workforce, the Secretary's Commission on Achieving Necessary Skills (SCANS), and the Wingspread Group on Improving Higher Education. He is Founder and Chairman of The Brock Offices, a firm specializing in international trade, investment, and human resources.

JUDY B. CODDING
President and CEO, America's Choice, Inc.

Judy B. Codding is President and Chief Executive Officer of American's Choice, Inc. Before assuming her present position, Dr. Codding was Vice President for the National Center on Education and the Economy and, prior to that, the award-winning principal of Pasadena High School in Los Angeles, a large urban, comprehensive high school serving predominantly low-income African American and Latino students. Previously, Dr. Codding had been a teacher and principal of Bronxville High School and Scarsdale High School in New York. Dr. Codding was a founder of the Coalition of Essential Schools, a national high school reform effort. She was an Associate in Education at the Harvard Graduate School of Education. She served as an education consultant to the Ministry of Education in the People's Republic of China and the U.S. Department of Defense schools. She served as a commissioner on the California Commission for the Establishment of Academic Content and Performance Standards. Dr. Codding is coauthor with Marc Tucker of *Standards for Our Schools: How to Set Them, Measure Them, and*

Reach Them (1998), with David Marsh of *The New American High School* (1999); and with Marc Tucker of *The Principal Challenge* (2002).

MICHAEL DOLAN
Executive Vice President and Chief Financial Officer, Viacom

Michael Dolan has served as Executive Vice President and Chief Financial Officer of Viacom since January 1, 2006. Prior to that, he was Executive Vice President and Chief Financial Officer of the former Viacom Inc., a predecessor of the company. Before joining Viacom, Mr. Dolan served as a senior advisor to Kohlberg Kravis Roberts & Co., a private equity firm. Previously, Mr. Dolan served as Chairman and Chief Executive Officer of Young & Rubicam, Inc. from 2000 until his retirement in 2003, as its President and Chief Executive Officer during 2000, and as its Vice Chairman and Chief Financial Officer from 1996 to 2000. Mr. Dolan also serves as nonexecutive Chairman of America's Choice and serves on the Board of Directors of Mattel, Inc.

DAVID P. DRISCOLL
Massachusetts Commissioner of Education

Commissioner Driscoll has a 40-year career in public education and educational leadership. A former mathematics teacher at the junior high school level in Somerville, Massachusetts, and at the senior high school in Melrose, he became Assistant Superintendent in Melrose in 1972 and Superintendent of Schools in Melrose in 1984. He served as the Melrose Superintendent for nine years until his appointment in 1993 as Deputy Commissioner of Education in Massachusetts. In July 1998, he was named Interim Commissioner of Education, and on March 10, 1999, he was appointed by the Board as Massachusetts' 22nd Commissioner of Education.

PAUL A. ELSNER
President, Paul Elsner Associates

Paul A. Elsner served as Chancellor of the Maricopa Community College District in Arizona from 1977 until 1999. Dr. Elsner served as Chair of the Board of the Educational Testing Service, President of the Board of Trustees for American College Testing, and President of the Board of the League for Innovation in Community Colleges. Among the many awards he has received are the Anderson Medal for co-founding "The Think Tank," the AACC Community Colleges' Leadership Award, and the Harold W. McGraw, Jr. Prize in Education. He is Founder and President of the Sedona Conferences and Conversations, Paul Elsner and Associates, and Los Vientos, Inc. — organizations dedicated to worldwide education.

JOHN ENGLER
President, National Association of Manufacturers

John Engler is President of the National Association of Manufacturers, the largest industry trade group in America. Mr. Engler is a former three-term Michigan Governor, first elected in 1990. Prior to being elected Governor, Mr. Engler was a member of the Michigan State Senate and House of Representatives. In 2005, Mr. Engler was named Vice Chairman of the President's Advisory Committee for Trade Policy and Negotiations, the U.S. government's senior trade advisory panel.

STEVE GUNDERSON
President and Chief Executive Officer, Council on Foundations

Steve Gunderson is President and Chief Executive Officer of the Council on Foundations, an association of more than 2,000 grant-making foundations and corporations. Prior to joining the Council, Mr. Gunderson served as the Senior Consultant and the Managing Director of the Washington office of The Greystone Group, a strategic management and communications consulting firm. Mr. Gunderson served for 16 years in the U.S. Congress and three terms in the Wisconsin State Legislature. During his tenure in Congress, Mr. Gunderson was a recognized leader on agriculture, education, employment policy, health care, and human rights issues. Mr. Gunderson's career also includes leadership roles on AIDS policy, modernization of our nation's employment policy, lifelong learning, community learning centers, and job training policies for a global high-tech economy. Recently, he served as the lead author of the book *The Jobs Revolution: Changing How America Works.*

CLIFFORD B. JANEY
Superintendent, District of Columbia Public Schools

Clifford B. Janey has been Superintendent of Schools in the District of Columbia since September 2004. Prior to his selection as School Superintendent for the nation's capital, Dr. Janey served as Vice President for Education at Scholastic, Inc., a $2 billion multimedia education publishing company in New York City. From 1995 to 2002, Dr. Janey served as Superintendent of Schools in Rochester, New York, an urban school system of 55,000 students. As Superintendent, he increased reading and mathematics performance on state assessments and reduced the achievement gap between black and Hispanic students and their white counterparts. Before serving as Superintendent of Schools in Rochester, Dr. Janey held a number of positions in the Boston Public Schools from 1973 to 1995. These included Chief Academic Officer, East Zone Superintendent (K–8), Community District

Superintendent (K–12), Principal of Theodore Roosevelt Middle School, and Reading Teacher at the George Bancroft School. He also served as a principal in the Salem (MA) Public Schools and as Director of Black Studies at Northeastern University.

SHARON LYNN KAGAN
Virginia and Leonard Marx Professor of Early Childhood and Family Policy, Codirector of the National Center for Children and Families, and Associate Dean for Policy at Teachers College, Columbia University and Professor Adjunct at Yale University's Child Study Center

Sharon Lynn Kagan has helped shape early childhood practice and policies in the United States and in other countries throughout the world. Author of over 200 articles and 12 books, Kagan's research focuses on the institutions that have an impact on child and family life. She consults with numerous international, federal, and state agencies; Congress; governors; and legislatures. She is a member of 40 national boards and panels, and is Past President of the National Association for the Education of Young Children and Family Support America. She is currently working around the globe with UNICEF to establish early learning standards in Armenia, Brazil, Cambodia, China, Ghana, Jordan, Mongolia, Paraguay, Turkmenistan, and Vietnam. She is the only woman in the history of American education to receive its three most prestigious awards: the 2004 Distinguished Service Award from the Council of Chief State School Officers, the 2005 James Bryant Conant Award for Lifetime Service to Education from the Education Commission of the States, and the Harold W. McGraw Jr. Prize in Education.

JOEL I. KLEIN
Chancellor, New York City Public Schools

Since 2002, Joel I. Klein has been Chancellor of New York City's public school system. As Chancellor, he oversees more than 1,350 schools with over 1.1 million students, 140,000 employees, and a $15 billion budget. Prior to being appointed Chancellor, Mr. Klein was Chairman and Chief Executive Officer of Bertelsmann, Inc., one of the world's largest media companies. Prior to that, Mr. Klein was Assistant Attorney General in charge of the U.S. Department of Justice's antitrust division. His appointment to the U.S. Justice Department came after he served two years (1993–1995) as Deputy Counsel to President Clinton.

DAL LAWRENCE
Past President, Toledo Federation of Teachers

Dal Lawrence is Past President of the Toledo Federation of Teachers (TFT) and a consultant to both unions and superintendents on teacher quality issues.

He was President from 1966 to 1996. During his tenure, Mr. Lawrence created The Toledo Plan, the nation's first peer-review teacher evaluation system, implemented in 1981. He led two strikes against the Toledo Public Schools in 1970 and 1978. He served as a Vice President of the American Federation of Teachers from 1988 to 1996, and was President of the Toledo Area AFL-CIO Council from 1994 to 1998. Mr. Lawrence also authored 133 monthly columns about public education in the Toledo *Blade*. Mr. Lawrence is retired and currently serves as Assistant to the TFT President. Monterrey, Mexico, and Syracuse, New York, and Chicago are currently establishing peer review evaluation programs with Mr. Lawrence's assistance. Mr. Lawrence is also a founding member of the Teacher Union Reform Network (TURN). He taught history at DeVilbiss High School in Toledo, Ohio.

RAY MARSHALL
Professor Emeritus and Audre and Bernard Rapoport Centennial Chair in Economics and Public Affairs, LBJ School of Public Affairs, The University of Texas at Austin

Ray Marshall holds the Audre and Bernard Rapoport Centennial Chair in Economic and Public Affairs, The University of Texas at Austin, and served as President Carter's Secretary of Labor. He chairs the National Center on Education and the Economy's Board of Trustees, was a Trustee of the Carnegie Corporation, and served as a member of the Carnegie Forum's Advisory Council. He is coauthor with Marc Tucker of *Thinking for a Living: Education and the Wealth of Nations*, winner of the Sidney Hillman Prize for 1992. Secretary Marshall's board memberships include the Institute for the Future (former Chair), German Marshall Fund, the USX Corporation, Spelman College, and the Quality Education for Minorities Network. With Secretary Bill Brock, he chaired the first Commission on the Skills of the American Workforce.

MARC H. MORIAL
President and Chief Executive Officer, National Urban League

Marc H. Morial is President and CEO of the National Urban League. Prior to being selected to lead that organization, Mr. Morial briefly practiced law after leaving office, having served two distinguished four-year terms as Mayor of New Orleans from 1994 to 2002. He also served as President of the United States Conference of Mayors in 2001 and 2002. Mr. Morial served two years in the Louisiana State Senate, where he was recognized as Conservationist Senator of the Year, Education Senator of the Year, and Legislative Rookie of the Year for his accomplishments.

BEVERLY O'NEILL
Former Mayor, Long Beach, California

Beverly O'Neill was Mayor of Long Beach, California's 5th largest city, from 1994 to 2006. Dr. O'Neill was a major force in changing the Long Beach economy into a diversified mix of international trade, tourism, emerging technologies, and expanding retail. As a member of the U.S. Conference of Mayors, Mayor O'Neill chaired the standing committee on Jobs, Education and Workforce for four years. She led efforts to focus attention on the issue of the nation's skill gap and co-hosted Mayor's Skills Summits. In June 2005, Mayor O'Neill was elected President of the organization. Prior to becoming mayor, Dr. O'Neill spent a 31-year career at Long Beach City College, beginning as a music instructor and women's advisor. In the succeeding years, she advanced to Campus Dean, Dean of Student Affairs, Vice President of Student Services, and spent her last five years as Superintendent-President.

RODERICK PAIGE
Chairman, Chartwell Education Group LLC

Roderick Paige, former U.S. Secretary of Education (2001–2005), cofounded the Chartwell Education Group on his departure from the government. The group assists both public and private enterprises focused on pre-K, K–12, and postsecondary education in the United States and abroad. Prior to his tenure at the U.S. Department of Education, Paige served as Dean of the College of Education at Texas Southern University, where he established the university's Center for Excellence in Urban Education. Following his time there, he was Superintendent of the Houston Independent School District, and in 2001, he was named National Superintendent of the Year by the American Association of School Administrators. Secretary Paige was a Public Policy Fellow at the Woodrow Wilson International Center for Scholars in 2005.

THOMAS W. PAYZANT
Former Superintendent, Boston Public Schools

Thomas W. Payzant served as Superintendent of Boston Public Schools from 1995 until 2006. Prior to his Boston superintendency, Dr. Payzant was appointed by President Clinton to serve as Assistant Secretary for Elementary and Secondary Education. Dr. Payzant's teaching career began at Belmont High School, Belmont, Massachusetts, in 1963. He then went to Tacoma, Washington, to teach at Gray Junior High School. His first superintendency was with the School District of Springfield Township, Montgomery County, Pennsylvania, from 1969 to 1973. Subsequently he was Superintendent of the Eugene, Oregon, Public Schools from 1973 to 1978; the Oklahoma City Public Schools from 1979 to 1982; and the San Diego Unified School District from 1982 to 1993. In 1992, Dr. Payzant was awarded the Harold W. McGraw, Jr. Prize in Education and in 2004 was awarded the Richard R. Green Award in Urban Excellence from the Council of the Great City Schools.

CHARLES B. REED
Chancellor, California State University System

As Chancellor of the California State University System, Charles B. Reed is the chief executive officer of the country's largest senior system of public higher education. Dr. Reed provides leadership to 44,000 faculty and staff and 405,000 students on 23 campuses and 7 off-campus centers. The system's annual budget is more than $5 billion. Dr. Reed became Chancellor of the California State University System in 1998. He was the Chancellor of the State University System of Florida from 1985 to 1998. He served as Chief of Staff in the Office of the Governor of Florida from 1984 to 1985, and Deputy Chief of Staff, Director of Legislative Affairs, and Education Policy Coordinator from 1979 until 1984. Prior to serving the governor, Charles Reed was the Director of the Office of Education Planning, Budgeting and Evaluation in the Florida Department of Education. Dr. Reed began his education career at George Washington University where he was an Associate Professor of Education.

RICHARD W. RILEY
Senior Partner, Nelson Mullins Riley & Scarborough LLP

Secretary Riley served as U.S. Secretary of Education in the Clinton Administration from 1993 to 2001 and was Governor of South Carolina from 1979 to 1987. Now Senior Partner at Nelson Mullins Riley & Scarborough, Secretary Riley is also a Distinguished University Professor of Education at the University of South Carolina and a Distinguished Professor of Government, Politics, and Public Leadership at the Richard W. Riley Institute at Furman University. Secretary Riley is the recipient of numerous honorary degrees from American universities and schools abroad.

HENRY B. SCHACHT
Managing Director and Senior Advisor, Warburg Pincus LLC

Henry B. Schacht returned to Warburg Pincus in 2004. He first joined the firm in early 1995, leaving later that year to become the founding Chairman and Chief Executive

Officer of Lucent Technologies. Prior to his tenure at Lucent, he was CEO and later Chairman of Cummins Engine Co. Mr. Schacht is a Director of ALCOA, Lucent Technologies, and formerly The New York Times Company. He is a Trustee of The Metropolitan Museum of Art, former Chairman of the Board of Trustees of The Ford Foundation, and a former Trustee of Yale University. He is a member of The Business Council and a former member of The Business Roundtable.

SUSAN SCLAFANI
Managing Director, Chartwell Education Group LLC

Susan Sclafani served in the Bush Administration as the Assistant Secretary for Vocational and Adult Education from 2003 to 2005 and as Counselor to the Secretary. Previously, Dr. Sclafani worked in a variety of roles at the Houston Independent School District, culminating in Chief of Staff for Educational Services. Prior to that, she was a teacher of mathematics, a magnet school leader, and a central office administrator in the departments of technology, curriculum development, and construction management. She is a charter member of Superintendents Prepared, an initiative to identify and train the next generation of urban superintendents. Dr. Sclafani is Senior Advisor and Codirector of the State Alliance for High Performance at NCEE.

HARRY A. SPENCE
Commissioner, Massachusetts Department of Social Services

Harry A. Spence was appointed Commissioner of the Massachusetts Department of Social Services, the state agency that is charged with the care and protection of children, November 2001. Mr. Spence formerly served as Deputy Chancellor for Operations for the New York City Public Schools, the nation's largest school system; Receiver for the bankrupt city of Chelsea, Massachusetts; Lecturer in public policy at the Kennedy School of Government at Harvard; court-appointed Receiver of the Boston Housing Authority, which became a model for public housing intervention across the nation; and Executive Director of the Cambridge Housing Authority.

SARA MARTINEZ TUCKER*
Former President and CEO Hispanic Scholarship Fund

Sara Martinez Tucker recently resigned as President and Chief Executive Officer of the Hispanic Scholarship Fund (HSF). In 2005, *Time* magazine named her one of the 25 most influential Hispanics in America. Ms. Martinez Tucker is a founding board member of the National Center for Educational Accountability and the National Scholarship Providers Association. Since 2001, she has served on the seven-member

North American Diversity Advisory board of Toyota Motor Corporation to raise employee awareness and provide counsel on diversity issues. Prior to joining HSF in 1996, Ms. Martinez Tucker spent 16 years at AT&T, becoming the first Latina to reach the company's executive level. In her last assignment at the company, she served as a Regional Vice President for AT&T's Global Business Communications Systems.

*Sara Martinez Tucker, on her nomination by President Bush to the position of Under Secretary of Education in the U.S. Department of Education, resigned from the Commission on September 6, 2006.

A. WILLIAM WIGGENHORN
President of Consulting Services
Educational Development Associates

A. William Wiggenhorn is responsible for EDA's consulting business, including custom-designed executive development strategy, systems and programs, as well as talent management strategies and systems. Prior to joining EDA, Mr. Wiggenhorn served as a senior learning and development executive at Xerox and as Chief Learning Officer at Motorola and Cigna. Perhaps best known for establishing Motorola University (MU) as the benchmark corporate university, Mr. Wiggenhorn expanded MU's international reach to encompass 101 education offices in 24 countries. He currently serves on the Center for Creative Leadership Board of Governors, the Rochester Institute of Technology President's Council, the University of Tennessee Business School Advisory Board, the Villanova University Engineering School Advisory Board, and the Institute for Work and the Economy. Mr. Wiggenhorn also serves as Vice Chairman of the Asia-based Global Education Management Corporation (GEM), which manages institutions of higher learning in Malaysia and China.

COMMISSION STAFF AND ASSOCIATES

EXECUTIVE STAFF

Marc S. Tucker, Director
Ray Uhalde, Deputy Director
Betsy Brown Ruzzi, Associate Director
    and Director of Communications
Carolyn Carey, Administration
Suzie Sullivan, Administration

LABOR MARKET AND ECONOMIC STUDIES STAFF

Anthony Carnevale, Director
Sam Harake
Kathryn Jessup
Gbemi Oseni
Zamira Simkins
Jeff Strohl

EDUCATION STUDIES STAFF

Marc S. Tucker, Director
Betsy Brown Ruzzi, Deputy Director
Judy B. Codding, Senior Advisor
Gretchen Cheney
Jackie Kraemer

INDUSTRY STUDIES STAFF

Mark Troppe, Director
Aziza Agia
Peter Carlson
Barbara Rivard
Ellen Scully Russ
Peggy Simpson

WORKFORCE SYSTEMS STUDIES STAFF

Gerri Fiala and Ray Uhalde, Codirectors
Tim Barnicle, Senior Advisor
Mary Clagett

ADVISORS

Pat Fahy
Barbara Kauffman
David Marsh
Karthik Muralidharin
Susan Sclafani
Ben Vickery
Yong Zhao